The Digital Photolab

ADVANCED BLACK-AND-WHITE TECHNIQUES USING PHOTOSHOP

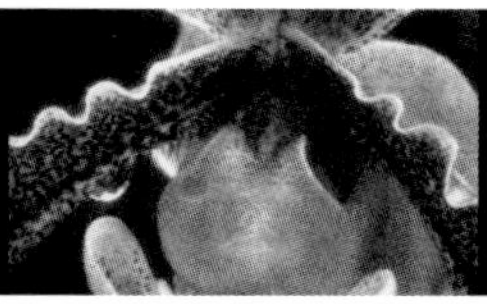
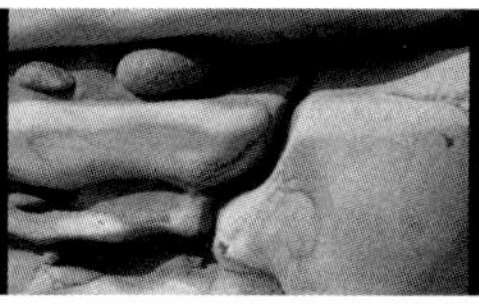
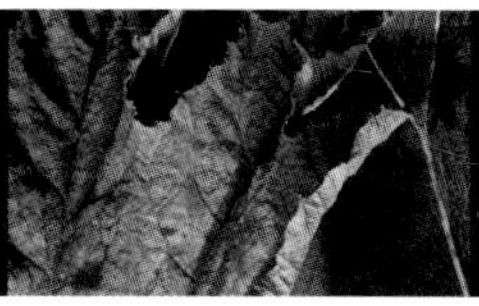
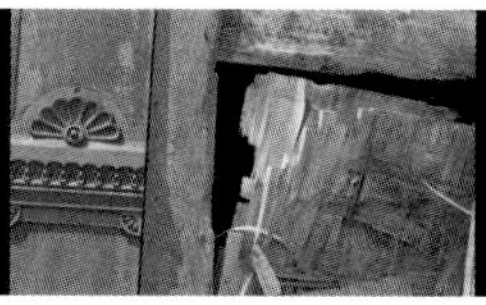

GEORGE SCHAUB

SILVER PIXEL PRESS

The Digital Photolab

ADVANCED BLACK-AND-WHITE TECHNIQUES USING PHOTOSHOP

WRITTEN BY GEORGE SCHAUB

Published by
Silver Pixel Press®
A Tiffen® Company
21 Jet View Drive
Rochester, NY 14624 USA
www.silverpixelpress.com

ISBN 1-883403-75-8

Design by Sandy Knight

Printed in China

Library of Congress Cataloging-in-Publication Data

Schaub, George.
The digital photolab : advanced black-and-white techniques using Photoshop / George Schaub.
p. cm.
ISBN 1-883403-75-8 (pbk.)
1. Adobe Photoshop. 2. Computer graphics. I. Title.
T385 .S28515 2002
778.3—dc21
2002002136

The Digital Photolab

ADVANCED BLACK-AND-WHITE TECHNIQUES USING PHOTOSHOP

GEORGE SCHAUB

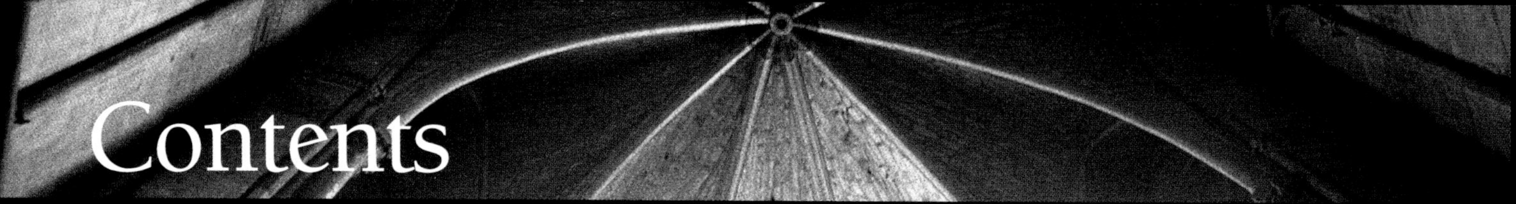

Contents

7 **Introduction**

11 **Calibration, Setup, and Materials**

12 Calibrating Your Monitor
12 Contrast and Color Cast
13 Procedure
14 Setting Up Your Printer
14 Tonal Values
14 Shadow Detail
14 Creating a Step Wedge
15 Acquiring an Image
15 Image Sources for Black-and-White/Duotone Printing
17 Digital Cameras
17 Digital Scan Backs
18 Photo CD and Picture CD
19 Scanners
20 Flatbed Scanners
22 Film Scanners
22 Drum Scanners
22 Scanning by Photo Labs
23 Resolution and Output Specs
23 Scanner Ratings
23 Making the Calculations
25 It's All Relative
26 Getting the Best Output
27 Saving and Opening Scans
27 Creating Contact Sheets
28 Paper
28 Types of Paper
29 Silver Gelatin and Digital Processes
30 Choosing a Paper
30 Paper Handling and Storage
30 Matching Paper and Printer Settings
31 Ink
31 Mixing and Using Inks
31 Grayscale or RGB?
32 Duotone Mode
32 Metamerism
32 Drydown
33 Longevity
33 Let's Get to Work!

35 **Image Workshops**

36 Variations
38 Contrast
38 Workshop 1—Contrast Basics
41 Workshop 2—Contrast Control Using Levels
44 Workshop 3—Working with Flat Negatives
46 Workshop 4—High-Key Effects
48 Workshop 5—Color Conversions
50 Workshop 6—Tonal Blending
53 Burning and Dodging
55 Workshop 1—Burning and Dodging Basics
56 Workshop 2—Exploring Burn and Dodge Controls
60 Workshop 3—Enhancing Infrared Photos
64 Workshop 4—Selective Tonal Control

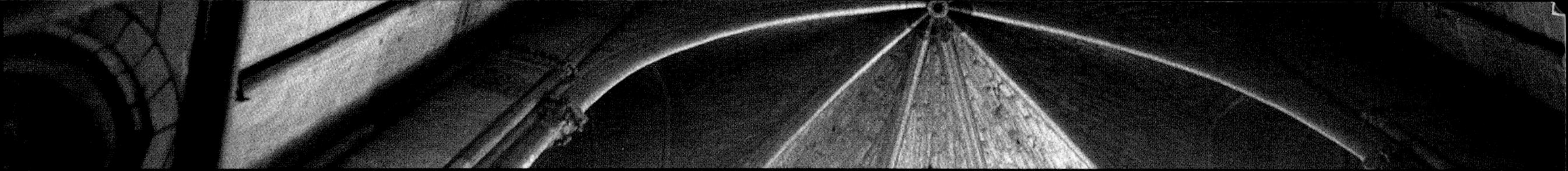

66 Selection Tools
67 Workshop 1—Color Range Selections
70 Workshop 2—Magic Wand
73 Workshop 3—Magnetic Lasso
76 Workshop 4—Elliptical Marquee
79 Workshop 5—Polygonal Lasso
81 Retouching and Restoration
82 Workshop 1—Minor Restoration
85 Workshop 2—Glass Plate Negatives
88 Workshop 3—Restoring Faded Photographs
91 Workshop 4—Retouching
92 Workshop 5—Retouching Scratched Slides
94 Creative Options
94 Workshop 1—Duotone and Tritone
98 Workshop 2—Detailed Subject
101 Workshop 3—Blending with Soft Light
104 Workshop 4—Converting Color Photographs to Black and White
107 Workshop 5—Tonal Controls
112 Workshop 6—Infrared Simulation
115 Refining the Image
115 Workshop 1—Subtle Tonal Corrections
119 Workshop 2—Correcting for Overexposed Highlights
122 Workshop 3—Discontinuous Tonal Borders
125 Workshop 4—Converting Colorization Using the Channel Mixer
128 Workshop 5—Creating Visual Drama
130 Workshop 6—Adjusting Contrast
132 Workshop 7—Heightening Effects
138 Emulations and Effects
139 Workshop 1—Albumen Print
141 Workshop 2—Brown Tone
143 Workshop 3—Cyanotype
146 Workshop 4—Hand Coloring
149 Workshop 5—Metallic Toning
152 Workshop 6—Paper Negatives
154 Workshop 7—Platinum/Palladium Prints
156 Workshop 8—Sepia Tone
159 Workshop 9—Modernist Approach
161 Workshop 10—Softening the Image
164 Workshop 11—Creating Mood
168 Workshop 12—Obscuring Details
170 Workshop 13—Gravure
174 Workshop 14—Electrifying an Image

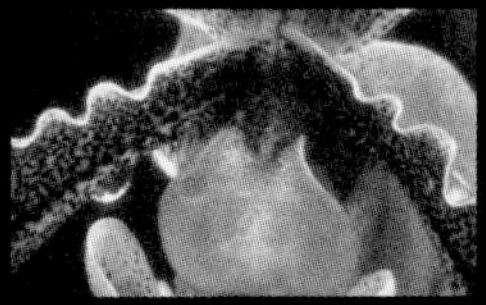

Dedication

This book is dedicated to all those who strive to express themselves through their images, and who labor long and hard to find the path. My visual journey could not have been undertaken without the dedication to the craft of those who taught me to see and to print, both through their words and through their images. It is also dedicated to my wife, Grace, who understands that creativity is the answer.

Many people, including Mimi and Marti at Silver Pixel Press and the folks at Epson America, who provided material support and encouragement for the work, aided this project. I'd also like to thank Sandy Knight, who created the flow and design of this book.

Introduction

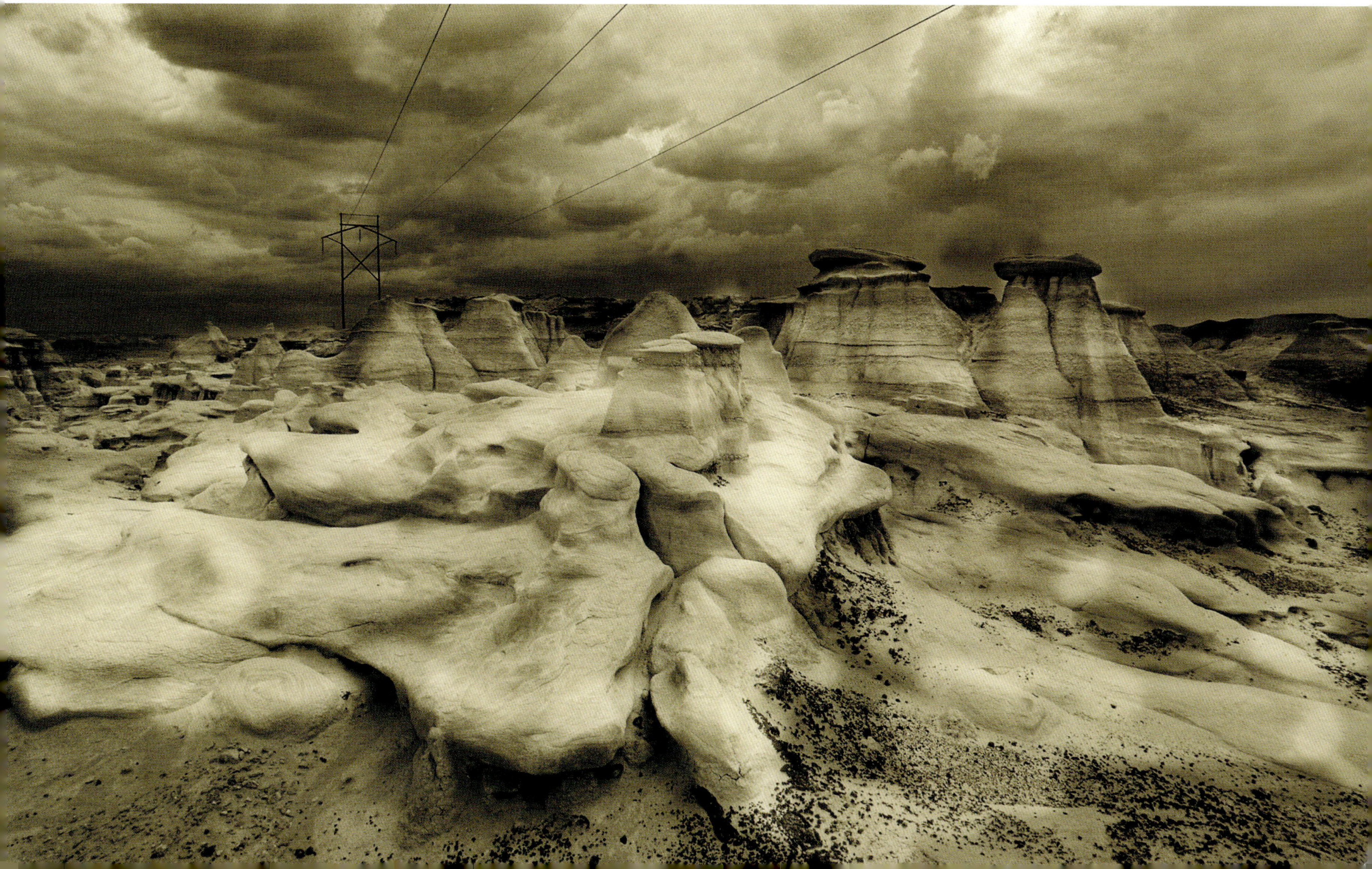

When I first started exploring the digital darkroom for black-and-white photography, in 1996, I had no idea where that exploration would take me. I considered myself a dedicated black-and-white photographer and chemical darkroom printer. I had worked as a custom black-and-white printer for 12 years; studied with Dennis Simonetti and George Tice; marveled at the work of Paul Strand and Minor White; and considered black-and-white printing to be the practice of the true faith in photography. My father, an excellent and professional darkroom craftsman, had showed me that first print coming up in the developer when I was about seven years old. In my twenties I returned to the darkroom and began to study and work in what I then considered my chosen craft. Since that time, I've written books and many magazine articles on black-and-white silver photography; I've also taught workshops and in colleges on black-and-white photography and tonal control.

So when I first began to take notice of digital imaging and how it might affect photography, I looked at it with a good deal of skepticism. It certainly was interesting, but the imagery looked hyped up and geared to the surrealism of low-end advertising. The prints I saw all had video edges—they looked like badly tuned TV sets—and they lacked the depth of silver tones. Friends who worked in digital imaging seemed to be plugged into something, but their results appeared more static than live, with no breadth and little spark. The images just sat there, as if waiting for something else to happen.

Then digital imagers started going beyond imaging tricks. They began to put good images on interesting paper. They became concerned with tonality, not just surface gimmickry. They started printing on something called an Iris printer. It sounded like it was getting serious, so I began to explore the possibilities and found that these prints were very expensive and not many places that offered them could relate to black-and-white photography. I figured that, for me, fine printing would still have to be achieved in the chemical darkroom.

Still, I was curious, so I got one of the first Power Macs, installed Adobe Photoshop, and borrowed a dye-sublimation printer. I had my images scanned onto Photo CDs.

I soon learned how techniques used in the darkroom, such as burning and dodging, were easily applied in the computer environment. I saw how testing and experimentation with images could be done without going through stacks of paper and gallons of chemicals. I also saw how experience in the chemical darkroom heightened a sense of what to do with images in the digital realm.

Then one day it hit me: I could make all of my functional prints using my computer and printer. As I mentioned, at that time it was a dye-sublimation printer—not the inkjet printer I use today—but I found I could make images that closely matched those I could produce on resin-coated glossy paper. If I had to get an image out for an article, I could just scan it and knock it out on the computer. If I needed some images I already had scanned to Photo CD, I could get the printout immediately, without mixing chemicals or setting up and breaking down the darkroom. For me, a dedicated black-and-white darkroom worker, this came as quite a shock.

The next shock appeared as I continued to work. I found that I could do certain things easier and at times better in the computer environment than I could in the darkroom. Tonal control, always an issue, became absolute, as did contrast variation. I could burn and dodge in areas that would be next to impossible in the darkroom. I could do toning variations, split contrast printing, posterization, and special effects—all the tricks of the darkroom craft, in fact—with a greater sense of freedom and ease.

The time and effort I spent experimenting resulted in the conversion of much of my printing work to the digital darkroom and to my first book on the subject, *The Digital Darkroom: Black-and-White Techniques Using Photoshop,* which was published by Silver Pixel Press in 1999. Written from the point of view of a photographer and a photographic printer, it offers a solid grounding in the subject and is a good starting point for those who have little or no computer-imaging experience.

Though this new book includes some of the techniques and technical information covered in the first one, it really takes off where the other ends. It represents further study in this field, and it is an attempt to address more than functional matters in this area of expression. It considers the black-and-white digital darkroom as a place where an artistic statement can be made; it reflects appreciation and respect for the aesthetic and visual considerations of fine-art black-and-white printing; and it explores the digital emulations of what some call "alternative processes," proposing a method of obtaining these effects in a fashion less hazardous than currently available—and by hazardous I mean in terms of health and social welfare, rather than visual timidity.

What has allowed me to take up such matters are the changes that have occurred in the field. New equipment and materials as well as a growing acceptance of this medium as a valid form of expression have changed the way many black-and-white printers view the potential of the digital darkroom.

Reasonably priced, photo-quality inkjet printers are now the norm, and they have opened up the use of a whole new class of papers and substrates. Perhaps the most important progress are the advances made in ink stability. We now have inks that rival silver paper longevity, given the usual care and proper storage. In short, the materials of the digital printing craft have caught up with the expectations of printmakers. Those wishing to make the transition will find a variety of superior materials available, and they will enjoy high-quality results from affordable printers.

Since the publication of *The Digital Darkroom,* I have had the opportunity to teach a number of workshops and seminars on this subject. Many of the participants were experienced and quite excellent black-and-white silver printers. While I cannot speak for them all, many shared my feeling of excitement about the digital darkroom as a newly found tool for artistic expression. In these workshops I often learned as much as I taught, and I came away marveling at the vision and artistic intention of the participants.

We know that silver prints have a delight and beauty all their own. Yet, given the right image, the right direction, and the right tools, the digital darkroom can open new doors for creativity and expression. While I also learned that the digital darkroom is not always the answer, it is an excellent way for black-and-white photographers to complete the process that began when they released the shutters on their cameras. Of course, in a purely practical sense, it is the future, and it should be understood by all those who either make their living with or express their creativity through black-and-white photography.

I therefore offer this, the second volume of *The Digital Darkroom,* as a summation of what I have learned in the last two years of work and study, and as an exploration of the new tools that have come along to further refine the craft. As in the first volume, I will try to convey information by example. This is how I learned, and I hope it will prove fruitful for you. I cover a number of different types of printing, including various duotone options. I discuss contrast control, burning and dodging, and other important techniques. I explore various types of image emulation and create prints that are based on various alternative processes. And I explain retouching and restoration methods that can be used to rescue damaged prints. But as you see what I've done, remember that the best way to understand and explore this medium is through *doing it yourself.*

Adobe Photoshop, photo-quality inkjet printers, and the high-powered computers of today make the digital darkroom an exciting place in which to work. I hope that this book inspires you to begin or continue your exploration of your own vision and sense of craft. We are all engaged in this experiment. We are continuing and, we hope, extending a legacy of visual expression that goes back many years.

With a tip of the hat to those aboard and a salute to those who have gone before, let's begin.

George Schaub
Taos, New Mexico
July 2001

Calibration, Setup, and Materials

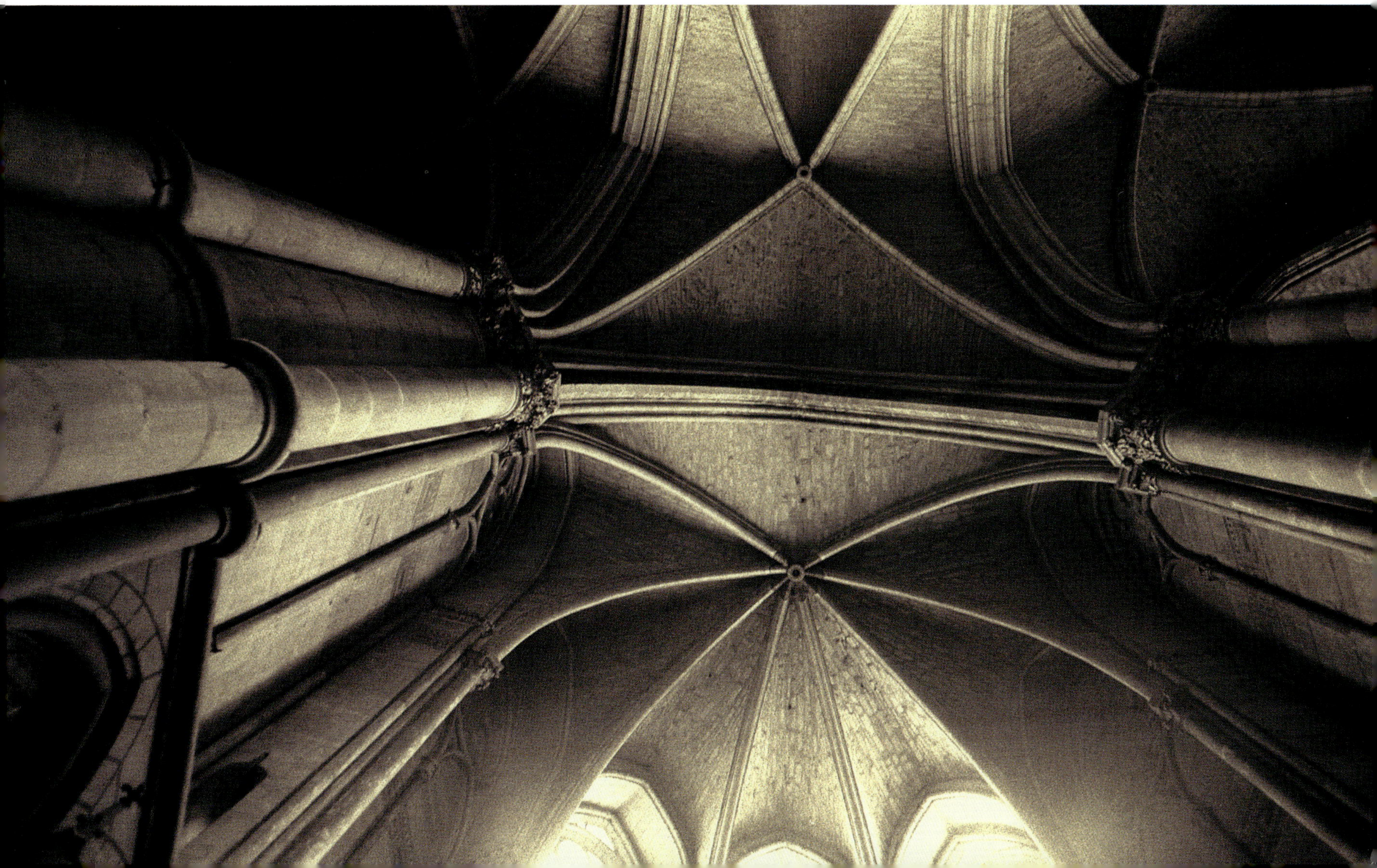

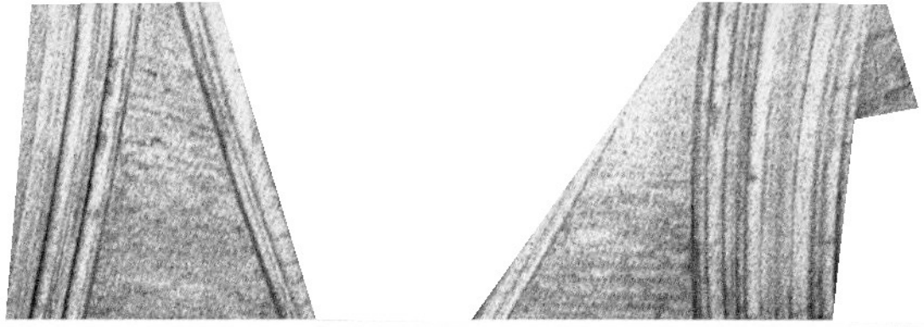

CALIBRATING YOUR MONITOR

Before you can start to make prints, or even acquire images from film and other sources, you must first pay close attention to calibrating the printing system. If you are working on your own closed-loop setup, this will be fairly easy using the steps discussed below. If you are working in a department with networked printers or monitors, it will be more difficult, and I won't address that knotty problem here. Consult any internal computer people available to you before beginning.

By closed loop I mean when it's just you and your desktop hardware: your computer, printer, and scanner or scanners. By networked I mean that there is more than one setup feeding into a printer or pulling images from a central server, images that are worked and sent back again. Every time I teach or work in a networked environment, my first task is to observe how each monitor reads the same image. Some read warm, some cold; others have a very different rendition of image contrast. Although the human eye and brain adjust to these different renditions, the central printer cannot possibly be expected to do the same. Despite the best efforts of smart technicians, this problem bedevils just about every multi-computer, shared-printer setup I've ever seen.

The goal of calibration is to get WYSIWYG (what you see is what you get) results. The image on the monitor should be more than an approximation of the output of the printer, just as the image information from the scanner should match what lands on your hard drive or other storage medium. Having worked on systems where I had to always factor in a 20% contrast difference or 10 points of yellow, I can assure you that calibration is worth the time and effort it might take.

Contrast and Color Cast

There are two aspects to calibration that are extremely important for the black-and-white printer. The first is *contrast*. If you are doing conventional printing, for example, and the paper you use is marked as a #2 grade and it prints as a #3, you would be right to be upset. But if the #2 always prints as a #3, you can adjust your thinking and selection accordingly. You can never be sure, however, that the #1 grade of that brand is actually a #1 or a #2. In short, you'd be okay with one set of circumstances but perhaps not so well off for many others, and this lack of consistency would get in the way of your creativity.

It's the same with contrast adjustments you might mentally need to make with a poorly calibrated monitor. They might work with one set of inks or type of paper and with one type of image, but not with any other set of materials or conditions. This is a situation that will lead only to frustration.

The second aspect is *color cast*. Much of the printing done here involves more than just black ink. In fact, the work is rarely done with black ink alone, relying instead on the effect of mixing color inks with black. When printing an edition set or series of images with one type of image color, such as sepia-tone emulation, having a monitor that's cooler (bluer) or warmer (more magenta) than what is required can be very frustrating. Yes, the color can be tweaked after the first print is made, but probably those tweaks won't be just right for other images and ink combinations.

In short, monitor calibration is very important for your work. Once you have attained calibration, though, you probably won't have to change it unless you alter the room lighting or someone manually adjusts the contrast and brightness settings. If you know this has happened, the first task you should perform is recalibration.

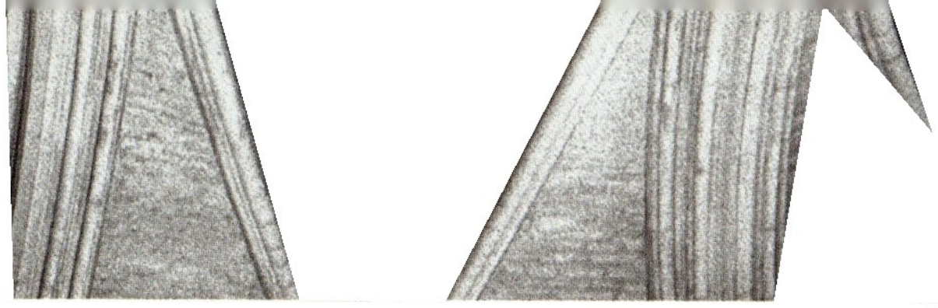

Procedure

Fortunately, Photoshop makes it easy to calibrate your monitor using ICC profiles and color management setups that coordinate the software with the hardware devices. For the most part, this works very well and requires little or no intervention on your part. If something's not right, though, the best way to attain calibration is to work within the Adobe Gamma utility.

Just follow the steps in the Photoshop manual. Here's a summation of what you have to do:

- Turn on the monitor and let it stay on for about half an hour. Start the Gamma utility, located in the Control Panels folder or the Photoshop/Goodies/Calibration folder.
- You will be presented with a dialog box with a gray square, under which sits a slider bar (Image 1). Follow the instructions in the dialog box to get a neutral gray.
- An option is to uncheck the View Single Gamma Only box. Another dialog box comes up with three color squares (Image 2). Move the sliders back and forth, and you will see how the color cast changes. Again, your best bet is to make the monitor as neutral as possible using your visual judgment. This may take some time, but you can play with the sliders until you get it right.
- Go to the White Point part of the dialog box in either option and click on Measure or select a default (I find bright white is best for my work). When you click on Measure, a dialog box appears. Click on Next or Continue, and the screen will go black and three neutral gray boxes will come up. Click on the box you think is the most neutral. For me, it's easy to see when a box is cool blue, but more difficult to see when it gains a warm color cast. Follow instructions on how to get the most neutral gray in the center and then click on it.

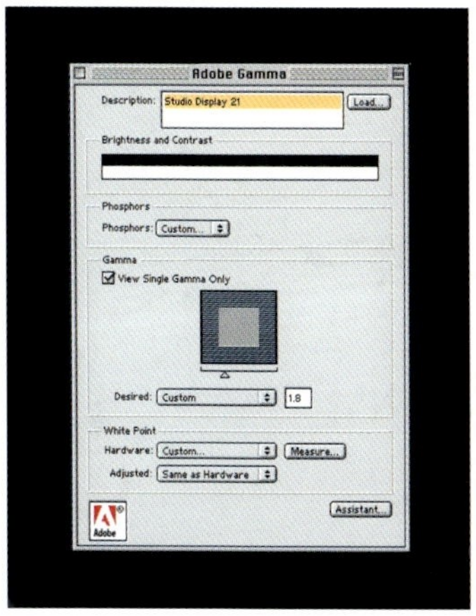

Image 1

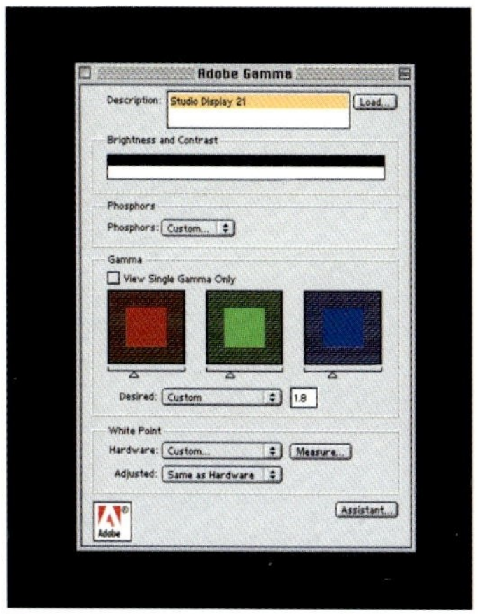

Image 2

That's most of what's involved with monitor calibration for your private printing setup. Once you've done it, the system should handshake with all the other devices, such as a scanner or printer, you might run through the monitor.

Of course, the proof is in the printing, so check your monitor image with your prints to make sure they are close enough so you don't have to second-guess every time you want a print to turn out the way the monitor displays it. Be particular about this. If the results are off, go back and calibrate again until one agrees with the other. Now is the time—before you begin the actual work—to eliminate frustration and wasted time and materials by calibrating your monitor.

Note that some versions of Photoshop may have different calibration steps, as do third-party calibration systems. Don't let this throw you. Just follow the setups described with your software or system and test it against the output.

SETTING UP YOUR PRINTER

Once you've calibrated your monitor, you should have agreement between it and your printer and your scanners. But there's one more very important step that helps you match monitor to output print, and that's checking the range of your printer so that the monitor shows you what will actually land on the paper.

Tonal Values

Think of how conventional (silver) printing compresses tonal values. Even though your negative may have a full tonal scale, you compress that scale of, say, nine stops in the negative to less than six stops on paper. In addition, after printing, you are viewing the image on a sheet of paper reflecting light rather than via light transmitted through film. That's a big difference alone in being able to see tonal scale. True, you can work within the range of that nine-stop scale to get your five-plus range of stops on the print; that's expressive printing's field of play. But you are still compressing that scale when you make a print. The same is true of digital printing. The advantage of digital printing, though, is that you can pretty much see on the monitor how that tonal scale will be compressed.

In the search for print snap or liveliness in silver printing, the tendency is to use too high a contrast grade. The same is true for digital prints. Too much contrast means loss of highlight detail and a harsh-looking print. But with digital printing you can predict and even measure when no ink will land in a spot, helping you avoid getting paper base rather than ink showing in any part of the image.

With conventional paper printing, you can fog the highlights slightly to add tone. In digital printing, you create highlight density through a thin shot of ink. If you can train yourself to watch for the highlights, to measure for them, and to preset your printer to catch them, you'll go a long way to solving one of the main problems of digital printing.

Shadow Detail

You may see the shadow details on your monitor, but when you make a print they lose tonal detail. Or, all the lower values bunch up and overlap. This type of print output is unacceptable, especially when it is so easy to overcome. Of course, if the digital image files do not have these tones (gray levels), then you cannot get them on the print. Burnt-up highlight pixels will just go gray and lost shadow detail will reproduce as dark tones. But if the detail's in the scan, it should be on the print—if you so choose.

Creating a Step Wedge

To check how the printed image matches the screen image, let's create a grayscale step wedge and print it out. Open a new file and make it 10 x 3.5 inches at 72 dpi. Choose Image >Mode >Grayscale. Double click on the Gradient tool and set the default to Black, White. Turn off Dither. Now hold on to the Shift key and draw a line with the mouse from one end of the New File window to the other, making sure it is a straight line and that it stops at the edges of the box. Now go to Image >Adjust >Posterize and type in 21. Look at the scale on the screen and see if you get separation between the tones and if your white has texture. If you've done it right, you should see the 21 steps on the screen.

Check where you begin to lose information in the step wedge. How many steps back do the white and black areas begin to differentiate—in other words, where does the tonal separation start to take place? Each step in the step wedge equals 5% of the output grayscale. With the settings I use, I recognize that a step is lost in the shadows and that highlights are good at 255 when going from my screen image to my printer. I adjust for that by previewing my image in the Levels dialog box at 10 and 255 output (output settings are at the bottom of the Levels dialog box).

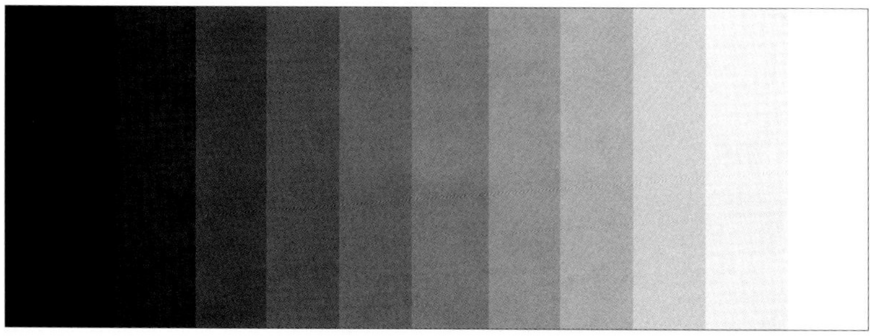

A step wedge helps you balance your monitor and printer and is an excellent way to judge what your printer can deliver. This scale holds 11 steps; you can break it up into as many steps as you require. You can also open the step wedge file and keep it on your screen as you print. Open a new file and use the Gradient tool to draw a line across it, then go to Image > Adjust > Posterize and choose the number of steps you want.

Will these settings work for you? Monitors, printers, the way each of us•scans—it all makes a difference in how images are previewed. The important thing is to recognize that calibration is vital to getting digital printing right. Keep whatever you have as a personal setup locked in.

Save the step wedge you've made and call it up once in a while. Some digital printmakers keep it as a constant companion on their screens, although I find that there's enough screen info to deal with without the step wedge sitting there.

TIP

To remove dialog boxes and other tool boxes and controls from your screen, press Tab. Press Tab again to bring them back. This is a great way to give yourself time for some unobstructed visual thinking with just your image displayed.

ACQUIRING AN IMAGE

In order to work on an image in Photoshop, or any imaging program, it must be in digital form. You can do this yourself with a scanner or a digital camera, or you can have an outside lab or digital service bureau provide the scans from any type of film. Our focus in this book is making digital output from film, but increasingly people will be working with files captured digitally right in a camera. Some are now calling digital cameras sources of *first generation* digital images, and film images that are scanned as *second generation.* This would be fine if today's digital cameras matched the quality of film cameras. The more expensive ones are getting close, but most of the under-$2,000 cameras have a way to go. In time, though, digital cameras may increasingly become good image sources as well. Digital is very ecumenical. As long as the image is digitized and the software can read the format, there's little difference in quality between sources.

Image Sources for Black-and-White/Duotone Printing

Any type of image source can be used for black-and-white and/or duotone printing. You can use black-and-white or color prints, black-and-white slides and negatives, and color slides and negatives. Converting all to monochrome is a push-button affair with Image > Mode>Grayscale, Image>Adjust>Desaturate, or Image>Channel Mixer. You might think that the preferred sources are black-and-white negatives and slides, but I have gotten excellent source images from color transparency film as well. If you need to get a black-and-white print from a color negative, scanning and converting is so much easier than working with panchromatic paper in the darkroom.

It is usually better to scan an original black-and-white negative than a print from that negative, even if the print has received a great deal of attention and handwork. The print may be great, but it also represents a compression of tonality that may be difficult to capture accurately on a flatbed scanner. Use the print as a guide for working with the negative and create a digital file from the original master image. Of course, if no negative exists, the print will have to do.

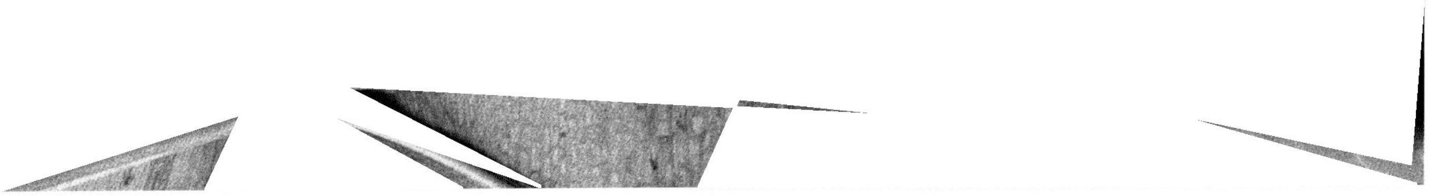

The most troublesome types of images for the digital darkroom have very high contrast; are overexposed (especially if the negatives are also overdeveloped, a common problem with mass photofinishing labs); are flat (low contrast and/or underdeveloped); or have any halation problem caused by flare or fogging. But these negatives, prints, and slides are also troublesome when working in the conventional darkroom. Although in many cases you can certainly fix problems easier in Photoshop, it is not a cure-all. I have seen many photographers frustrated by their inability to fix something in Photoshop because they think the program can do everything. True, it is pretty amazing, but it too has to play catch-up to turn a poor source image into something passable.

TIP
If you are working with contrasty negatives, make your tonal adjustment first in scanning and adjust it further in Photoshop. Try not to give Photoshop a straight scan of a problem negative.

I have changed the way I expose when shooting since I've gotten involved with digital printing, particularly in developing a critical eye when editing older images. I have become much less expressive in my exposure techniques, and rather than work for a certain previsualization of tones I do my best to photograph to get a good tonal spread without overexposure. I used to expose black-and-white negative film without worrying about overexposure too much, at least up to a stop or two, as I knew I could handle the negatives later in the darkroom. Now I tend to shoot in lower contrast conditions. If it is very contrasty I expose black-and-white film like slide film—that is, I bias exposure toward the highlights. If high-contrast conditions exist, I cut back on developing time to control the highlight density. This should be familiar ground to black-and-white photographers who process and print their own negatives.

If negative tonal control is new to you, check out books by Lootens, Feininger, Adams, and Zakia on such matters. I have also done books for other publishers on this topic—see the Internet for resources.

I also shoot a lot more with black-and-white slide film. I really like the way it scans. Agfa Scala is one such film. It offers excellent tonal scale and makes editing easy. I also have begun to shoot a lot more chromogenic black-and-white film, like Kodak Portra 400, as it handles contrast very well. When I develop black-and-white negatives I follow what I have always done: cut down developing time at least 20% from the manufacturer's recommendations.

I used to print with a cold-light head in the darkroom. This allowed me to work with more contrasty negatives, as this source eliminates the Callier Effect. This effect shows up with condenser enlargers and tends to emphasize negative contrast, as light rays penetrate the highlight areas less than the shadow areas. The cold-light head allowed me to overexpose a bit (great for shadows but sometimes tough on highlight rendition) without having to compensate in development. Some of these negatives are difficult to scan today, although working with the Curves control (tonal gradient) in the scanner can really help.

A NOTE ON FORMAT
When I describe where I accessed the tool or control, I write it as Tool > Burn > Highlights, Opacity 40%. This means I got the control from the toolbox and chose the Burn tool and modified the tool to work on highlights. The opacity is the degree of the effect, with a higher opacity meaning more of an effect.

If I write Image > Adjust > Hue/Saturation, 58/12/0, it means that under Image on the menu I chose Adjust and then Hue/Saturation; a dialog box came up and my settings were 58/12/0. If I write Image > Mode > Duotone > Tritone, black, Pantone® 1345CVC, Pantone 413CVC, I have converted an image using Mode under the Image menu and then set my three ink colors (two of them Pantone colors) as indicated.

DIGITAL CAMERAS

While digital cameras are quite convenient for quick prints, only those costing several thousand dollars are capable of delivering image quality good enough for making enlargements comparable to those made from film shot in even the most modest 35mm SLR. Those of you who can afford or who have access to the more expensive digital cameras should photograph using uncompressed TIFF or Raw mode and meter as if you have transparency film in the camera. In other words, avoid overexposure (overexposure can be checked on these higher-end cameras through use of the histogram feature after the photograph is made; in some, the LCD preview also shows blue or red "flecks" where the image has been overexposed).

Point-and-shoot digital cameras today can produce 10 to 12 MB files in Uncompressed mode and can yield good 5 x 7-inch or 8 x 10-inch prints. But Uncompressed mode eats up the camera's memory, and the lens and exposure-control systems often produce images that, to my taste, lack the visual pleasure of digitized film images. If you do work with a JPEG-capture digital camera, use only the lowest compression mode (usually 1:4) and always use Fine or the highest image quality recording mode.

The image resolution and file size are key when making prints, but they're just part of the equation. Exposure, lens sharpness, and file format have as much of a role to play. Of course, by the time this book is in your hands, all will have changed (again), and there might be an affordable digital camera that blows film out of the water. But even with such advances, most film photographers still have all their great film images yet to be printed.

Digital Scan Backs

Digital scan backs are similar in size and function to interchangeable film backs on conventional cameras. Such backs have allowed those with Hasselblad, Mamiya, Contax, Rollei, Bronica, and other medium-format cameras, or Toyo, Cambo, Sinar and other large-format cameras, to adapt to digital capture without purchasing new camera bodies. They also use the same lenses and accessories, albeit with some change in focal length coverage.

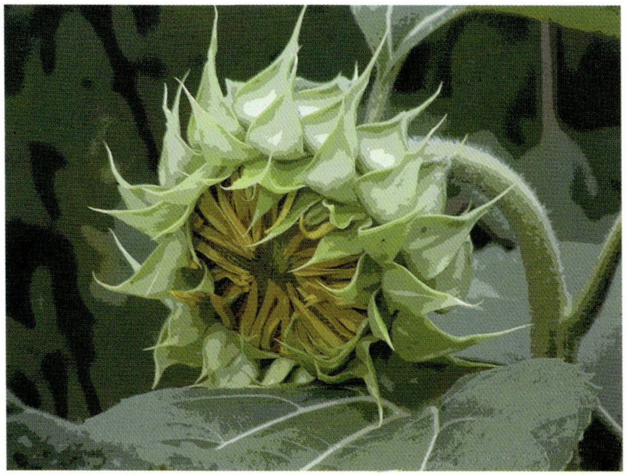

Although I work almost exclusively from scanned images—mostly film, occasionally prints—I have begun to explore the possibility of using a digital camera for source images.

This shot was taken with a Sony Mavica CD-R digital camera that creates a JPEG file opening at about 5.5 MB. Here is the original file. I "solarized" the image using a special-effects digital filter when I took the photograph.

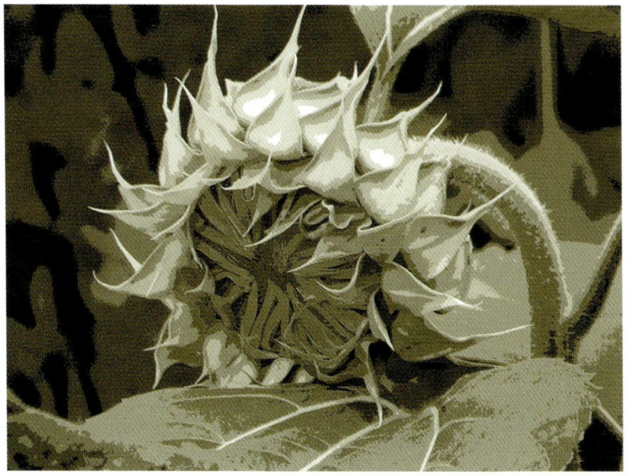

I desaturated—got rid of the color—by using Image > Adjust > Desaturate and then Image > Adjust > Hue/Saturation set at 58/12/0. That's a warm brown color at low color saturation.

These backs are quite expensive, but are a good choice for those who make their living from imaging and already have the front-end equipment. Some people have described these backs as drum scanners with lenses. Quality is quite high and prints made using these backs are excellent.

Digital scan backs are superb for scanning oversized prints in the studio or making digital images in the field. While I still prefer starting with film, the logic of using digital scan backs for copying is inescapable. Many photographers have begun to use these backs on their cameras on field shooting expeditions, and they make prints directly from the captured files. Again, the present cost of these backs makes them accessible only to those who can justify their expense through earning income by their use—or to those who simply have the money and time.

TIP
When converting to Duotone, you must convert an image to grayscale first.

Photo CD and Picture CD

Photo CD remains for me a viable form of outside service scanning. If you get a scan via drum or scan back or even flatbed or film scanner from an outside source, the scan will usually be of one size and one file format. This is fine if you know the end use of the image. If you change the output later, however, you may require another scan, especially for larger file sizes.

The Photo CD format yields a hierarchy of image resolutions, and thus file sizes. You get a package from each scan that can be used to output images for a Web page or e-mail (smallest to small resolution); up to an 18 MB file from 35mm images; and up to 72 MB for larger format images. The file format is proprietary but translates with no problem to Photoshop. The maximum output will depend on the type of printer you use and how it spreads ink, but the Epsons I work with do a very good job of producing the print size/file size output ratios given on page 26.

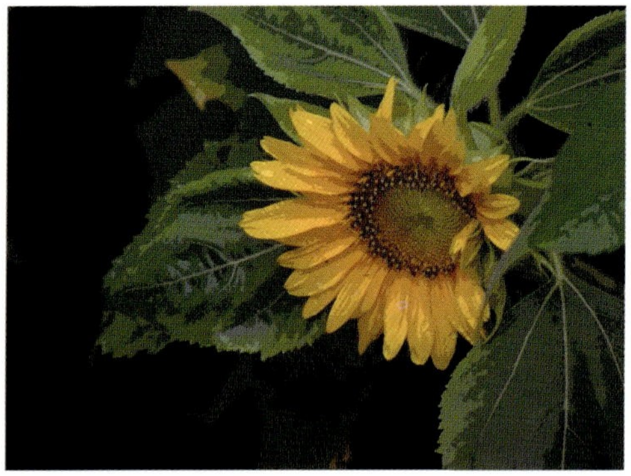

Another color photograph made with the Sony Mavica.

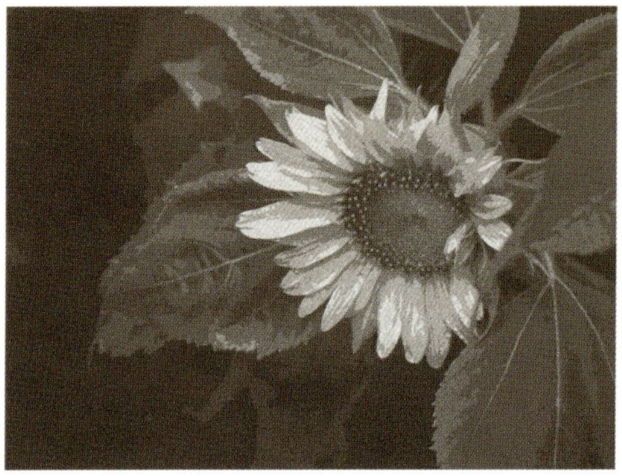

The image was converted to grayscale via Image > Mode > Grayscale and then to a tritone image via Image > Mode > Duotone. I chose a warm brown in Tritone with black, Pantone 1345CVC, and Pantone 413CVC.

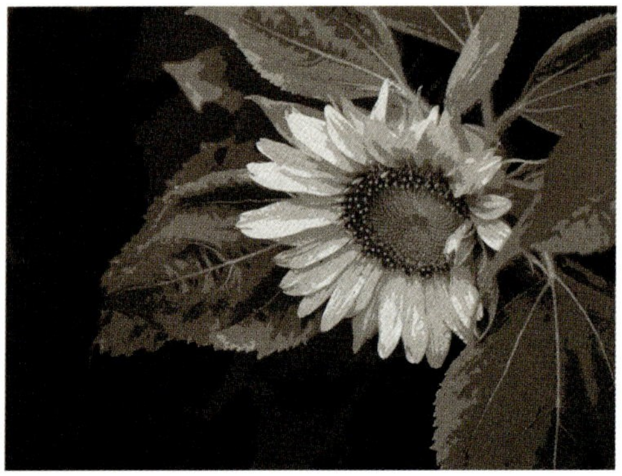

Finally, I opened Layer > New Adjustment Layer, Levels and worked with the middle gray slider to get the look I desired. This enhanced the contrast and completed the vision—all in three simple steps. To do such enhancement in the conventional darkroom would have been a long process, with many steps. The digital darkroom provides an easier route into such creative processes. It is a great medium for experimentation, as it allows for visual trial and error.

You get Photo CDs from labs and service bureaus with a Photo CD workstation and order them just as you order reprints. But there is no cropping or fine-tuning of the images, as you might do if you scan the images yourself. All scans are performed as color files, even those of black-and-white negatives and slides. Starting with a color scan and converting to monochrome is simple enough. A conversion from RGB to Grayscale/Duotone mode reduces the image file size by two-thirds (from 18 MB to 6 MB, for example), but the image resolution remains the same. Photo CD scans of color transparencies are a very good source for black-and-white printing.

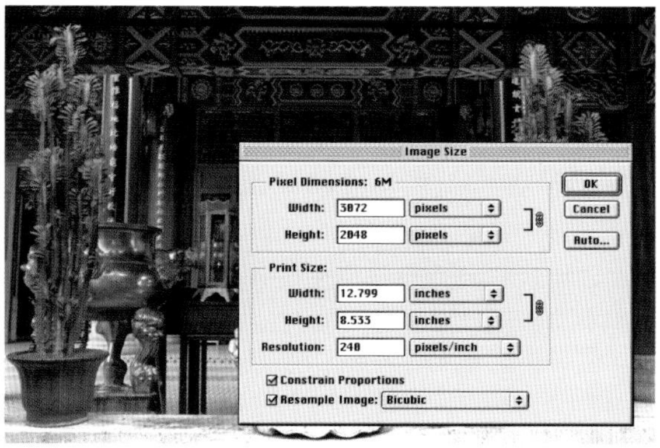

Photo CDs offer a set of resolution choices from each scan. The different file sizes available are expressed as pixel resolutions. I chose 3072 x 2048, an 18 MB RGB file. When converted to grayscale, the file size is 6 MB, good enough for a 13 x 8.5-inch print.

The Picture CD is another matter. This is the photofinishing industry's answer to image digitization, one that now comes as an option on every 35mm and Advanced Photo System film processing order. Each image is scanned at about 1.5 MB in size, too small a file format for making other than 4 x 6-inch snapshot-size prints. As of this writing, Picture CD scans are not available from black-and-white, slide, or chromogenic film, or as a reprint order.

SCANNERS

A scanner is essentially a copy machine. If you deliver a poor copy to Photoshop, you will have to work so much harder just to get it to where you can begin to think about being creative. If all the prints, negatives, and slides in the world were just right, a very functional and straightforward scan would be fine. But many prints and negatives have some problems—underexposure, burned-up highlights, faded areas, scratches, and so forth. The scanner software can be used to fix some of these problems before the image is delivered to image-editing software.

There are two stages to scanning: a preview (preliminary) and a final scan. Before making the preliminary scan (a quick appraisal scan that is used for cropping and other adjustments), you set up the software for the image at hand. Each software program is different, so I'll try to be as generic as possible here. I also encourage you to read more about scanning in texts dedicated to the subject and online help sources. If you are going to be doing image adjustments other than basic cropping and resolution setting when scanning, you must make tests and gain experience before you start scanning every negative in your files. You should not assume that everything will work out fine using the same procedures for each image.

TIP
Competition has driven most poor-performing scanners and scanner companies out of the marketplace, but you still get what you pay for. Higher priced scanners may have better software bundles, more facility for multiple print scanning on the same glass plate, or other desirable features. As with all equipment, check sites on the Web for end-user appraisals.

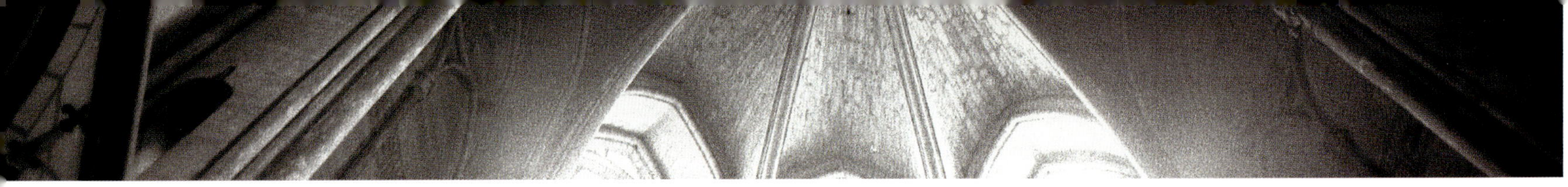

Flatbed Scanners

A flatbed scanner looks and works like an office copy machine—that is, a CCD array passes across the surface of the print or object and digitizes it, line by line. The flatbed can be used to scan printed material, photographs, old prints, glass negatives, tintypes, daguerreotypes, and images mounted on cardboard.

Flatbed scanners come in all sizes and resolutions. The least useful for copying old photographs and image objects is the sheet-fed variety, which more resembles a fax machine. Because this type of scanner passes the image over a reading surface, rather than passing an array over the image, it won't work for fragile or mounted images.

Grayscale and RGB. Most scanners offer either Grayscale or RGB color mode. They may also offer black-and-white scans; avoid them. Black and white to a scanner or in prepress means just that: black and white. No grayscale, no tonal distribution. It's fine for graphs and text, but useless for photography.

Grayscale usually means you'll get an 8-bit scan and a file size to match, even though the scanner may in fact be scanning in RGB and converting to grayscale before it hits the monitor. Those 8 bits are what happens on the output side. If you begin with a higher bit scanner, such as 36-bit, which captures 12 bits per channel, that 12 bits of information will revert to 8 bits on output, although you have more room to play in image manipulation before output. Just as a negative always has more tonal information than a print, the fact that there is more tonal information in the scan means that there's more room for interpretation in the digital print. That's why full-scale negatives are best for scanning, and are always better than those exposed expressly for a given dramatic effect.

The bigger the tonal space, the greater the room for interpretation later. If you put yourself in a tonal or contrast box from the beginning, you paint yourself into an expressive corner. It may be a good corner, but it might not always be where you want to finish with that image. Although you may sometimes know exactly where you want to take an image when you scan, you'll find that you may change your mind from time to time.

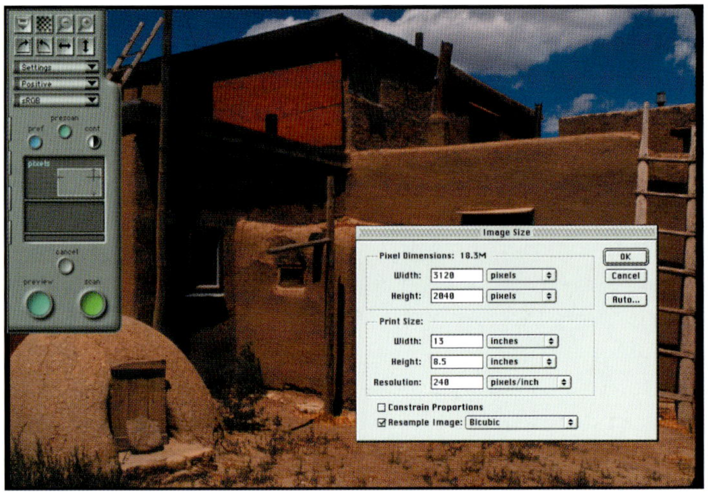

Scanner software will generally help you decide how to set up the numbers for the scan, but you have to know just what it is you want to do with the image first. I plugged in two sets of numbers: the resolution I wanted (240 ppi, to match the desired resolution for my printer) and the image size I wanted, about 13 x 8.5 inches. The scanner calculated the rest and gave me an 18.3 MB file.

Some people scan grayscale images in RGB and then choose a channel from the RGB for grayscale work. Or they scan in RGB and then construct their grayscale using the Channel Mixer in Photoshop. I have tried this, and yes, there are different renditions in each channel, but I can also get them by working with contrast in Levels or Curves. The Channel Mixer is fun, and I encourage you to try it. It takes some time to get right, but you can get excellent translations of RGB to Grayscale files with it.

One reason that you might choose to work in grayscale rather than RGB scanning for black-and-white prints is the resultant smaller file size. An RGB scan of the same image at the same resolution and size is three times the size of a grayscale scan: for example, a 6 MB scan in grayscale equals an 18 MB scan in RGB. Both of these scans have the same resolution.

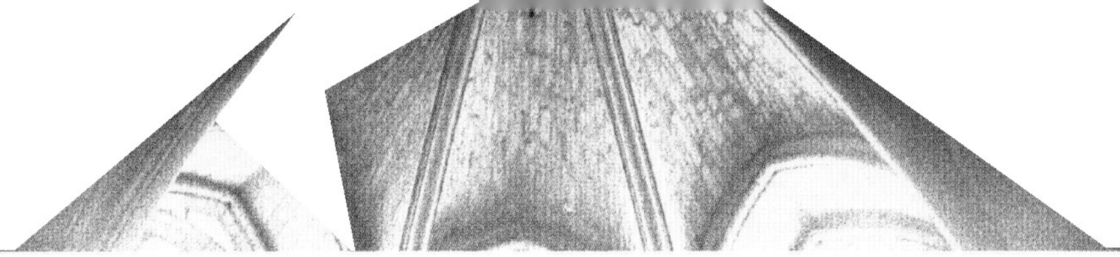

Smaller file size means faster working later, even if you have a revved-up computer. It also saves space on whatever storage media you're placing the scans. But if you do scan in RGB, it's a simple matter to convert to grayscale after you get the image into Photoshop.

Often the subject matter and its conditions determine the grayscale/RGB choice. If I am scanning an old print on a flatbed scanner that is in excellent condition, I might choose RGB so that all the nuances of image color and tone are captured. While ink mixing in Duotone mode can emulate virtually every color or tonality of old prints, the unique surface characteristics (patina) of an old image might be better captured by working in RGB. If that image were damaged, however, I would scan in grayscale and retouch and emulate the color after the digital repair. If I'm working with a hand-colored image I'll use the same criteria.

Most flatbed and film scanners come bundled with software that allows you to make adjustments to the image prior to importing it to Photoshop. There is a debate over just how much adjustment should be made in the scanner and how much adjustment should be left to Photoshop. I try to balance the two.

Settings. Scanners usually ask for some of the following settings: mode, original, input, scale, range, tone curve (gradation), speed, or quality. I always set scanners—and printers—to optimize quality at the expense of speed. As for material type, prints and other image materials are reflective (the image is read by reflected light); slides and negatives are transparent (the light passes through them).

Even if you decide to leave the scanner on the factory default settings, one thing that you should always do in the preview stage and in scanning itself is to crop out extraneous image information, including borders and uneven edges, from the image. Blank areas and print borders add to the file size, so when you crop out unwanted image area from the scan, you are decreasing the file size—always a good thing. Cropping is done in the preview stage by moving crop areas into the image. Most scanners have standard right-angle cropping tools; others may have ovals or other selection setups.

Some scanners may only scan in RGB mode. This is no problem for black-and-white images and prints, as they are easily converted later. Some scanners may not have a Grayscale or Monochrome mode, and therefore will have trouble with black-and-white negatives. With these scanners, the best method is to scan the black-and-white negative in Positive mode and then "flip," or reverse, it later in Photoshop.

Tonal Curves. Think of tonal curves as the "developing" stage of creating a digital image. In film developing, you can alter the contrast rendition of film by changing the time and temperature. In scanning, you can change the contrast by playing with the curves. You can also do this later in Photoshop with the Levels and Curves controls, but doing it at the scan stage delivers a working file right to the desktop. Some scanners allow for real-time curve previews, while others require you to apply the curves and hit the OK button before you see the results.

Play with the curve shape to see what happens when you move the shoulder or toe or shift the midtone area. In general, scanners are pretty well calibrated to pick up a good average of white-point and black-point settings and give you a good scan. If, however, your image is extremely light or dark, if there's excessive "silvering" or tarnishing, or if there are areas of specular highlights (bright highlights that can go paper-white), the scanner will react like any metering system and get thrown off.

If that happens, you will have to intervene and set the black and white points yourself. They may be called "Dmin" and "Dmax" settings. Just click on the option and follow the steps. Do not set the Dmin setting at the specular highlight, as this will drive down the other values considerably. Think of how you meter for scenes with a film camera, and this will guide you in your black- and white-point settings.

TIP
If you have both a negative and print of an image, scan from the negative, even if the print is perfect.

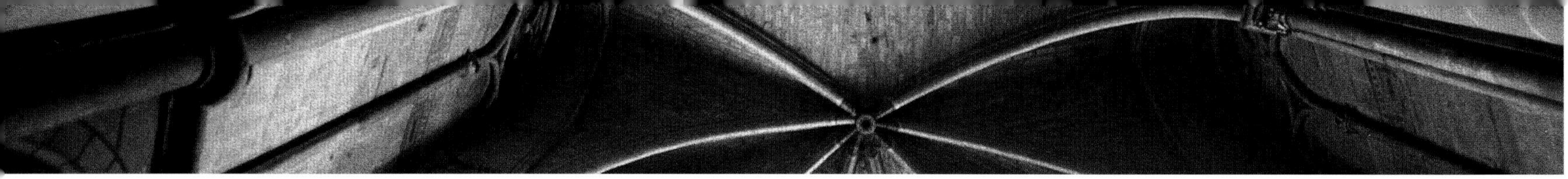

Calibration. You can calibrate scanners quite well by using test strip software or working with various film types. Any good full-scale image will do. Scan first at the default (factory) settings and compare the monitor image with the hard copy. Make sure that the scanner is set for 300 dpi, or whatever its true optical resolution.

TIP
If you do not calibrate your monitor, any changes you make to the scanner will only multiply your problems with a given image later.

Film Scanners

Much of what applies to making scans with flatbed scanners also applies to film scanners. The main difference is that the desktop film scanner has the capability to deliver much higher resolution from film images, which is necessary because the film will inevitably be enlarged. The film scanner I use can deliver a 28 MB RGB file from 35mm film. It also has a higher dynamic range than my flatbed scanner, which allows me to get more shadow detail and a broader range of tones overall. Although that tonal range and breadth is compressed when I make prints, it still gives me more room to play.

I am usually amazed at the detail my film scanner delivers, especially when I compare the image on the screen to a print I may have made previously in the darkroom. A number of printmakers have also reported the same amazement. Two things contribute to this difference. Few people have seen their images enlarged and backlit (meaning illuminated by the phosphors on the monitor), which brings out quite a bit of previously unnoticed detail. And even though the monitor image shows less range than is available in the scan, it does allow you to move around within those tones with ease.

When you open a film scanner window, you will be presented with a number of options for scanner settings, including color or grayscale mode, resolution and/or image size output, scale, tone curve, and black- and white-point settings. When you first begin, keep the tone curve at 45° or work with the factory defaults. As you gain experience, you probably will want to set the curve bowed slightly out or slightly in, depending on your negative and taste for scans. (Bowing out raises contrast, bowing in lowers it.) Your best bet is to experiment with different negatives and different tone curve settings to see results.

Drum Scanners

Traditionally, drum scanners have produced the highest quality scans and biggest image files, and thus they have been the choice for reproduction houses and Iris print shops. Most print-for-pay ateliers and service bureaus prefer drum scanners. Costs vary, but generally the drum scan is the most expensive you can get. There's no doubt about the quality, though, and if you are going to have an image made large and the work done by a service bureau or atelier, you won't go wrong with a drum scan. I don't know anyone except a very busy commercial photographer who can afford the cost of a drum scanner.

Scanning by Photo Labs

When you bring an image for digitizing into an Iris print shop or digital service bureau, it is handled according to its form and what you'd like to have done with it. If it is a negative or slide, it will be scanned using a film or drum scanner. If it is a print, it may be scanned with a high-end flatbed or drum scanner. If it is a large print, it may be scanned with a digital scan back on a medium format or 4 x 5-inch camera body.

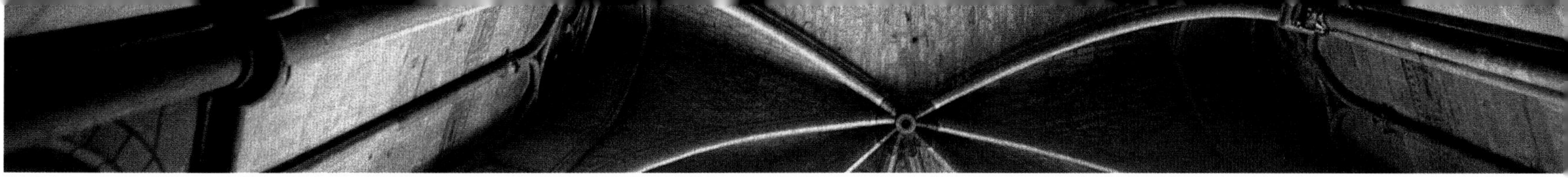

RESOLUTION AND OUTPUT SPECS

One of the main tasks in digital printing is setting resolution and output specs. This is where digital imaging asks you to think ahead. If you are scanning your own images, you must be aware of how you want to output them—and if you do not do this step correctly at the scan, you will have trouble when you make a print. It is therefore essential that you decide upon your output requirements when you scan your film. You can do this through either setting image size and resolution or simply setting file size.

Scanner Ratings

Like any digital capture device, scanners have a resolution level at which they perform best. This value is expressed in dots per inch (dpi). Generally, the higher the resolution capability, the finer the detail and the more subtle the tones the scanner can capture. The scanner rating should indicate *true* or *optical* resolution, as opposed to an interpolated (based on approximated digital file size expansion) rating; beware of any claim based on the unit's interpolated rating. Another scanner rating that should be checked is its dynamic range—the ability to pick up a certain tonal (and sometimes color) range in an image. For flatbed scanners, a dynamic range of about 3.2 is fine.

When using a scanner for print output (as opposed to output for the Web), use the highest optical resolution the scanner offers. While this may be more than you need for the print at hand, you can always change it later. Keep in mind, however, that if you double the resolution in scanning you are actually quadrupling the file size. Images also can be scanned at lower than maximum resolution when required; I use a 600-dpi scanner for most of my work, though I often set it at 300 dpi.

Making the Calculations

When you set up a scan, the easiest way to figure the numbers out is to consider the output dpi of your printer and the size at which you want to make the print. Then you can input those numbers, and the scanner software will calculate the file size and resolution specs for you.

In general, if you're working with a 300-dpi scanner, set it at 300 dpi. If in doubt about the resolution you need, just follow the formula given on page 26 for image size and use the calculator in the Image > Adjust > Image Size dialog box in Photoshop. Your scanner software probably has the same guides for input and potential output sizes.

Through experience I have found that I get excellent prints at about 240 dpi. Your printer may give you the best results at slightly higher or lower settings. When I make a film scan, I consider the size of the print I want to make. The print size I usually make on my Epson inkjet printer is 11 x 14 inches. I plug in those numbers. At 240 dpi at 11 x 14 inches output, I get about a 22 MB (RGB) file, or about 7 MB in grayscale. If I am doing general scanning, I'll use those numbers because I can always reduce the image size later. I can also get a bit larger in print size from this file.

If you want to change the tone curve, do so, but generally leave it at a straight 45° angle. If you have an underexposed print, you can change the curve shape to enhance contrast, but remember to reset it when you are done so it is not applied to the next image you scan.

Because resolution can also refer to the number of pixels per inch (ppi) in an image, it is a relational number—it exists in conjunction with a certain image size. So a 1 x 1-inch image at a resolution of 80 ppi has 6400 pixels. But that same image at 200 ppi has 40,000 pixels. More pixels mean more image information—as well as the ability to make a larger print that will hold continuous tone and not exhibit jagged edges.

The only time I'll rescan the image is if I need to send an electronic file to a magazine or book publisher. Before I rescan, I'll find out the resolution required and the size they usually reproduce on the page. A fine-art magazine, for example, requires 300-ppi resolution. This represents a relatively high line screen, as opposed to a newspaper or some other magazines that might use a lower line screen reproduction and thus require a lower resolution.

Be sure to check with the end user before you submit scans. Test your own equipment and see what resolution the user needs to get the best results. You will want to know what resolution they require in ppi and what size they anticipate the image to be on the page. Publishers are used to working in lpi (lines per inch). If that's what they give you, just multiply it by 1.5 to get the resolution you need to set at ppi.

Scanner and Photoshop software offers an easy way to handle all the math. Type in output sizes or numbers, and pixel dimensions are automatically calculated. In Photoshop you'll find the calculator at Image > Adjust > Image Size. There you can plug in numbers to your heart's content. If you do not set any resolution numbers, Photoshop, and perhaps your scanner, will save at screen resolution—72 ppi. This is not what you want for prints.

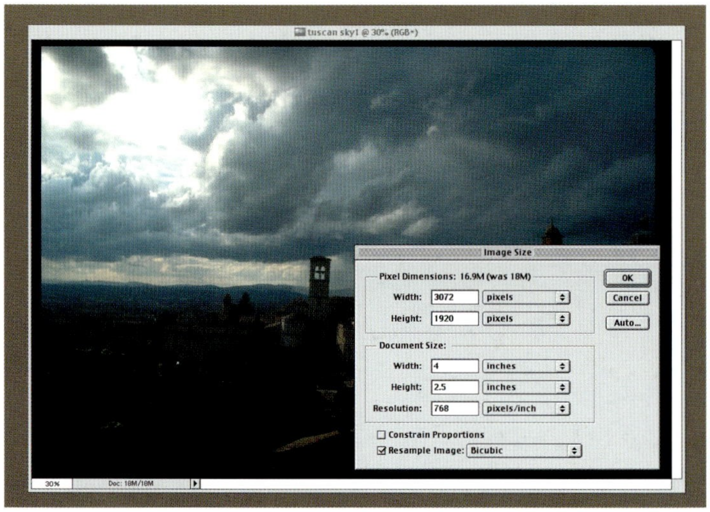

B. The output resolution at 768 dpi shown above seems impressive, and you would think that it would make a super-defined print. This resolution, however, is wasted on most printers. Besides, the print size is only 2.5 x 4 inches.

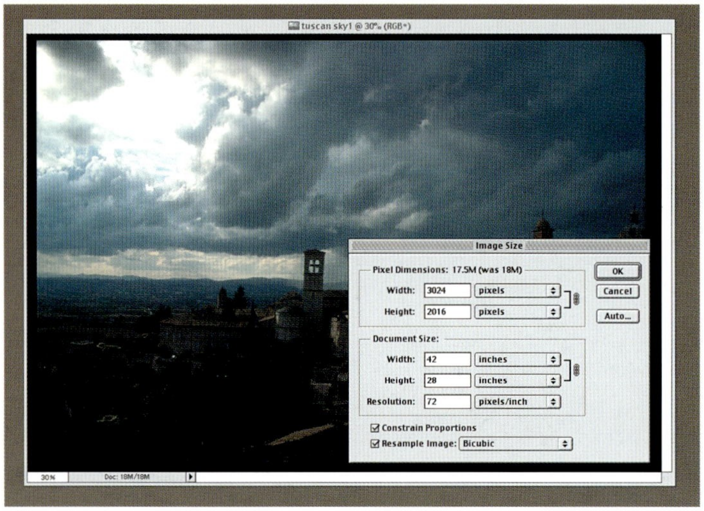

A. When you first open an image in Photoshop, it will read out the file at screen resolution, 72 ppi. At 72 ppi, this 18 MB image would read as 28 x 42 inches. That seems large, but it's screen resolution; it would look very bad as a print. Output resolution for a printer is usually between 200 and 300 dpi.

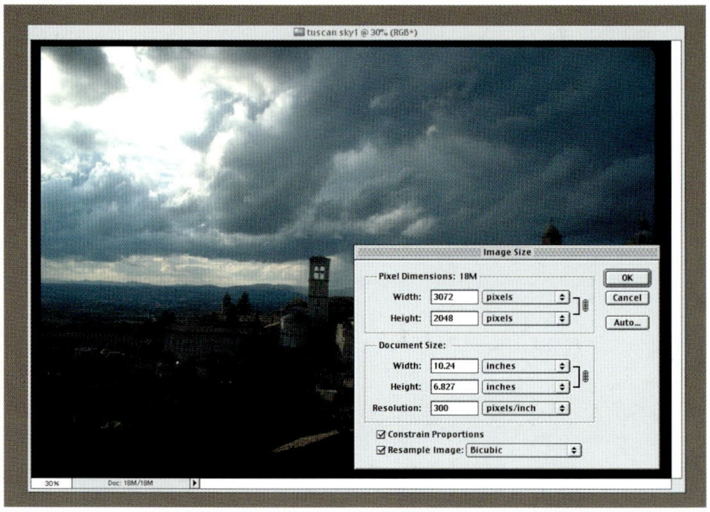

C. At 300 dpi, which seems optimum for some printers, you get about a 7 x 10-inch print.

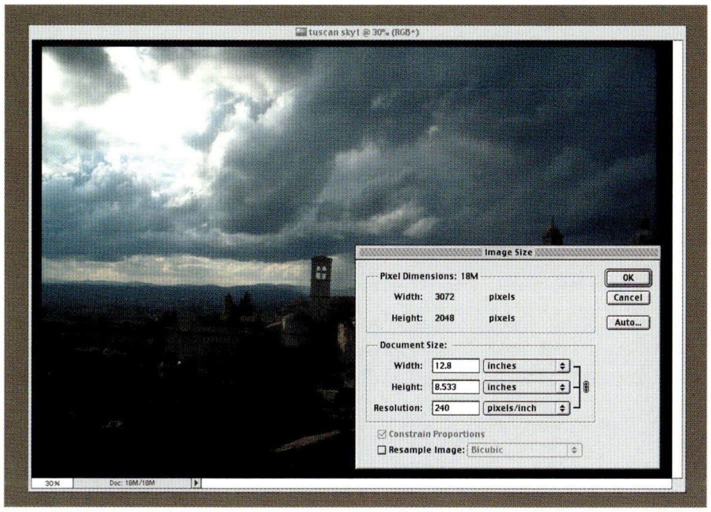

D. Tests have shown me that my Epson kicks out great prints at 240 dpi, and at that setting output is nearly 8.5 x 13 inches.

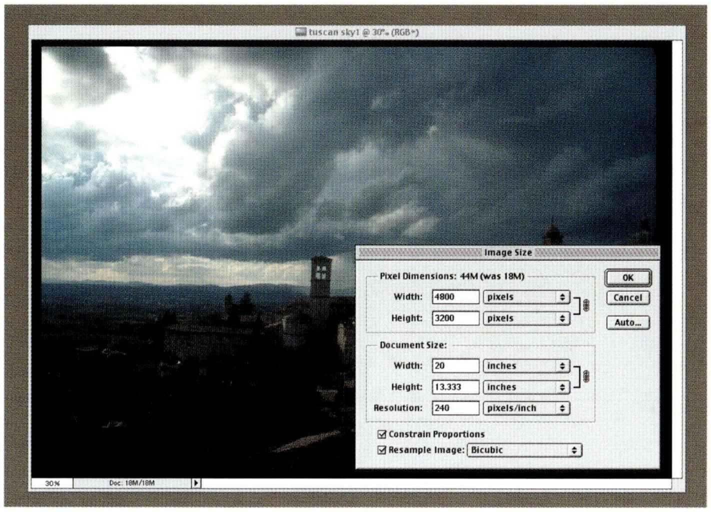

E. Although sometimes risky, you can squeeze out a bit more print size by resampling (adding or subtracting pixels) the image size. Check the resample box, and don't forget to constrain proportions, which means that the aspect ratio (relation of height to width of the image frame) will remain the same. Here, a resample up to 13 x 20 kicks the file up to 44 MB. Study and work with this dialog box and it will teach you all you need to know about the file size–print size relationship. Plug in any set of numbers and the others will automatically change for you.

It's All Relative

It bears repeating: The three output values—file size, resolution, and print size—are interrelated. File size, which relates to the resolution of the image at a certain print size, is the number that has a K (kilobyte) or MB (megabyte) attached to it. The larger the file size, the more likely you will be able to get a better quality print. If you have an image file of 6 MB and one of 18 MB, you will get a better 8 x 10-inch print from the 18 MB file, all other things being equal.

The Image Size dialog box is your guide to understanding the resolution–file size–print size relationship. Use it as a calculator before you scan (if your scanner software lacks it) or as a way to make choices from your scans.

But there's a catch. If you are making a 2 x 3-inch print from the same two files, the 18 MB file may not produce any better results than the 6 MB file. That's because the 6 MB file probably has enough information to give us a very good small print.

For printers, this only makes sense when you figure in the resolution of the printer you have and at what resolution that printer will yield very good results. The two are often different numbers. For example, it might be thought that because you have an X-dpi-capable printer that the best results will happen when you set that resolution in your Image Size dialog box. In fact, the dpi you can set is often considerably lower than the "ideal" number, whatever that might be.

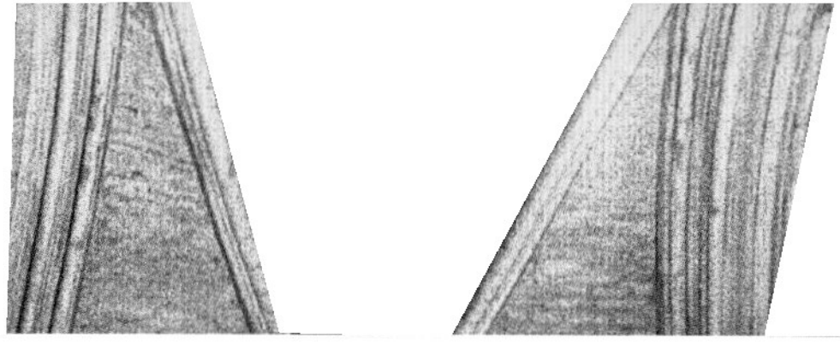

Getting the Best Output

Many photographers think it optimal to set some inkjet printers at 300 dpi. But the Epson printers I have worked with (the 1200, 1270, and 2000P) give me just as good results (that is, results I can't differentiate from higher settings) at 240 dpi, a 20% saving in resolution. And I've even resampled images as much as 30% to get a larger print size at 240 dpi and still obtained great results.

Twenty and 30% might not seem like a lot if you haven't worked with digital images before, but it is, and there are many ways it can save you time, money, and especially energy. Let's look at how the 20% difference in required printer resolution translates to being able to make larger prints with "smaller" file sizes, at least when compared with the "ideal."

Here's the formula: Pixel dimensions/resolution = image (print output) size. Say you have a 5.46 MB grayscale file with 1948 x 2935 pixels. You can see the file size if you open the image folder as a list (in Mac), as a preview, or at the bottom of the image frame when the file is opened.

At 300 dpi you get a 6.4 x 9.7-inch image; at 240 dpi you get an 8.1 x 12.2-inch image. If you resample the image up to 12 x 18 inches at 240 dpi, you get a 12 MB file at 2880 x 4339 pixels. Be aware, though, that the law of diminishing returns is in force with resampling, and there is a point beyond which the image will degrade. Resampling creates assumptions about new pixels, then creates them; success depends on the intricacy of the image you're working with. But I have done it to print larger sizes when I thought it wasn't necessary.

Don't worry. I'm not very good at math, and you don't have to be either. All this is figured out for us in the Photoshop Image Size box under the Image menu. Open the box and plug the numbers in yourself. What the dialog box will not tell you is just how much you can get away with and what numbers to start with. This will come from testing and understanding the capabilities of your printer.

As you begin to work, you will appreciate being able to squeeze larger print sizes out of smaller files and being able to use lower resolution numbers to calculate print sizes. Smaller files mean less space taken on your hard drive and faster processing times in every step along the way. Until someone figures out how to get fantastic prints from 100K files, this is what you have to do.

Below are the figures I use when I play with print sizes in relation to file size. They may or may not work with your printer, but try them out. I use these figures when selecting an image size from a Photo CD hierarchy or when making my own film scans.

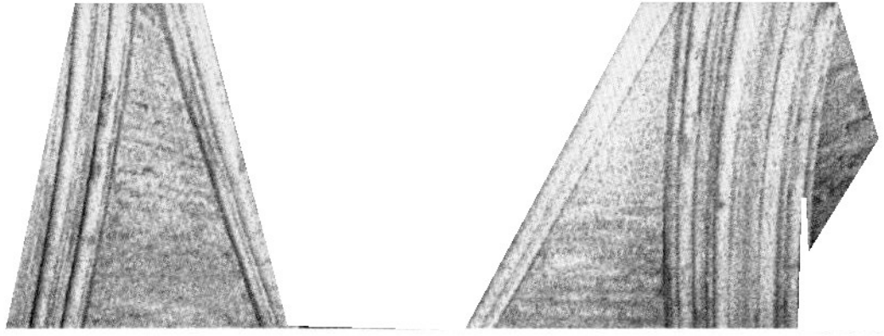

SAVING AND OPENING SCANS

You need to organize and save your scans for storage and easy retrieval. Choose the file format for saving scans with care. According to scanning mavens I've talked with, TIFF is the best choice, as it handles grayscale best. Most scanners acquire images right into Photoshop for you (if they don't, don't buy or use them), and you can then save them as TIFF or Photoshop files.

However you get your image to digital form, the first step in working with it is opening it on the screen in Photoshop. If you have saved your image to a CD or Zip or to your hard drive, open Photoshop first and then open your file from inside Photoshop. If you are reworking an image and have already saved it in the Photoshop file format, the program should automatically open when you open the image. If you are acquiring an image from a scanner or digital camera or other source inside Photoshop, it will come in through the Import > Acquire route under the File menu.

Once you have the file on your screen, it may or may not have a meaningful file name, depending on how you accessed and acquired the image. Some images will have just numbers on them. Before you do any work, I suggest you do a Save As on all images, identifying them so that you can find them easily. Place your renamed Save As files into folders that are organized and labeled for ready access and retrieval. The Save As files then become your working files. (If you work with a Photo CD, you can't do this, as you cannot write over the Photo CD with any changes you make on the image.)

Once you've saved your scan to a Zip or hard drive, it is a good idea to keep the original scan as is and make separate files for subsequent images. As you work, you can use Save a Copy in the File menu, or you can open the History palette and drag a copy of the document at any stage to the Copy or Duplicate area and name and save the file that way. I often do that when I want to keep a definite record of various stages of image work.

Those of you with computer experience know the importance of saving often, as freezes and crashes will destroy any work not saved—a source of much frustration and one of the more hateful aspects of working with computers.

Creating Contact Sheets

Think of an image file as a negative, one that you store carefully for both protection and later retrieval. When you begin you might not have many files to work with, but that will change and the files and storage media will grow. If you work with a Photo CD, you get an index (or thumbnail proof) print along with the scans. This is very helpful in locating images. Photoshop gives you a way (see screen and instructions, page 28) to make a similar contact sheet, one that can be stored with a Zip disk or CD you might create for images on which you have worked.

I use contact sheets for job folders as a way to keep track of specific essays, and I keep them just as I keep contacts with my negatives. I include the picture caption or name when I print out the contact. I always send a contact along with image files when sending work to magazines and publishing houses.

Before you create a contact sheet, you need to name your working files as Save As files and create a folder for them. You can do this when you scan or when you save images in Photoshop or TIFF format. I suggest that you place all similar images, all images from a portfolio or a job, in the same folder. Creation of a folder is essential, as the folder is the source for the contact sheet creator to find images.

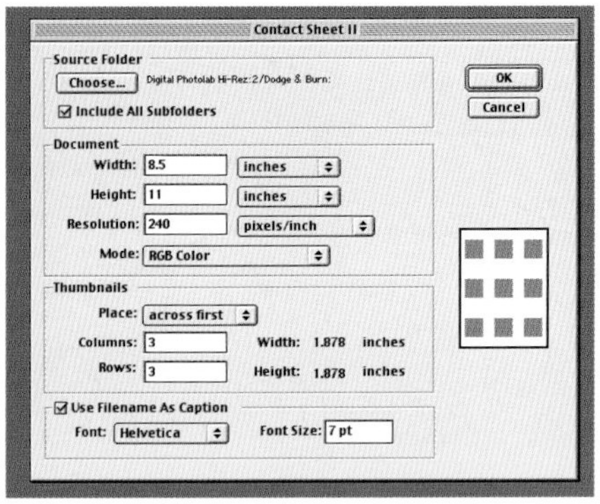

Creating contact sheets.

Go to File > Automate > Contact Sheet. You will get a dialog box asking you to choose the source for the contact sheet images. Go through the branches of your file tree to find just the folder you need and choose it as the source. The dialog box then asks you to choose a format for printing by rows and numbers of pictures in the row. Type in a few different arrangements; you'll notice that the image dimensions become smaller as you add more images to the sheet. Try to keep the images bigger than a 35mm frame, or 1 x 1.5 inches, so you can read them properly.

The contact sheet shown above holds nine images in 35mm frame size, good enough for filing and retrieval. I make contact sheets for every file folder of images that I burn to a CD.

Don't be concerned if there are more images in your folder than there are on a contact sheet page, as the program will just start another sheet of printing paper to continue the work.

PAPER

One of the great joys of working in the digital darkroom is the newfound and growing varieties of paper. The choice in silver black-and-white printing papers has become quite slim, in fact, with many surfaces and brands disappearing or becoming hard to find. While there are a few good papers left, they have become quite expensive for most people. RC (resin-coated) paper is fine for proof sheets and other functional images, but it has never been a favorite choice for the fine-art or even the avid hobbyist printer.

With digital printing, you can now work with fine-art papers of all sorts from many different manufacturers, ranging from smooth lustrous surfaces to watercolor buff stock. You can also work with functional photo-quality inkjet paper when required.

My love of printing has always involved the enjoyment of working with many different types of paper. My work with alternative processes had less to do with an interest in mixing my own emulsions than it did with having access to many different papers for printing. The digital darkroom has brought back paper choice as an exciting part of printing again.

Types of Paper

Here's a quick review of some of the printing papers I have used.

- ***Glossy, Photo-Quality Inkjet.*** This is the standard paper for printing color prints, snapshots, commercial work, and work for scanning from prints for reproduction. It yields the sharpest rendition of all the papers, which may be good or not so good for the image; it may be too contrasty for some work and eliminate some tonal subtlety. But it yields the deepest black and whitest white. If I am doing prints that will be scanned for reproduction, this is my choice.

- ***Matte Heavyweight, Photo-Quality Inkjet.*** The matte surface tends to tone down the contrast, yet still delivers an excellent tonal edge. It holds the ink as well as the glossy stock and is most suitable for nature, scenics, and even some portraits. It is probably not suitable for most commercial work, when the print will be scanned for reproduction, illustration, or some portraiture. Blacks are deep and whites are bright, but not as deep or brilliant as on glossy stock.

- ***Canvas, Textured, or Other Art Papers, Photo-Quality Inkjet.*** Even though textured papers with a rough surface are usually not a good idea with inkjet printers, there is a class of art papers with a textured surface that is designed to hold the inks well. Some of these papers are made specifically for hand coloring with photo oils, although most inkjet papers are not. Use these as you would use such surfaces when making photographic silver prints.

- ***Fine-Art Papers.*** Paper companies now make a great selection of high-end papers for inkjet printers. These papers come in a variety of weights and surfaces. Many add a luxurious feel to inkjet images and, because they are usually acid free, aid in the image's longevity. Iris printmakers often use these papers. They are considerably more expensive than stock or standard inkjet papers but may be worth the price for certain select images or editions.

- ***Generic Art Papers.*** The least expensive choice, generic art papers for standard printing may be used for inkjet printing if they are coated properly. Check with the seller or distributor. I have had very good luck with some of these papers and enjoy the variety and selection. Most come in a number of shades and base colors, something the branded papers have yet to pick up on. Keep in mind, though, that these papers do not offer the long-term stability of some of the others.

- ***Special-Effects Surfaces.*** You can also print on fabric (silk-like material), transparent sheets, and other types of media. This option may be attractive to those who use their images for multimedia projects.

Silver Gelatin and Digital Processes

The difference between a silver gelatin and a digital photographic print is in the nature of the image formation. In a silver gelatin print, the exposure and development of silver grains form silver images. When you look at a photographic print, you are looking at millions of these grains joined to create the illusion of a continuous tone. The difference in density or degree of exposure and development is the difference in tonal values.

Inkjet prints, on the other hand, are composed of dots that are literally sprayed onto the paper. Though "sprayed" implies a pretty random placement, in actuality the dots created are very, very small and are placed with amazing accuracy. The density and placement of these dots are what create the effect of a continuous-tone image.

The main difference in appearance between a digital inkjet print and a silver print is that the silver image seems to come up through the paper. The light-sensitive material in the paper that receives the image is what in essence creates the image. The silver halides are already coated on the paper, awaiting exposure by a light source projected through a negative.

Because inkjet printing starts with a blank receiving sheet that is then coated with ink, there is no inherent emulsion or light-sensitive material awaiting exposure. The only requirement for that blank sheet is that it is coated or treated so it can receive the sprayed dots into the paper without too much diffusion. In addition, the ink and paper should work together so that the ink does not smudge or require a very long drying time once it's applied.

But digital ink prints are not the same as silver photographic prints. A silver print is going to come only from a darkroom. The digital darkroom is a different visual—and at times visceral—experience.

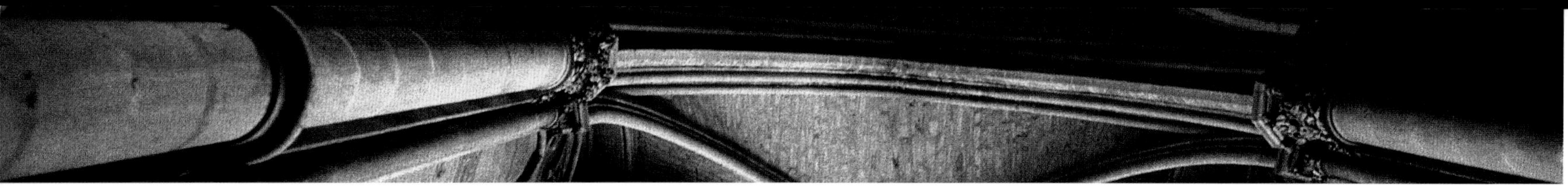

Choosing a Paper

The choice of printing paper can have a profound effect on results. I will often work an image differently according to the paper it will be printed on. Those who have worked in the darkroom, or who have done silk-screen or wood block printing, know what effect paper choice has. It is the same with digital printing—although inkjet printing has more to do with using inks than it does with photographic printing.

Failure to work with dedicated papers will certainly lower the quality of the printed image. I have used a number of papers, those branded and specifically designed for inkjet printing and more generic coated papers that are available in bulk in major art supply stores or on the Net. If you are shopping for a generic paper, ask a specialist in the store if it can be used for inkjet prints. If they give you a blank stare, use a touch test. Run your finger over the surface of the paper. If it feels hard or slick, it is probably okay for inkjet prints. Too soft a paper with high texture (and absorbency) will absorb the ink too much and diffuse it, thus ruining the print.

Papers can have a profound influence on the long-term stability of an inkjet print. Recent developments in dedicated inkjet paper along with specific ink sets have created ink/paper combinations that match standard photographic paper longevity. One- to two-hundred-year pigmented ink and paper sets, which certainly rival black-and-white prints processed to archival standards, are now available as well. Some papers and inks don't even come close to these standards, though, so keep aware of developments in this area. Keep tabs on Web sites dedicated to inkjet printers or type in "inkjet printers archival standards" on a search engine.

Paper surface and base color also have a great effect on the image. Just as in photographic printing, there are differences in how an image will look if it's printed on glossy or matte stock, or if that stock has a brilliant white or cream base color. I often print duotone or sepia images on a warm paper base stock to enhance the image. I always print commercial work or work for reproduction on glossy stock, but rarely use it for gallery works. Your personal choices will be based on taste and tests.

Paper Handling and Storage

Most branded papers I have worked with come with instructions advising against getting too many fingerprints on the surface prior to printing; that, of course, is just plain common sense. I have found, though, that the few moments after the paper emerges from the printer are critical. Have a space where you can set the print flat to let it "dry," and don't place anything on top of it. You can stack dried prints a few minutes after they emerge from the printer, but it's best to place them inside individual sleeves for best protection. Note that some papers require overnight "setting" before they can be stacked. Check the specifications that come in the paper packages for instructions and advice on this matter.

Care and storage of prints requires that they be kept in a safe place free from folds, bends, spills, and excessive handling. You can place prints in portfolios with acid-free backing and sleeves, or in print drawers with similar separators. Like all prints, avoid storage in areas of excessive humidity.

Matching Paper and Printer Settings

Check the instruction sheet that comes with your paper to ensure that you are properly matching paper type with the printer setup. Mismatches may cause poor ink dispersal or banding. If no instructions are included, test the various paper types in the Print Setup dialog box to see which works best.

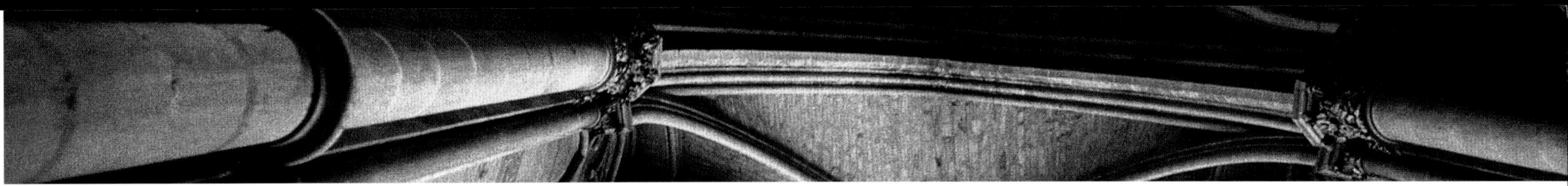

INK

The ability to emulate and even expand on potential image color possibilities in the digital darkroom is exciting. Anyone who has struggled to maintain consistent image color throughout an edition or portfolio, or who has tried a variety of toner dilution to get an image just right, will particularly appreciate it. The ink options available today are one of the most important elements in expressive digital printing.

The study of prints made by photomechanical means other than conventional darkroom methods also reveals the amazing image color possibilities of the photographic image. Platinum, palladium, cyanotype, Van Dyke brown, and even photogravure show very seductive image color effects. Some of these arcane methods, often referred to as alternative or personal processes, are kept alive by a dedicated core of artists. While digital ink mixing cannot hope to obtain the patina of the images obtained with such alternative processes, they certainly can emulate the look and visual feel—all without mixing dangerous chemicals.

The image color of even a conventional black-and-white silver print is rarely just black, white, and grayscale shades. It may be warm or cold, neutral or toned. Over many years, printmakers and chemists have created paper and developer combinations, as well as after-printing toners, to add additional color to monochrome prints. Image color variations might have been attained by using a warm-tone paper and warm-enhancing developer or a cold-tone paper and mild dilution of rapid selenium toner for a harder bright white, deep-black effect.

Some companies make ink sets that could be described as "warm tone" or "neutral" black. These have a mix of inks that can be used to give a beautiful black-and-white silver-print emulation.

Inkjet inks are made by a number of manufacturers with varying claims for fidelity and longevity. This is a technology that changes all the time, but happily the trend is toward longer-lasting ink-and-paper combinations. Inks must be replaced quite often and are quite expensive. I generally use the inks made specifically for the printer itself and try to avoid refills and other options, as inkjet heads are geared toward working with a particular consistency of ink.

Mixing and Using Inks

Although this book is about grayscale printing, I find that using black ink alone lacks the tonal vigor of printing with color inks. There are times when I use black ink alone, but it is becoming a rarer experience. I usually make my prints in RGB printer mode. This may sound like a contradiction, but I have taken to mixing inks in Duotone mode to get a better image "color" and more vivid tones on the prints.

In fact, I have never considered black and white a strictly grayscale visual experience. Every paper has an image color that makes it anything but a grayscale set. The papers I mention are in some cases no longer available, but their beauty was as much in the image color as in their tonal scale rendition. Agfa Portriga in Kodak Dektol had a somewhat green cast, one that defined a visual mood and set; in Kodak Selectol Soft, it had a luxurious warm tone. Agfa Brovira in Kodak Dektol with a touch of selenium toner was a cold blue, a hard, steely look—not really neutral. Kodak Ektalure in Selectol had a soft, warm aura. In the past, albumen papers had a look in the lighter tones that approached ivory. Warm-tone papers combined with warm-tone developers were creamy (almost yellow) white and an umber black. Toners created a whole rainbow of possible image colors from blue to copper. Cyanotypes, ambrotypes, tintypes, platinum—all these images had a coloration that was and is anything but grayscale black and white.

Grayscale or RGB?

There are two choices when working with black-and-white images. One is to print using the Grayscale mode and the other is to print using RGB, or color mode. This might be a matter of taste, but if you are working with a file in Grayscale mode, you can print in either, depending on how your printer works. Some images look fine in grayscale; others create a weaker looking print than one printed as RGB. If you have converted your grayscale file to duotone or have scanned a toned image into RGB, then work with the printer in RGB mode. I print almost all my work using RGB inksets.

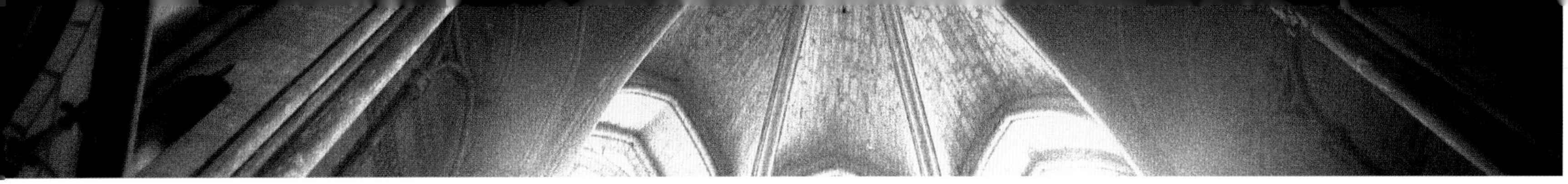

If the only prints you've seen are in books and magazines you might think I've lost touch, but those who have made fiber prints or who have studied the work of other printers by looking at actual prints will understand exactly what I mean about image color. The best resources for this visual feast are museums and collections, original prints and books that pay attention to this subtlety of color and tone. Books printed with black ink alone show the history of the image content, but they rarely match the beauty and sensuousness of the print. It's this beauty and depth that I always hope to obtain in my digital prints, and that's why I rarely print in Grayscale mode.

Duotone Mode

When you work in Duotone, you actually have a choice of working with two inks, three inks, or four, called, respectively, duotone, tritone, and quadtone printing. These inks can be composed of black and colors, such as Pantone, or black and shades of gray. You can build these colors and black and gray combinations yourself, or you can easily pick from the Adobe set in a folder that comes with the program. I like to mix my own, then save them as fixed combinations (sets). This comes in handy when I'm making edition copies and want consistent colors from one print to the next.

The first ink in the setup should be black, followed by other color choices. To choose the other colors, click on the color boxes in the Duotone dialog box. The color picker will come up on the screen. You can choose from the overall or the Custom picker. Try both to see which best suits your needs. Once you open the color picker you can move the circle around the entire color range. If you see an exclamation point, it means the color is out of gamut (the range of color a device can reproduce) and usually will not reproduce as you see it on your monitor.

When you choose a color, you get to see what it will look like right on your screen image. You can choose one, two, or even three colors in addition to black. After you have chosen a color, you can play with how it distributes itself in certain tonal values in your image. You get to see this by clicking on the curve box that sits next to the color box in the Duotone dialog box. As you change the curve, your ink is placed in different ways. Move the curve around and you'll see the difference right in the screen preview. Change the curves. If you leave them all the same, you will not benefit from the effect. The degree of control you have with the duotone colors is incredible. You get to choose both color and color intensity in different tonal areas. Experiment with this control, and you'll be amazed at the variety of image color selections you have from the choices in the ink distribution in the various tonal areas in the print.

Metamerism

When using a pigment-ink printer, you may experience a color shift when viewing the print under different light sources. This effect, called "metamerism," is inherent to the nature of the inks themselves. When using these printers, keep in mind the conditions under which the print will be used, and work and test using similar viewing conditions.

Drydown

Some inksets have a "drydown" effect similar to that experienced with silver prints. Always let a print set before you do an edition to ensure that it matches your expectations. In addition, check the instruction sheet that comes with the paper and note whether the ink/paper combination needs to set before it's finished.

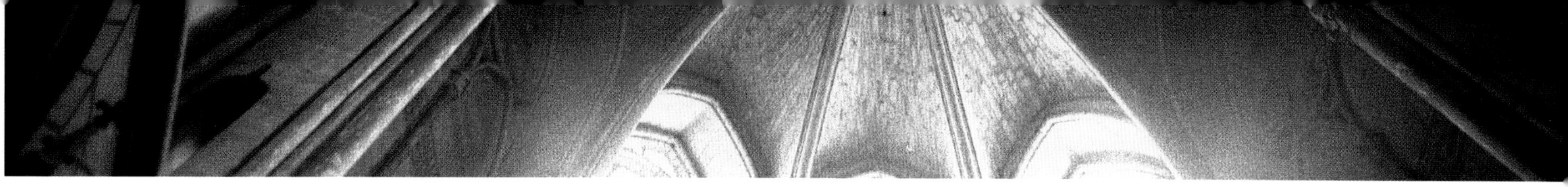

LONGEVITY

The need for a print to last a certain amount of time is determined by its end use. If you are making prints for reproduction or proofing, they need to last as long as the project. If you are experimenting with various printing techniques and want to maintain a catalog of results, you may want the prints to last longer. Keep in mind that the digital file will (usually) outlast the print, and it can always be used to create more prints. If you are selling prints, however, you need to make the buyer aware of how certain conditions speed print deterioration. You should also be clear about what your true expectations of image integrity and life span will be.

If you carefully process a black-and-white silver-halide print to archival standards, you can sell it with the confidence that if your buyer treats it right it will outlive both you and the buyer, even if you're 16 years old at the time of sale. That's not the case with many inkjet prints. Even the vaunted Iris print (especially those made prior to 1998) won't last for more than 15 or 20 years—although, as of this writing, new ink sets have added more years to the time.

There are two duties I have always considered important in this area. One is to make buyers aware that they have a part to play. If they display any print in a sunny room, it will fade. If they display the print in a room with high humidity or odd fumes (such as a beauty parlor or smoky bar), it will discolor. If they mount it on a non-acid-free board, it will discolor. If they store it properly in a dark area, however, it will last longer than even the tests predict.

Your other responsibility is to make buyers aware of just what they are purchasing. I do my best to find out what the expectations are for a certain ink and paper set or combination. I purchase and use the best materials I can. I lobby for longer lasting combinations and support those companies that do the research and development in the field. And I let buyers know the facts.

How you handle all this is up to you. Happily, the demand for longer lasting ink and paper combinations is having an impact on manufacturers. Keep in mind that many of these inkjet printers were first used as proofers rather than output devices for exhibition prints. The transition from prepress to printmaking device is moving forward at a fast pace. As of this writing, many print/ink combinations can easily boast a 30-year life span. Companies are doing research and have reportedly developed a 200-year ink-and-paper set. This is very exciting news for printmakers and the print marketplace.

Let's Get to Work!

I've covered a lot of ground here, but think of it as a preamble to what follows: working on images with the tools and techniques of the software. Some of what has been discussed may be clear to you already, while other aspects may be a mystery. As you work with your images, all the discussion of resolution, mixing inks, curves, and the like will begin to make sense.

Each of the image lessons that follows is intended to explore tools and techniques. Although I've tried to keep the information in neat categories, you'll notice that the tools and techniques tend to spill over into one another. That's just how this stuff (creativity and inspiration) works.

Apply these lessons to your own images and give yourself time to play and experiment. Getting digital images into your computer is fairly easy. Knowing what to do with the image once it's on the screen might be another matter. Printmaking, whether it's silver or digital, always comes to the point where the circle you began when you first snapped the shutter nears completion. It is an expressive process that usually reveals just as much about you and your vision as that split second of exposure when you first recognized and acted upon your visual instincts.

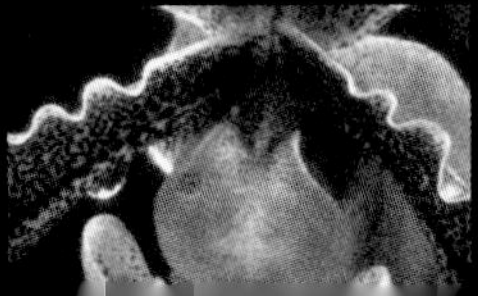
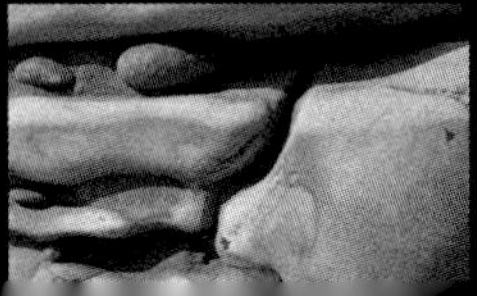
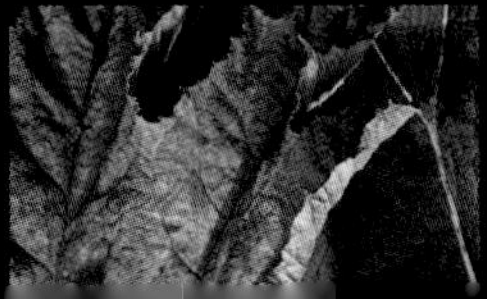

Image Workshops

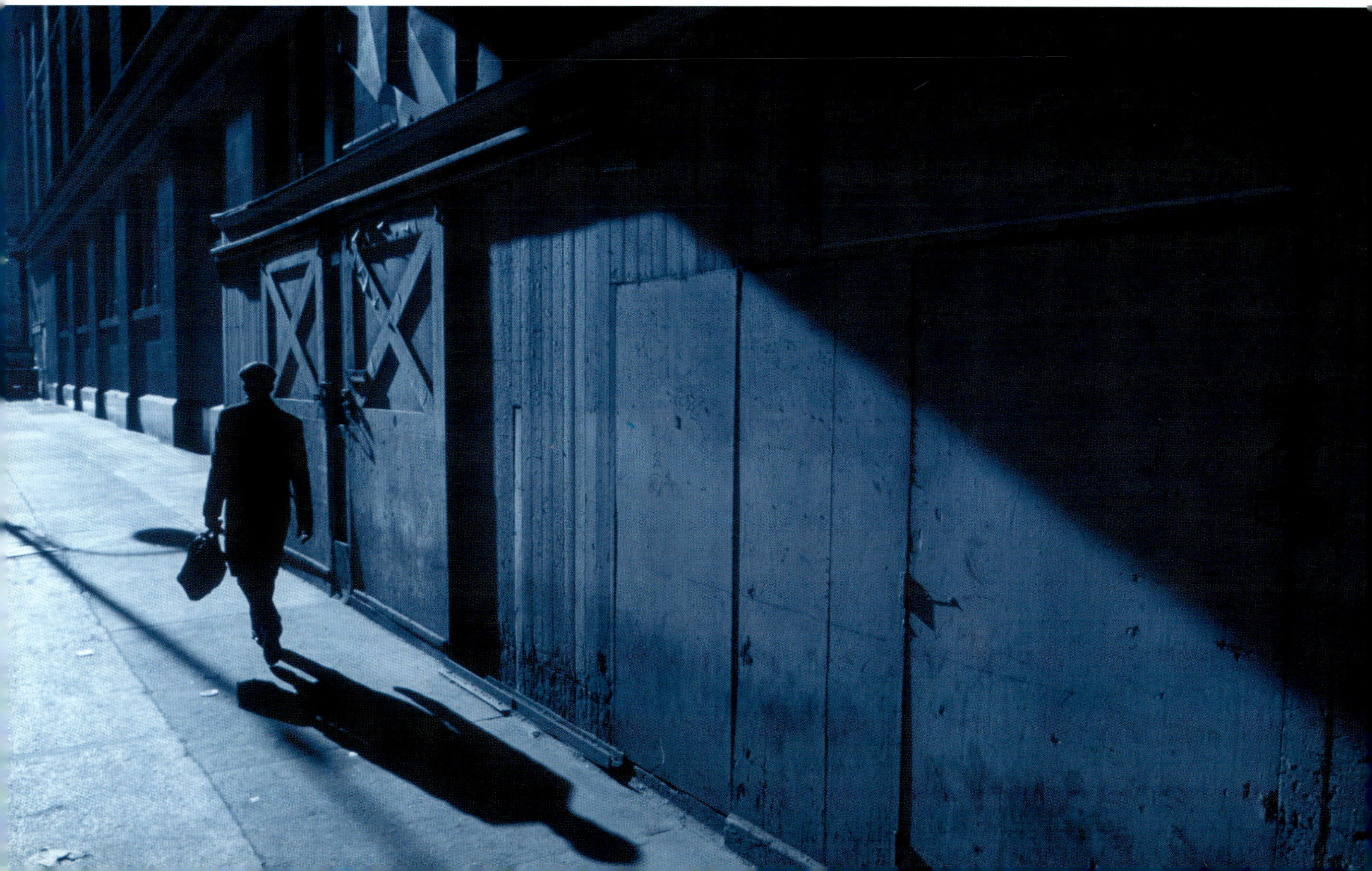

Variations

One of the quickest ways to make changes, and a great way to see just what you can do inside Photoshop, is to open and explore the Variations tools. You get to Variations by following the Image > Adjust>Variations route. This opens a dialog box with a "ring" around the image you have chosen. You'll see a number of adjustments, including a Fine to Coarse slider (an opacity control for the effects) and choices for lighten and darken in the highlights, midtones, and shadows (Variation A). In some cases, all you might need to do for an image is open Variations and make a few adjustments.

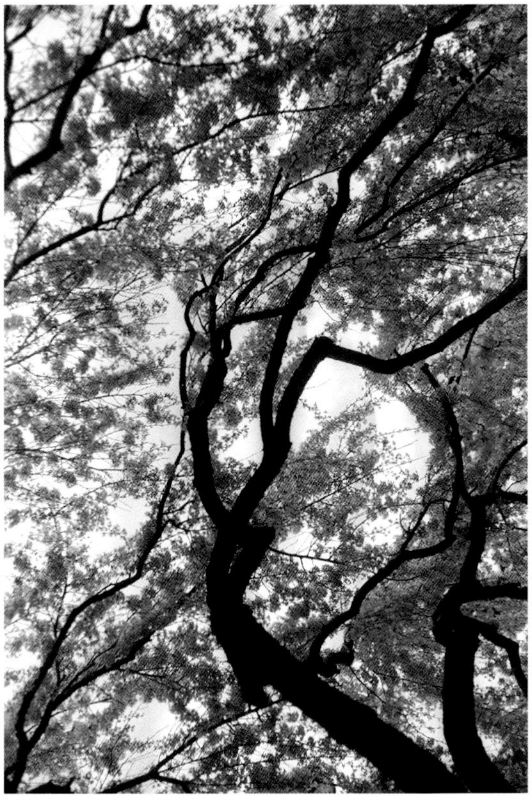

A

VARIATION A

I recommend Variations to anyone who wants to see how an image can be changed. In this sequence, you'll begin with a scan from a 35mm black-and-white negative.

VARIATION B

I have made this print several times in the darkroom and usually work with a lower grade paper to alleviate the harsh tones and create a more delicate, airy feel to the leaves. With Variations, I accomplish the same thing by choosing the Lighter variation on Midtones. When you choose a variation, the software shows you the original and the present state of the image.

VARIATION C

I liked the changes but wanted to take it a step further, so I chose Lighter Midtones for three clicks. Then, I pressed the Lighter square of the image three times. Each time, the present state changed.

VARIATION D

Because working with Variations is so easy, you are encouraged to experiment. Here's another version, done by switching the selection to Shadows. I did three clicks on the Darker square control to get this effect and finished up with another two clicks on the Lighter square, with Midtones chosen.

TIP

You can work with Variations as a layer to try out the effects before flattening the image. Open the Layers dialog box by going to Window > Show Layers and then click and drag the Background to the Copy Layer symbol (the one that looks like a folded piece of paper) at the bottom. This will create a background copy for you to try out your effects. You can also alter the degree of the effect by dragging the Opacity slider in the Layers palette from 100% down.

B

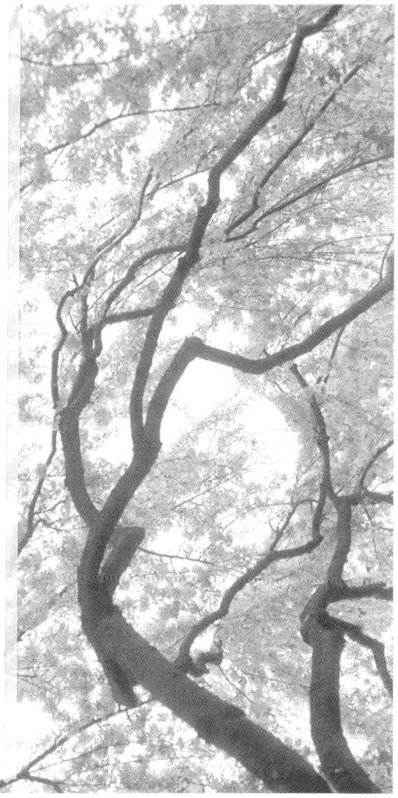

C

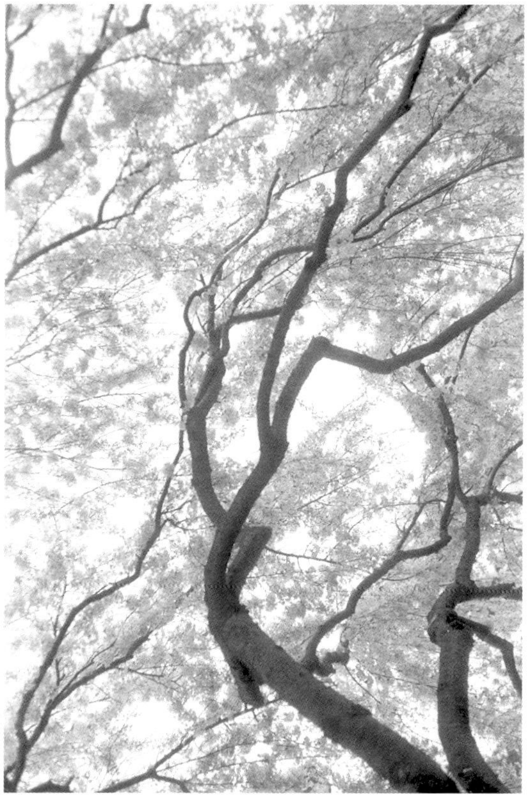

D

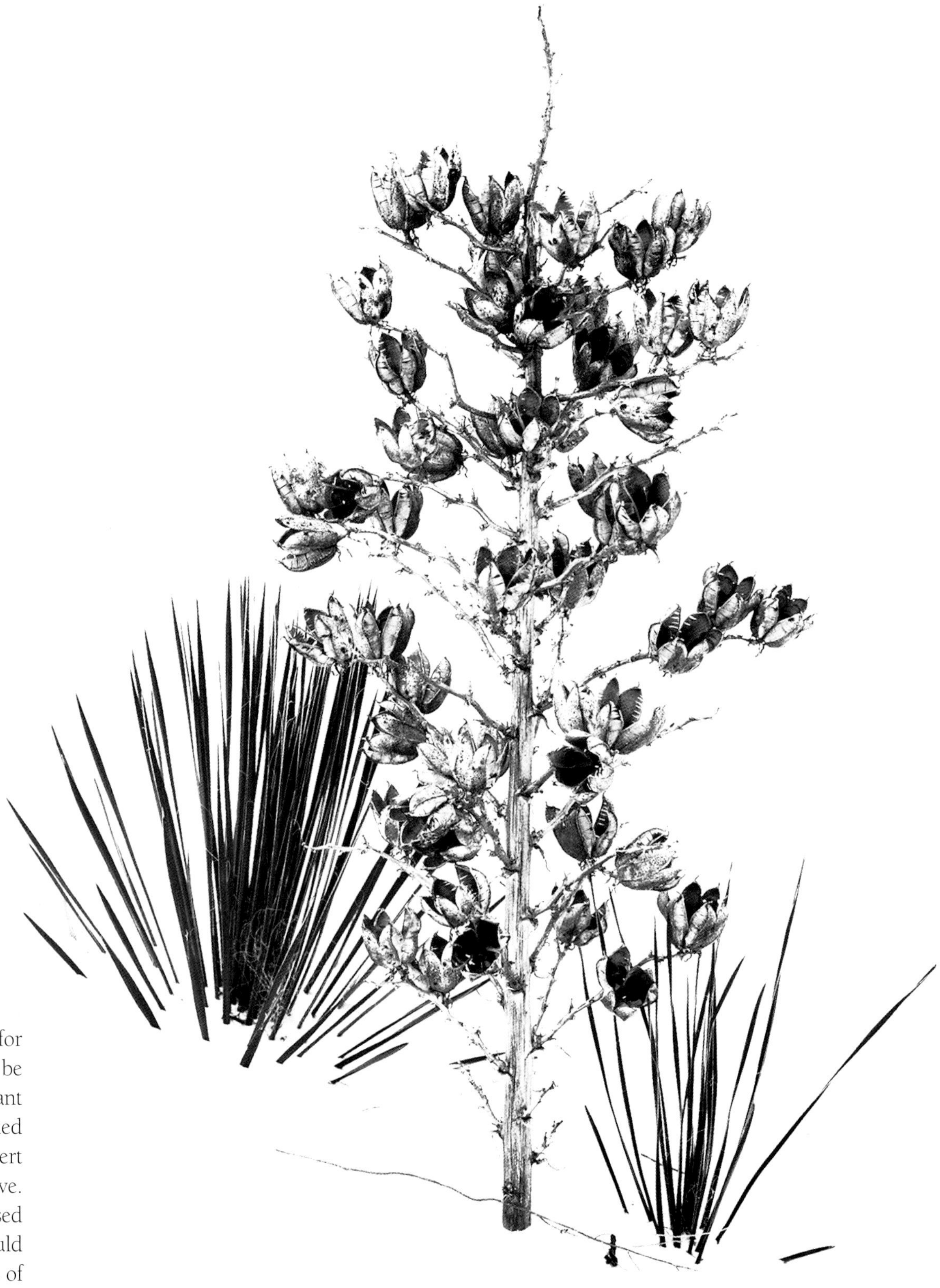

IMAGE 4

Although I would not choose this rendition for this image, I wanted to show what else could be done. When the background is where you want it, you can use Select > Reselect (if you deselected the last version) and/or Select > Reselect > Invert so that the plant and not the background is active. Opening Layer > New Adjustment Layer, I used Levels to render a high-contrast effect. I could modify the layer and try out different degrees of contrast as well by using the Opacity slider in the Layers palette.

WORKSHOP 2 **CONTRAST CONTROL USING LEVELS**

SHIP'S DECK

There are certain negatives that haunt photographers. No matter how they try, they cannot get a good print from these negatives, usually because of excessive or insufficient contrast. Having had my share of such negatives, I wondered whether Photoshop could do any better with them. Although I have more to discover, I can say that in many cases Photoshop can help you do more than you'd be able to do in the conventional darkroom, and in less time. One of the main reasons is the program's ability to control not only the overall contrast but also the specific contrast of areas. Another plus is the fact that you can maintain overall contrast (black and white points) while altering the middle gray values.

IMAGE 1

This exposure, scanned without adjustment in the scanner software from a 35mm negative, poses some interesting problems. The highlights are overexposed and the shadow areas are somewhat thin. If the highlights are suppressed on the input (scan) side, the whites go a bit too flat. If there is an attempt to alter contrast by weakening the deep areas (blacks), detail is lost in those areas. The first step in working with such negatives is to analyze how best to proceed. The plan here is to first tackle the shadow detail and then work on the highlights. This is done by using one command and one dialog box.

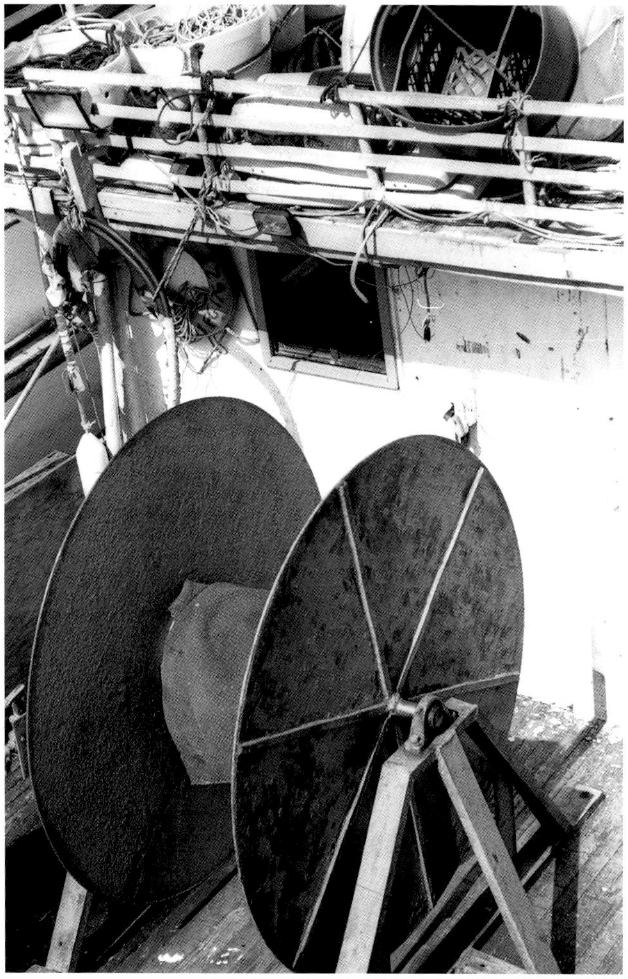

1

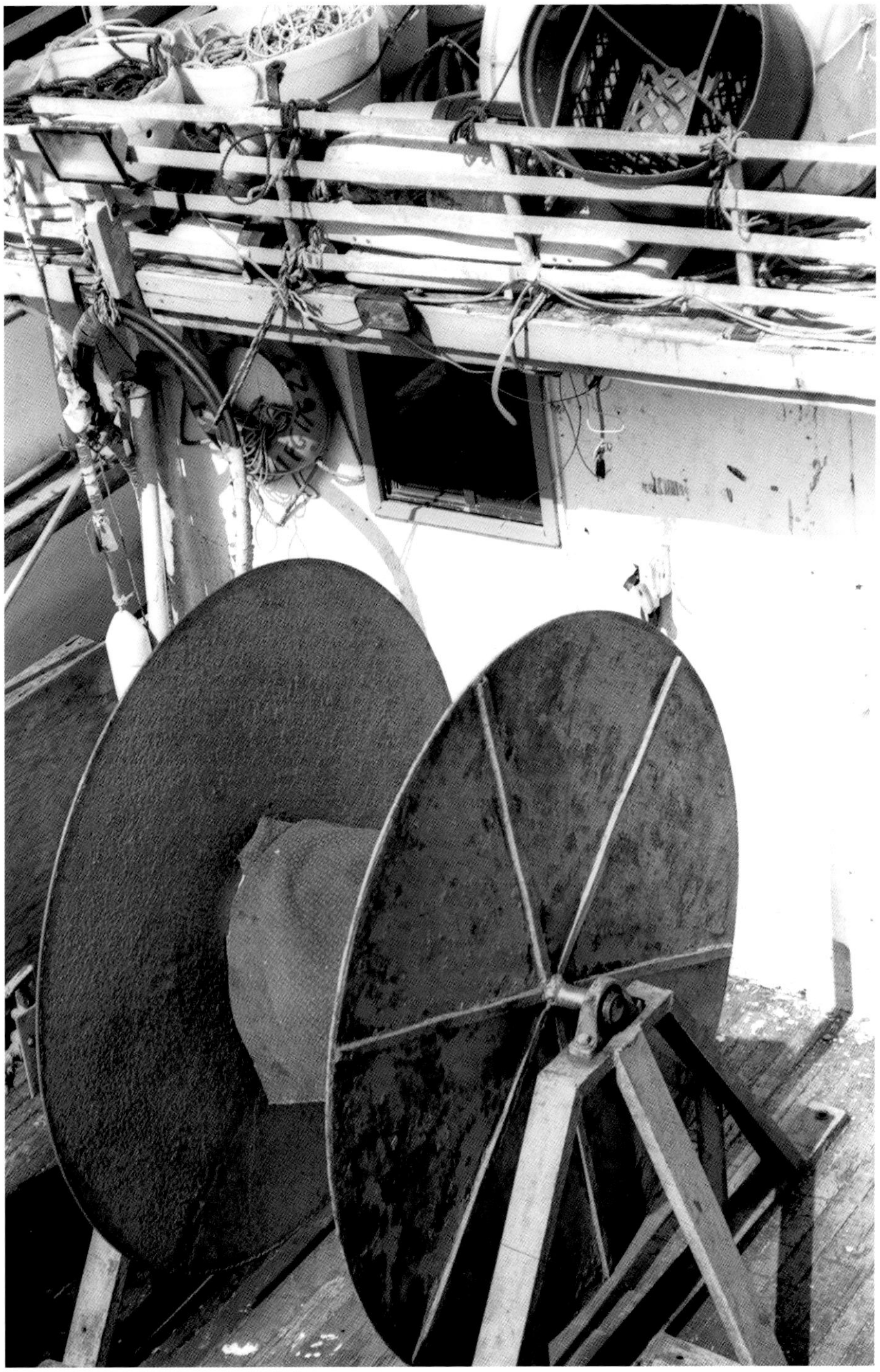

2

IMAGE 2

I opened the Levels dialog box with Image > Adjust > Levels. On the Input Levels slider, I moved the middle gray to 1.38, creating the effect here. This opens up details in the grays and darker areas while keeping the integrity of the deeper dark areas. But there is still a hot highlight.

IMAGE 3

If you were to make a print of Image 2, you would have a highlight area that is harsh and near paper-white (or whatever the base color of the paper). To solve this problem, suppress the highlight slightly on the Output Levels slider, down about 5%, or to 240. This may give a false tone, but it keeps the highlights under control on the print without having them go gray.

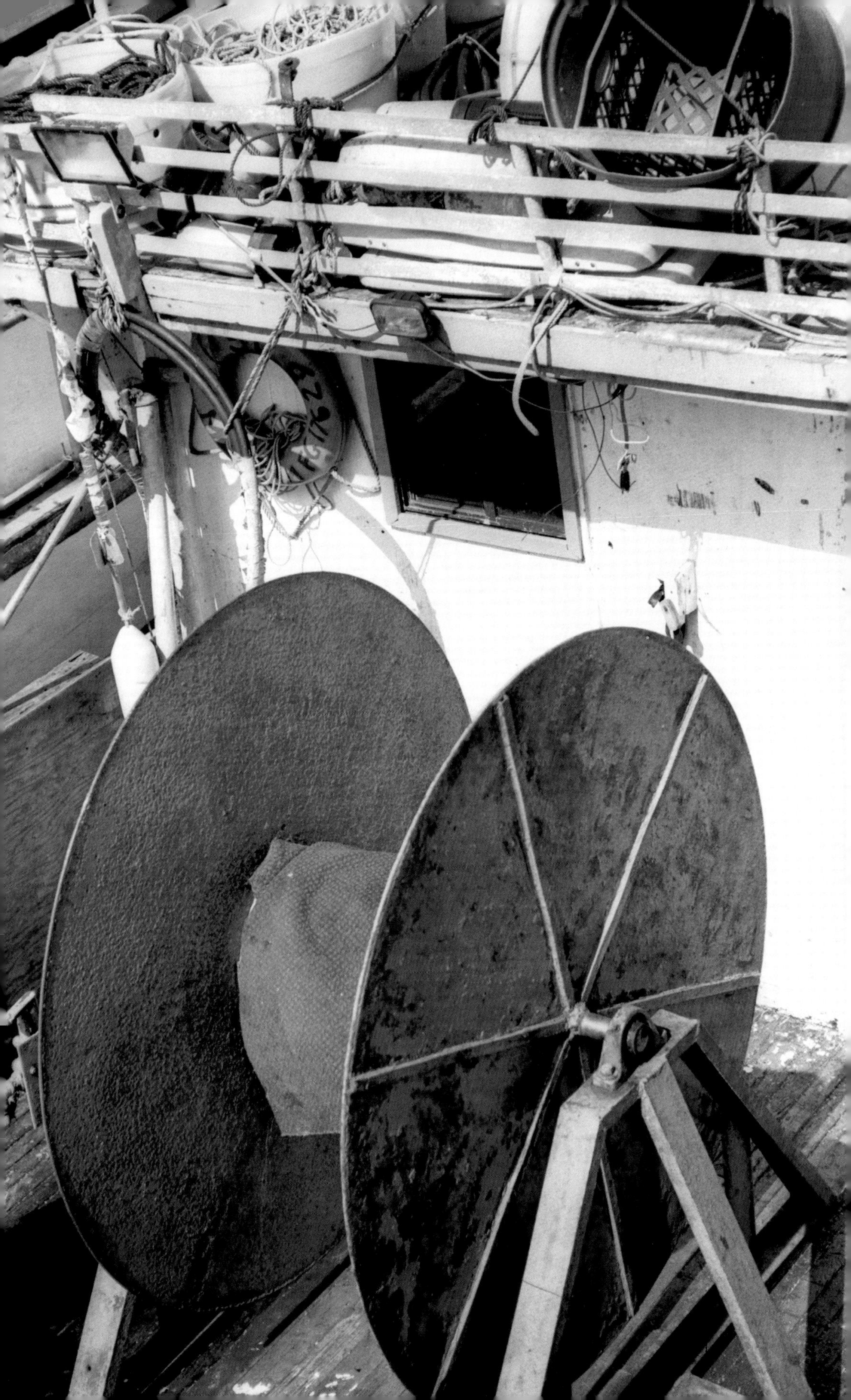

WORKSHOP 3 **WORKING WITH FLAT NEGATIVES**

WHITE SANDS

The reason I and perhaps many other photographers tend to overexpose is that we have seen how poorly underexposed, flat negatives print. But if we try to enhance the image through forcing more contrast on it we get a harsh image; if we try to burn back the contrast we get harsh grain. The result is that we tend to print those negatives only if necessary. Here's one way to finally get something out of those underexposed negatives.

IMAGE 1

This negative is hardly the worst example, but it is weak. Underexposure and probably a bit of underdevelopment make it a tough print assignment.

1

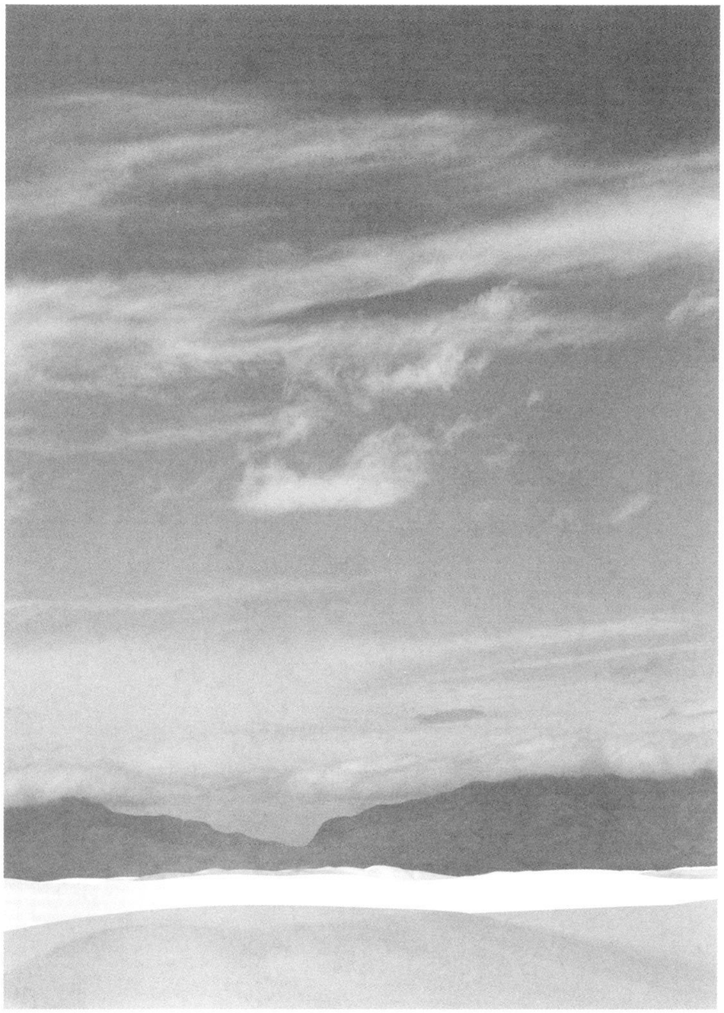

2

IMAGE 2

Here's a quick and immediate fix that might be all you need to do. Go to Layer > New Adjustment Layer, Levels and choose the Overlay Blending mode. This heightens image contrast immediately without loss of tonal texture. You can also try Multiply, applying this layer as many times as needed. With old faded prints I've scanned, I have used the Multiply layer and Overlay Blending mode with three or four hits.

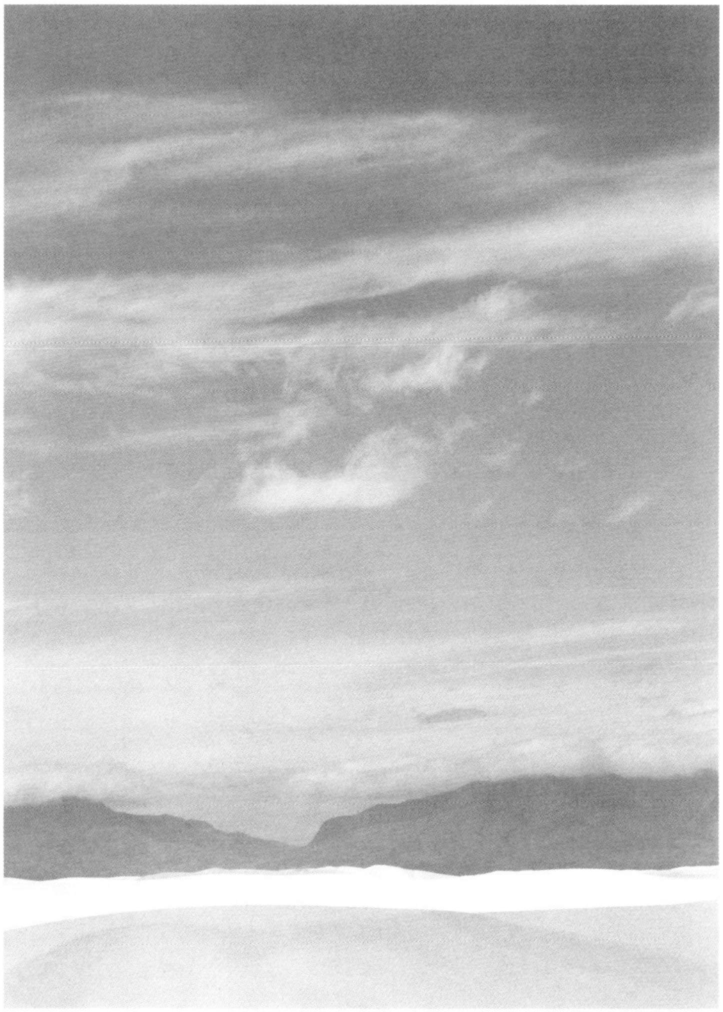

3

4

IMAGE 3

The grain has jumped up a bit from the effect, though, so you need to soften it without losing contrast. (Note that if you sharpen such an image, the grain might get objectionable.) Here, the Layers palette was opened and the image was dragged into the Duplicate icon to make a dupe layer. The next step was Filter >Blur >Gaussian Blur 2%, with the Opacity of the effect at 40%. The blur softened the grain just slightly, enough to make a difference but restrained enough to have virtually no effect on focus.

IMAGE 4

The final stage is an overall kick on the contrast using Layer >New Adjustment Layer, Levels to tighten up the black and white points. The Layers palette allows for further modifications to any of the effects that were applied.

WORKSHOP 4 **HIGH-KEY EFFECTS**

CATTAIL

There are a number of analogies between music and photography. One is the "key" of the image, with high key meaning those images that play in the higher, lighter tonal values and low key meaning those that work mainly with the lower or darker tonal values. Both have a great deal of charm.

Some images lend themselves naturally to one of these interpretations and might need just a slight nudge to complete the effect. When going for high key, for example, you want to maintain the lightness of tonality without resorting to increased contrast. Indeed, increased contrast would just deepen any darker tones that exist in the image, the exact opposite of what you're trying to achieve. The same goes for low-key images, where increased contrast would compress the darker tones. You want to reveal the beauty of those low tones, not obscure them with contrast.

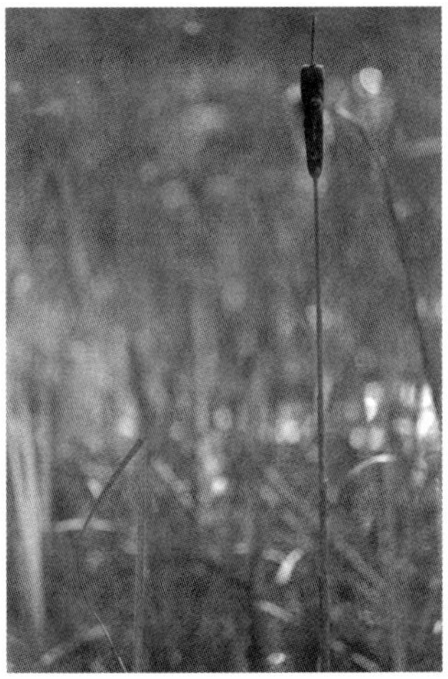

1

IMAGE 1

This is a good example of an image that can be printed in a high-key fashion. I scanned it from a 35mm negative. The scan represents the values that existed in the scene and in the negative. To bring the image into a high-key mode, increase the lightness and openness of the tonality without raising contrast.

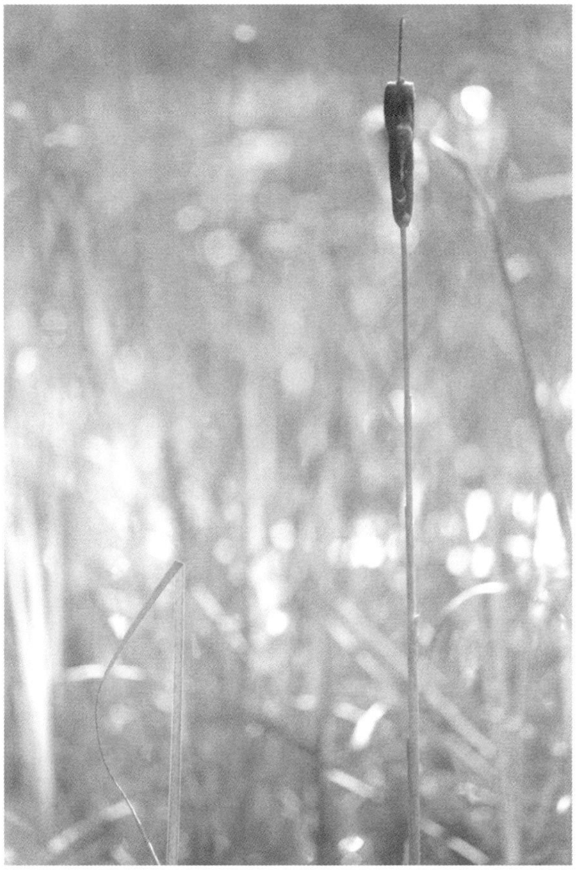

2

IMAGE 2

This is quite easy to do using a Layer Blending mode. Create a new adjustment layer and use Screen mode on the layer. This is an instant high-key creator.

TIP

When working on an image, you can save the image on the screen at any stage of the work by going to File>Save a Copy. You then name the version and place it in a folder for safekeeping.

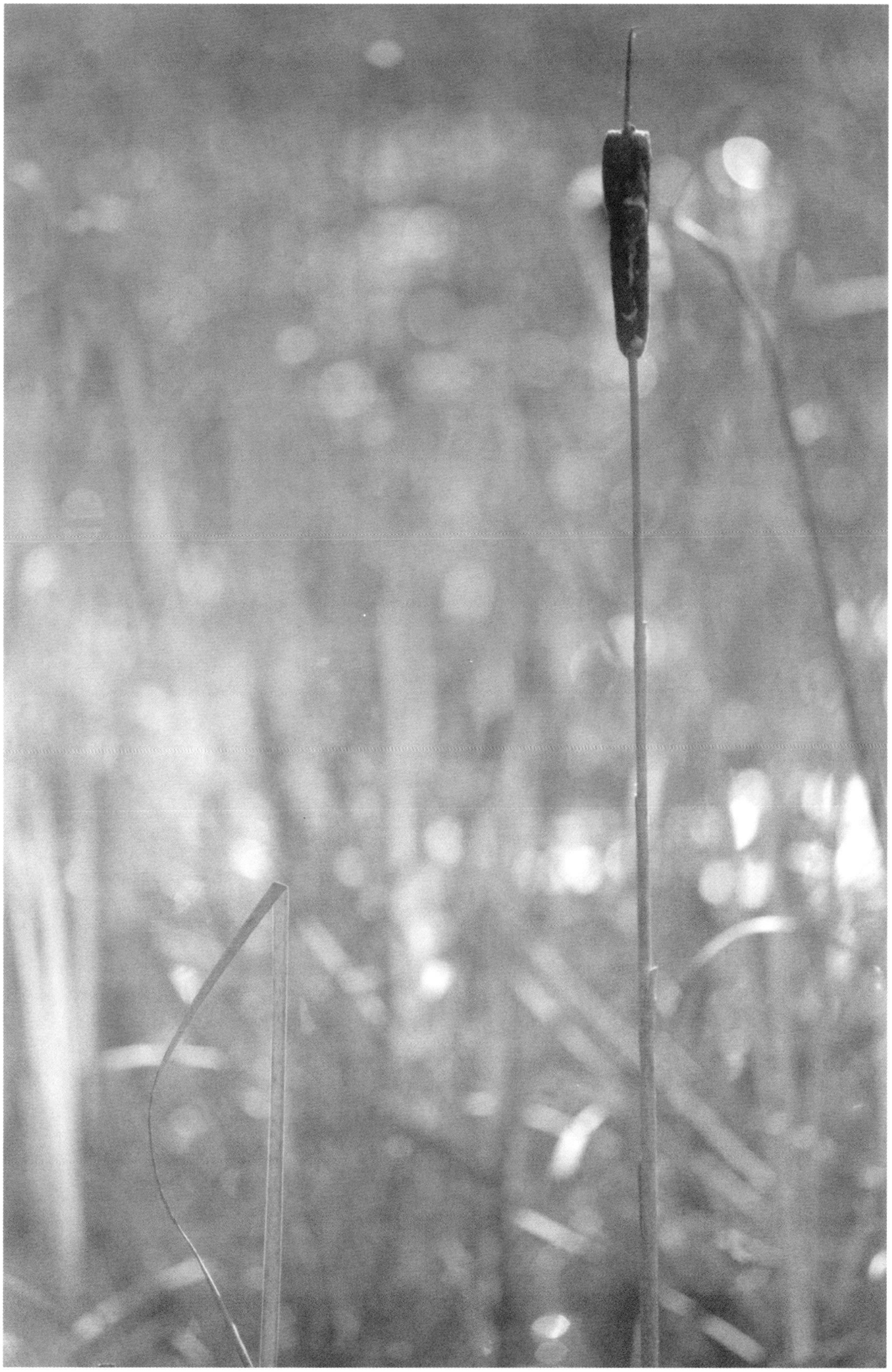

3

IMAGE 3
The advantage of working with a layer is that you can try different variations using the Opacity slider. You can activate and deactivate the layer in the Layers palette to compare it with the original image; you can also do this with the History palette. Moving the Opacity slider back to 50% created this image.

WORKSHOP 5 **COLOR CONVERSIONS**

ORCHID

One of the happier discoveries about working in the digital darkroom is that you can easily make conversions from color to black and white without sacrificing tonal quality. This has opened up a whole new set of images for black-and-white printing, so all those apparently foolish times I photographed in color can now be forgiven and perhaps redeemed. Color slides are particularly suitable for conversion; because they usually are exposed in a way that controls highlights, converting them digitally (as all reproduction houses know) reveals so much more than any typical photomechanical conversion can provide. Having tried to convert color slides in the darkroom, and having stumbled through panchromatic paper printing when making black-and-white prints from color negatives, I can attest to the great benefits of digital conversion.

IMAGE 1

I scanned this image from a 35mm color slide in RGB. It is a bit dark, but there is good separation between the different values. Try to convert the image in a number of ways that allow you to make different print interpretations.

IMAGE 2

One way to convert from color is to use the Channel Mixer, located at Image >Adjust >Channel Mixer. When the dialog box opens, check the Monochrome box. This conversion was made at Red +76, Green +98, and Blue -58, with no change in the Contrast setting. This opens up the image values without producing excessive contrast.

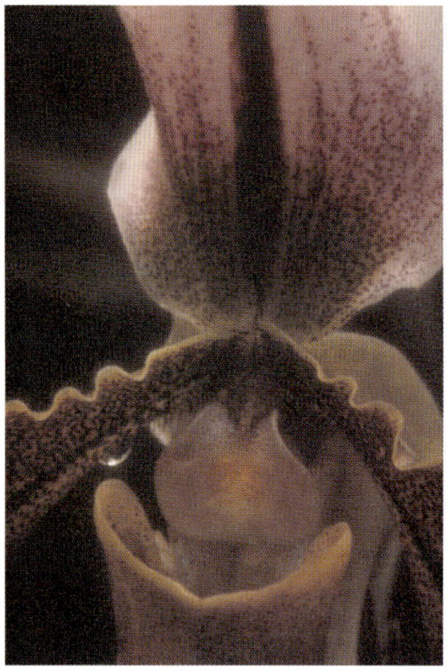

1

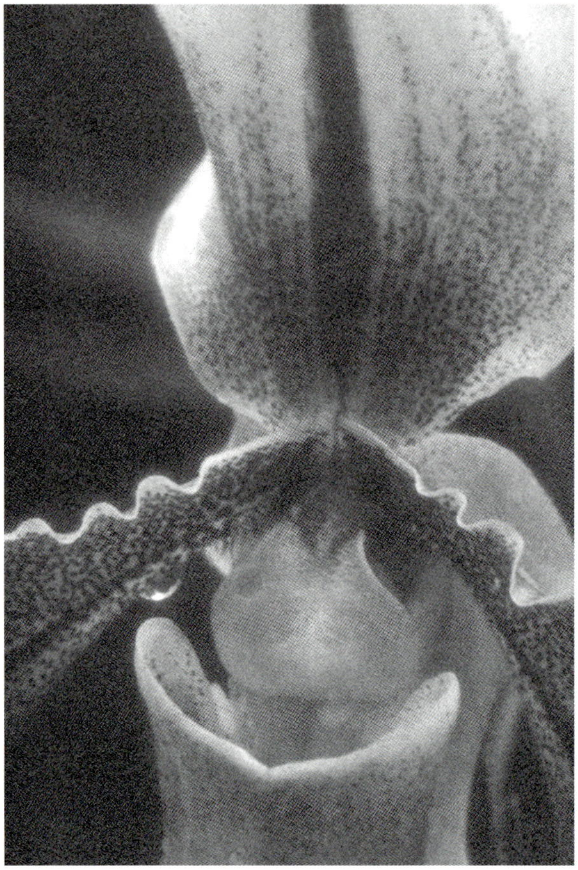

2

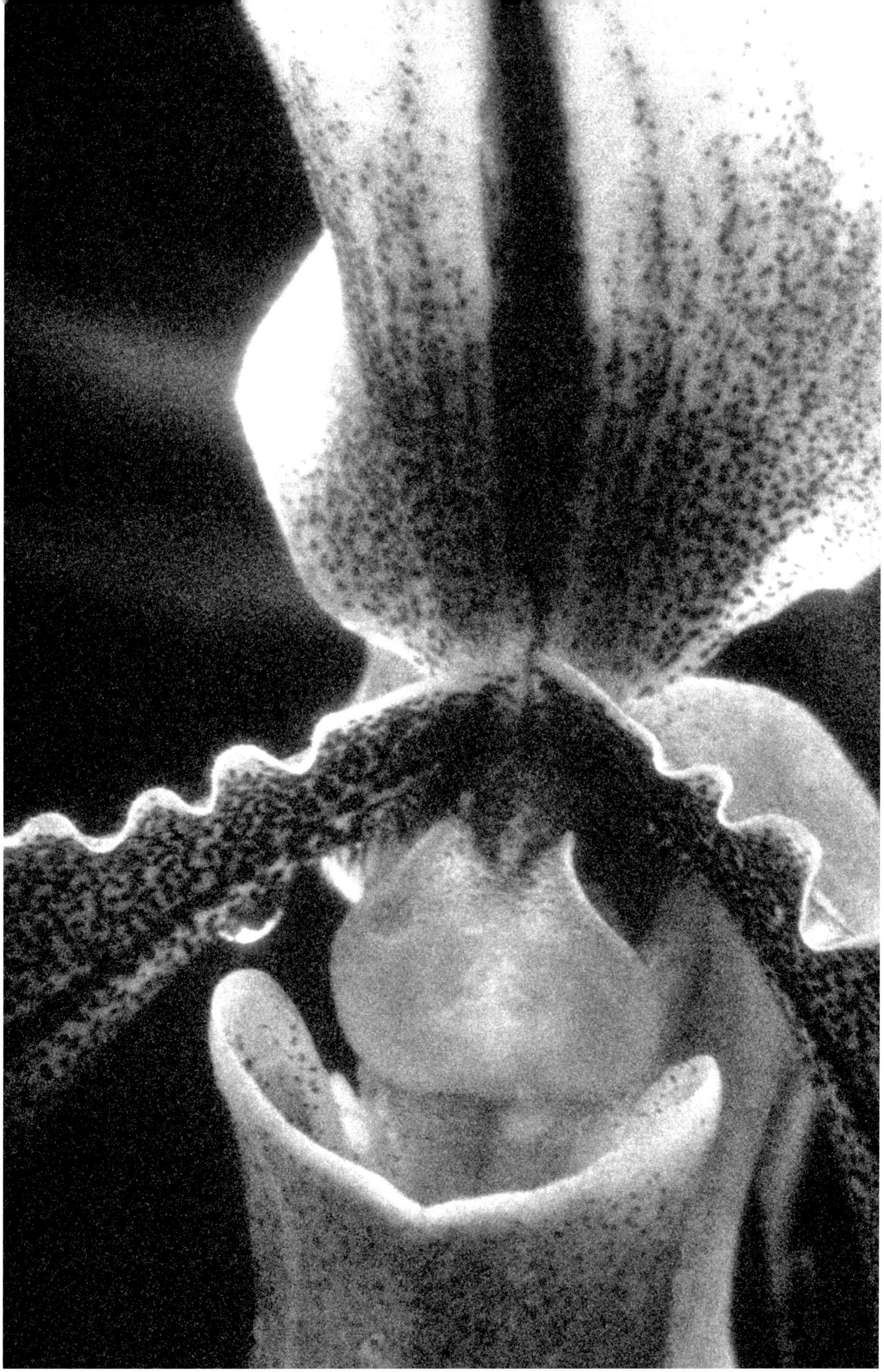

IMAGE 3

You can get a higher contrast version by setting the Channel Mixer at Red +84, Green +20, and Blue -16, and the Constant at -54. As you can see, you can move these interpretations all over the tonal map.

WORKSHOP 6 **TONAL BLENDING**

CEMENT MIXER, ELBA

Tonality is a chief concern for every printmaker. The ability to create a smooth blend of tones and to "spread it like butter" through the print is one of the challenges and rewards of printing. There are many routes that you can take to achieve this, including Levels, Curves, and methods of converting from color to black and white. This exercise explores some of these options. Each image you work with will dictate the best path.

IMAGE 1

I have always wanted to make a black-and-white print of this 35mm slide, but every conversion I made in the darkroom came up too contrasty. There are a number of ways that the conversion can be made in the digital darkroom: by using the RGB>Grayscale mode conversion; by picking the image from one of the channels in the RGB channels; or by using the Channel Mixer.

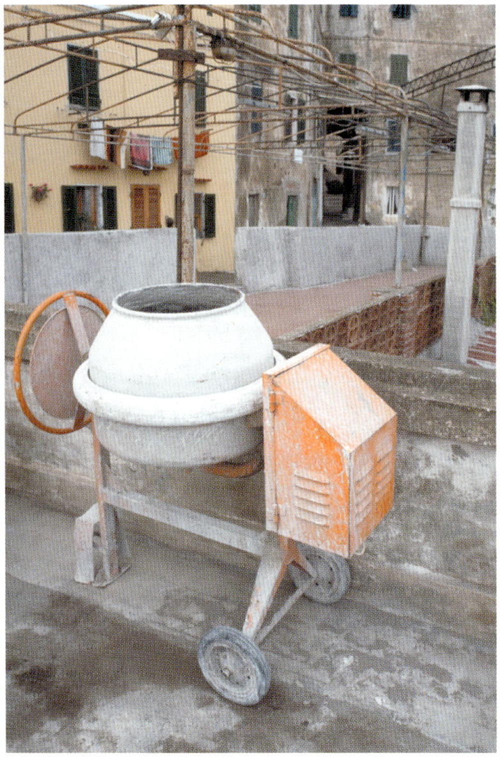

1

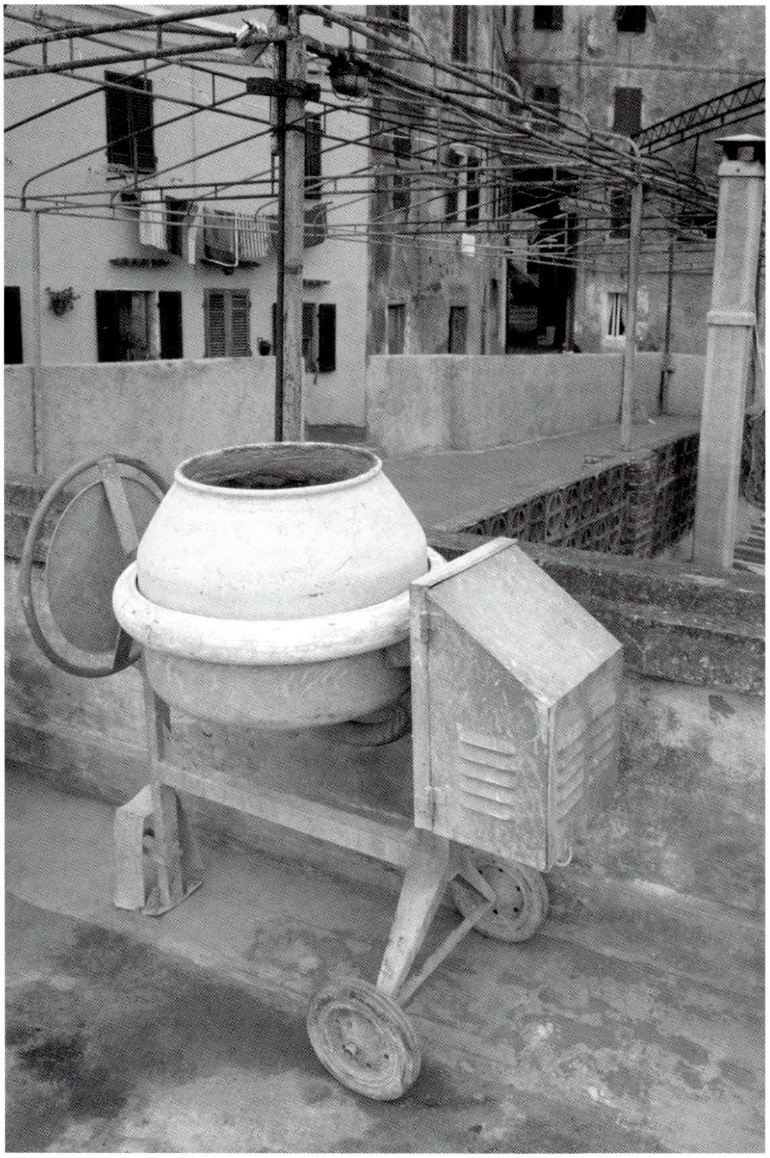

2

IMAGE 2

I took this conversion from the Red channel in the RGB channels (View>Show Channels). It is a bit "chalky" and had to be lightened using Levels. It is an option, however.

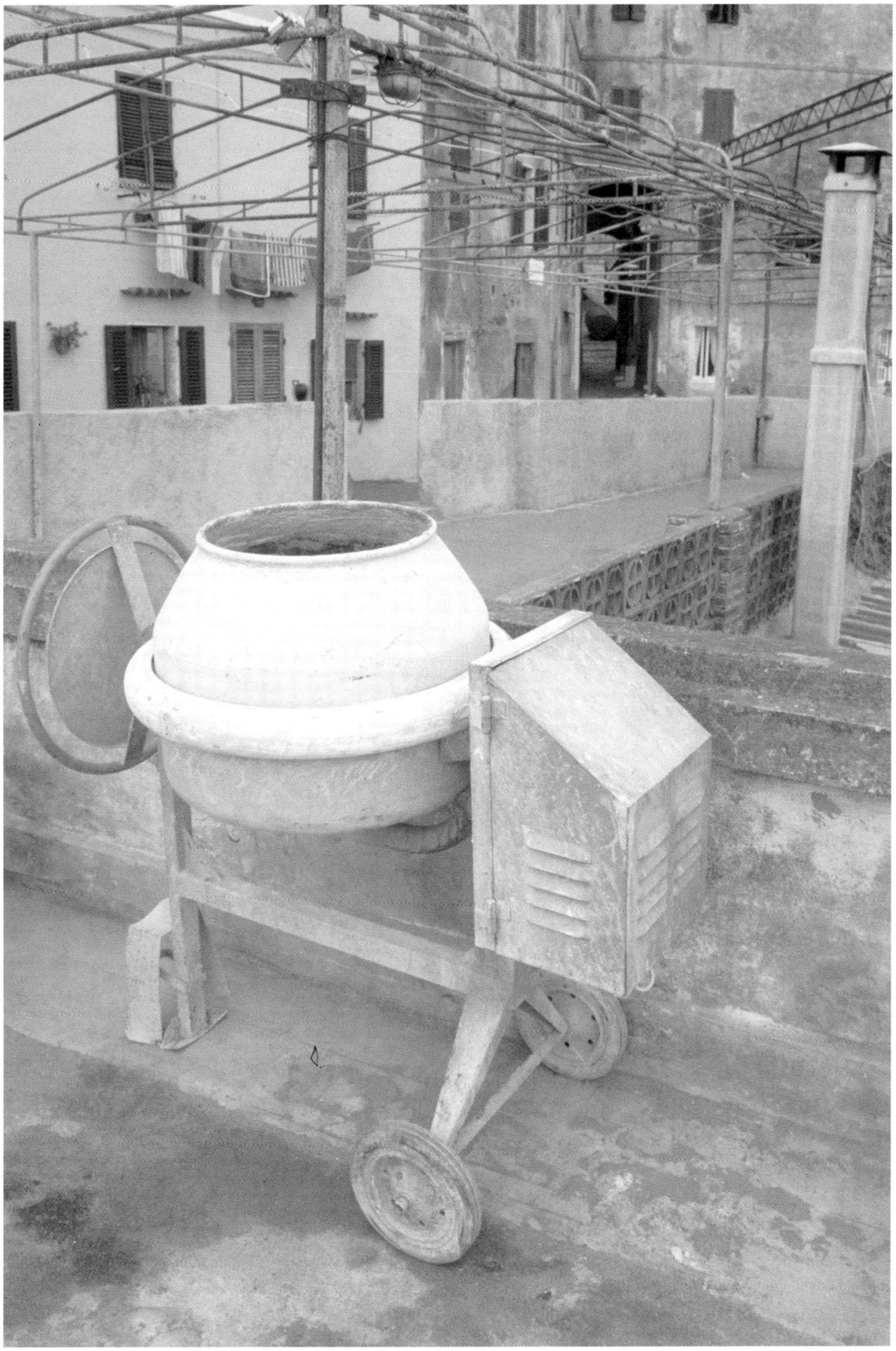

3

IMAGE 3
I made this conversion from the Green channel in the RGB channels. It is a fine tonal rendition of the scene and could be used as the foundation of a good print.

IMAGE 4

The Channel Mixer approach is the most customized and allows you to tweak every value carefully. It does take some practice, and certainly takes more time than the straight mode or channel conversions. I converted this image using Red +66, Green +98, and Blue +22, and Constant +2.

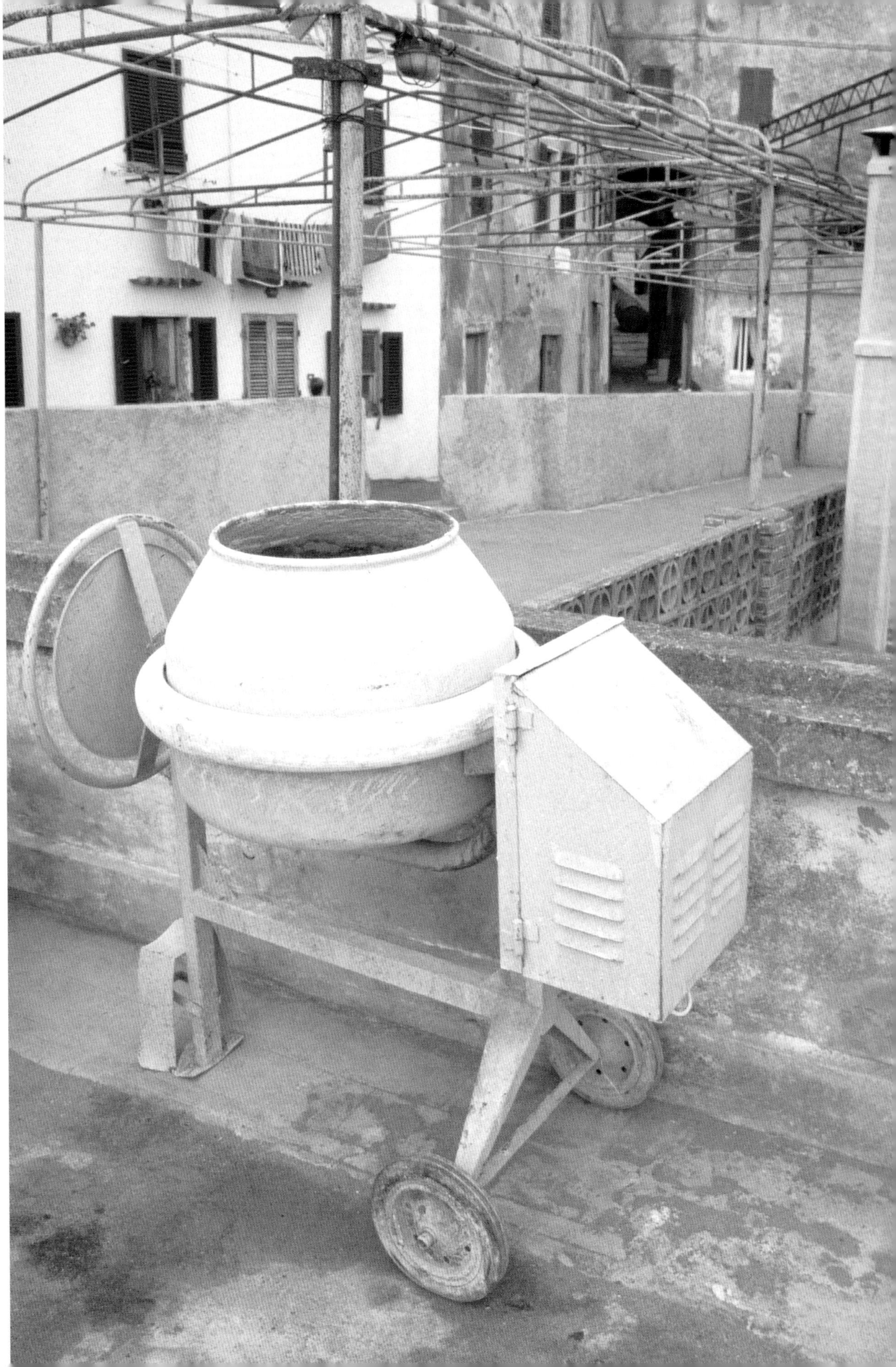

Burning and Dodging

One of the most exciting controls in both the conventional and digital darkroom is the ability to add and delete density from an area of the image—to burn and dodge. This manipulation of light is a subtle technique that takes some practice to get right. Handled correctly, it can create a dynamic sky and bold forms, and reveal detail in even the darkest shadow areas. Done without care, though, it can result in halos around dodged faces, apparent horizon lines, and a poor blending of adjacent tones.

A prime advantage of working in the digital darkroom is that you have excellent control over all aspects of good burn-and-dodge technique. You can, for example, easily adjust the overall image contrast (the relationship of light to dark values); you can create a good blend using the Feather settings in the Selection dialog area; and you can control the degree of burning and dodging as you apply them by working with the Exposure setting. Perhaps most exciting, though, is the amazing selectivity of the areas in which you can work and the edges you can define. Selection tools let you define the areas that will and will not be part of an effect, such as Burn or Dodge; using Brush Sizes, you can define exactly where you want the effect to take place and see graphically where the burn or dodge will occur. The Zoom tool lets you see into the tiniest part of the image.

Before you start using Burn and Dodge tools, however, there's an important step: creating a graphic for the tool that will show you exactly where it is working and how large or small the effect will be. Brush size is one of the best graphic features of the program.

Brush Size

Go to File>Preferences>Display and Cursors. You'll be presented with two choices: Painting Cursors and Other Cursors. For Painting Cursors, check off Brush Size. For Other Cursors, I leave it on Standard, but you can choose Precise if you like.

Next, go to Window>Show Brushes and pick a brush size; if you're using Photoshop 6, just pick a brush from the drop-down menu under the Tool dialog box. You can also toggle through the brushes using the space bar on the keyboard. Some like a fuzzy-edged brush, others a hard-edged brush. I like a softer edge, but what you choose will depend on the type of images you work with and your taste. Experiment with both kinds of brushes.

Next, open an image and select the Burn or the Dodge tool. You'll see that you get a circle or bracket of some sort. On your keyboard, find the bracket key (lower-case position). Press the bracket key on the right or on the left to expand or contract the brush size. The size you see on the screen is exactly the size and placement of the effect. When you zoom in, the size of the brush changes along with the zoom.

You can burn and dodge on the background image (the imported foundation image) or on a copy layer (but not on a new adjustment layer once a Blending mode is applied). I suggest experimenting with burn-and-dodge effects on a layer and then examining the layer later. This way, you can play with the effects before accepting them as final.

You also have great control over the effect itself. If you make a mistake or do something you decide you don't like, you can erase it using Undo (cancellation of an effect) or Command/Control Z. If you want to backtrack on a series of strokes, you can do so using the History tool (Window>Show History) and highlighting the state (previous step) you want to check out.

History Palette

In the past, Photoshop offered only one level of Undo. This meant that you had to Save As or Save a Copy periodically to lock in your work so that if you made a mistake you could revert to the saved copy. This was a waste of drive space and time. Now, with the History palette, you can be freer in your work and allow yourself to mess up a bit before thinking about it—a creative way to work, in my opinion. It is invaluable when working with Burn and Dodge controls.

In the History palette, you can choose anywhere from one to 100 states as an option. The default of 20 states should be enough for most images; saving more tends to hog RAM. Let's say you've made 20 burns and dodges on an image and want to review each before you go ahead. All you need to do to activate a state is to click on it, and the image at that state will appear. You can then click through the progression of states in the History palette to check your work and make any changes you want.

With the History palette, you can choose to work in a linear or non-linear fashion. Work with Linear History to revert to a previous history state, or non-Linear History to throw away a single step. If you decide to discard a state (by dragging it into the trash at the bottom of the History palette) and you're working in Linear, all the states after that one disappear once you continue working. If you're working in non-Linear, only that state is trashed.

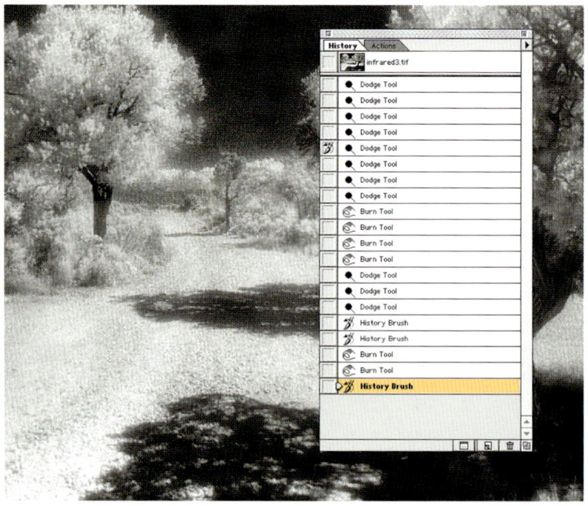

The History palette gives you the option to revert to a previous version (state) of the image, at any time. The palette shown above is set to remember twenty states of the image. It is possible to change the default number of states from 20 to up to 100, but your file size will increase drastically with this change. You can use the History Brush along with the History palette to selectively return to a previous state, or "paint in the past."

History Brush

With the History Brush, you can choose a state in your working progress or from a snapshot you made of a particular state and selectively eliminate certain steps and actions you don't like by "painting back" very selectively within the image. This is great, because you have much more tonal control than with a straight burn-and-dodge technique. The History Brush is also useful for retouching techniques.

TIP

You can toggle between the Dodge and Burn tools by clicking on the tool in the palette or using Alt/Option as a toggle in Photoshop 5.0 and 5.5. To show a tool's options, double click on the tool. To show brushes, choose Window >Show brushes or use F5. In Photoshop 6, the tool options open at the top of the image frame when you select the tool.

WORKSHOP 1 **BURNING AND DODGING BASICS**

TREE ROOTS

A negative or slide is often a sketch, one that is refined when a print is made. When you consider a negative a sketch, you aim for more open tonal values and know that you will complete the vision later. Changing tonal values selectively with burning and dodging is a classic way to interpret an image.

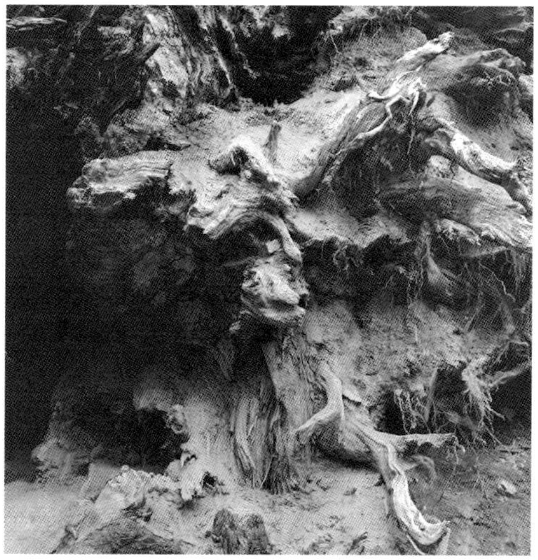

2

IMAGE 1

This is a straightforward application of Burn and Dodge tools. The scan revealed all the shadow detail within this image of an overturned tree stump. A standard printing practice would be to choose a paper with a higher contrast grade and to work the edges. You would have no idea, however, about density and the actual effect of burning until the print emerged from the developer.

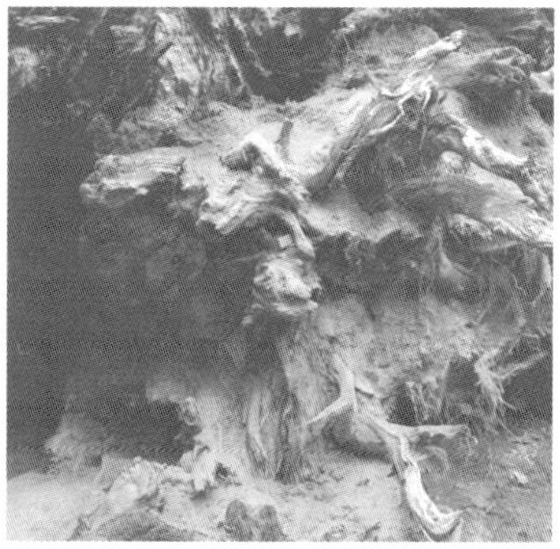

1

IMAGE 2

Here I chose a large brush size from Windows >Show Brushes, and then adapted the size using the bracket keys for each section. I chose the Burn tool with Shadows and Opacity 70%. Even if highlights were accidentally passed over, they would not be affected, as the tool is set to affect only Shadow areas. In some areas I selected a Dodge tool on Highlights and Opacity 15%, using a small brush size for the smaller roots. Zooming in allowed for very fine tonal control.

IMAGE 3

The final image—dramatic and finely detailed.

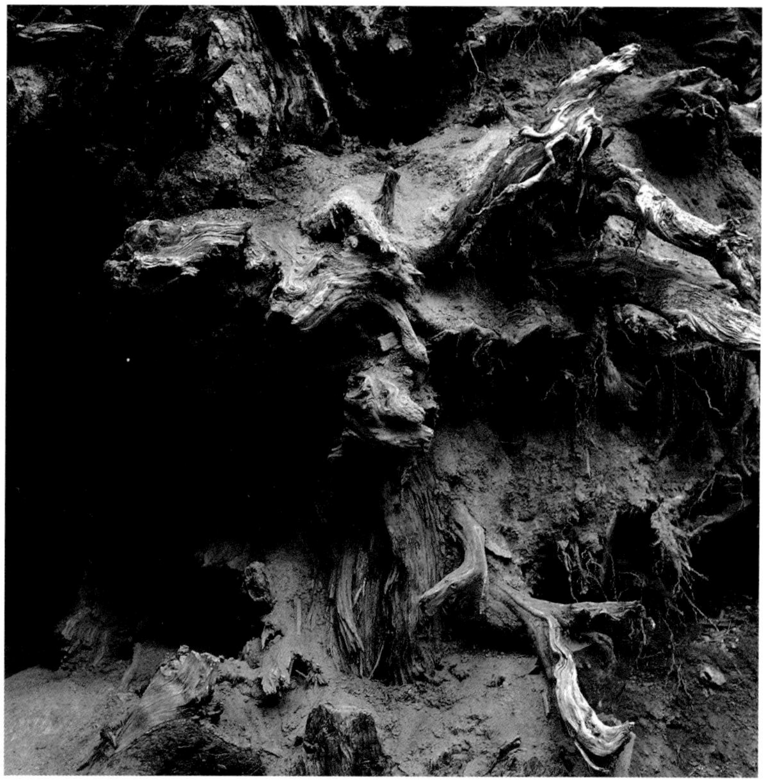

3

WORKSHOP 2 **EXPLORING BURN AND DODGE CONTROLS**

EVERGLADES POND

This image is a field trip for those of you who want to play with the Burn and Dodge controls. I have worked on this print many times, and each time I come up with another interpretation. The key to this image is creating an effect that plays with the reflection while exploiting the possibilities of light and dark rhythms.

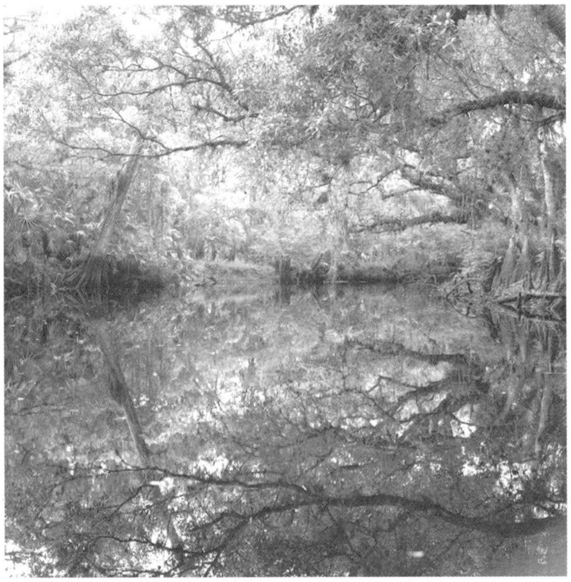

1

IMAGE 1

The scan of the negative shows good exposure and detail. When you consider a print such as this, look at how the tonal values are spread throughout and how some judicious burning and dodging can alter and enhance the scene. Judge the depth of shadows, the highlight play, and how altering the overall contrast through selective tonal control can make certain areas emerge and others recede into the image space. Although the lighting is fairly even in the original, the selective reduction and deepening of the values enhance the tonal play.

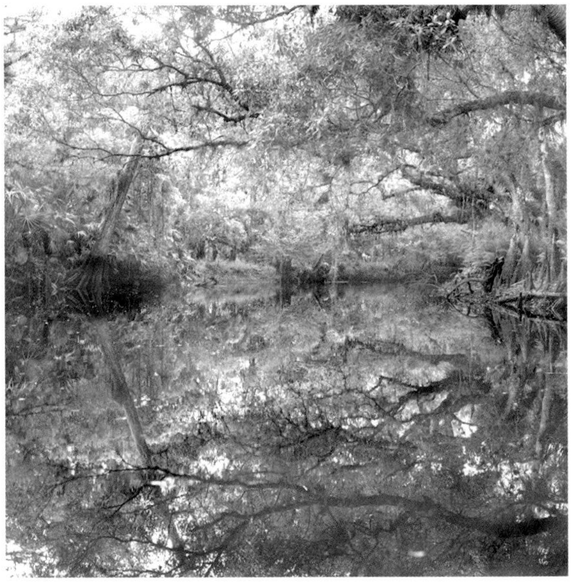

2

IMAGE 2

Begin with the shadow areas. In this image and others with such intricate detail, zooming in helps. Choose the Zoom tool (or press Z). On a PC, you can increase and decrease the size using the Alt key and the ± key; on a Mac, you can do the same with Command plus (+) or minus (–). Choose a brush size that's comfortable. To test your work, use a layer by opening up the Layers palette and dragging the background to the Copy icon at the base of the Layers palette, or use Command J (layer via copy). On this version, I set the Burn tool at Shadows, with an Exposure of 20%.

You can build density through repeated strokes; a lower opacity gives you more control with each stroke. If you make a mistake, you can go to Edit>Undo for one stroke. If you don't like a series of strokes, you can go to the Window>Show History and click back on the states.

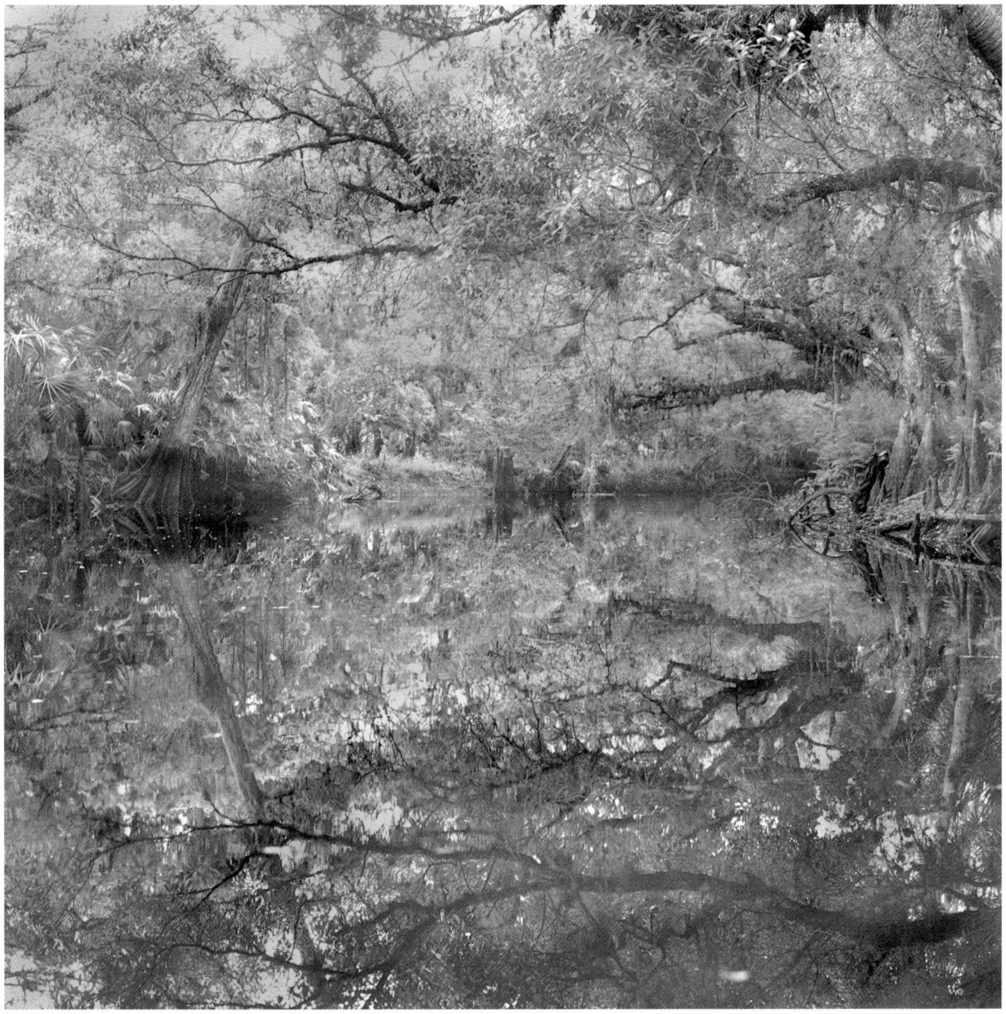

3

IMAGE 3

To work the highlights, try a different approach. Click on the History Brush tool and place the History Brush at an early stage of the work; this is the state that you will paint "back" to. In the History Brush palette, choose a Blending mode. Blending modes are great ways to modify effects and choose just the density you want. To lighten the areas, choose Screen. If the option says Normal, just click on it and the choices will drop down. This image shows the effect of Screen, History Brush on the areas that were worked.

TIP

When doing burning or dodging, work loose and free and in a combination of long and short strokes with the mouse or stylus. This will help with tonal blending and with creating a sense of rhythm in the print. Choppy strokes will not help the look of the image; what you're trying to do is heighten visual appeal through tonal differences.

IMAGE 4

Now you're going to deepen more of the shadow areas. You could go to Burn > Shadows, but instead try History Brush, Multiply. This darkens your areas. When you do this, you're going to open another layer and work on that. So, drag the Background to the copy icon on the Layers palette. Now work the areas with the Brush again. Once all the work is complete, go back to the Layers palette and click on each layer or a sequence of layers. This allows you to judge the work and to modify each area or density as desired—very helpful in the way the tones sit and blend with one another, as you can adjust each layer in relation to all the others and see the effect right on the screen.

IMAGE 5

This image shows that to complete the picture I switched from Grayscale to Duotone mode and chose a warm yellow/brown tone.

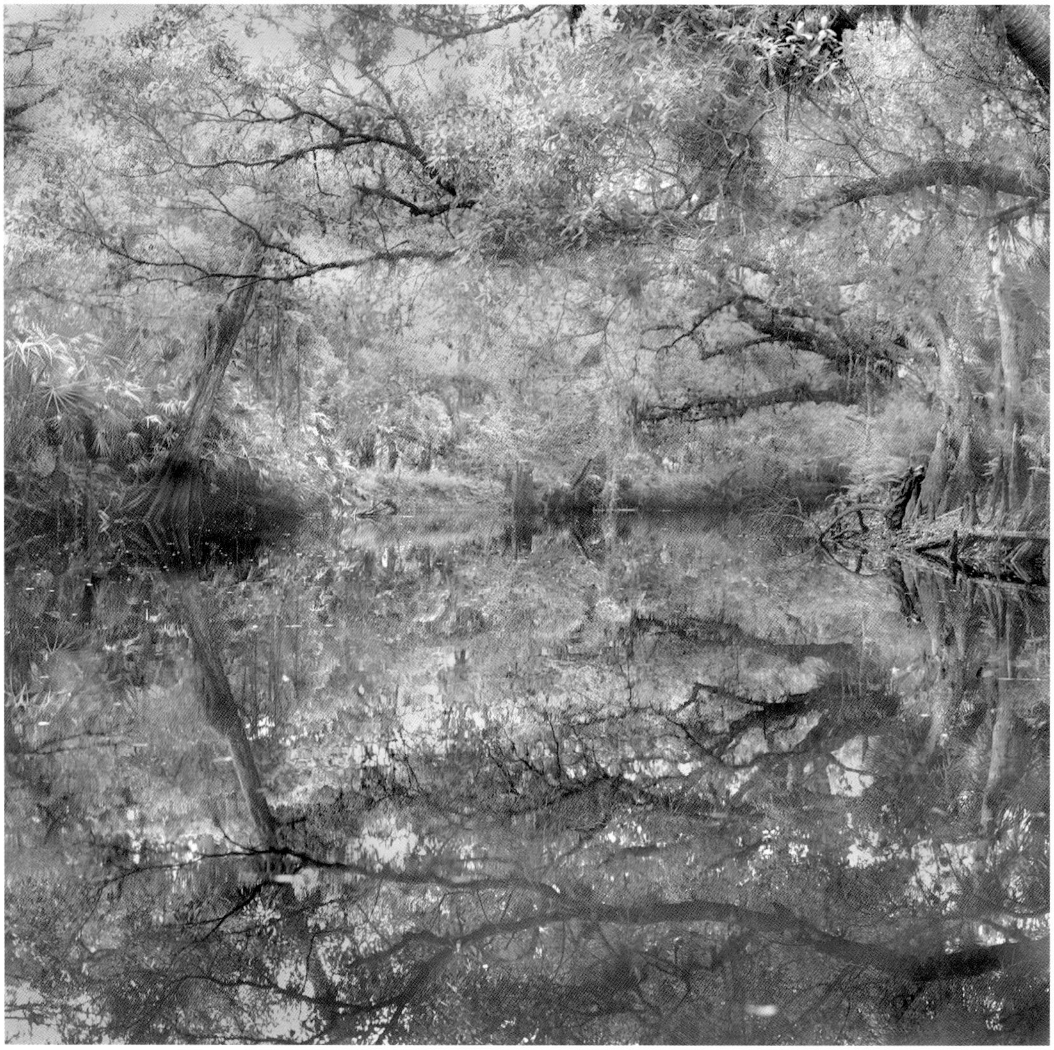

4

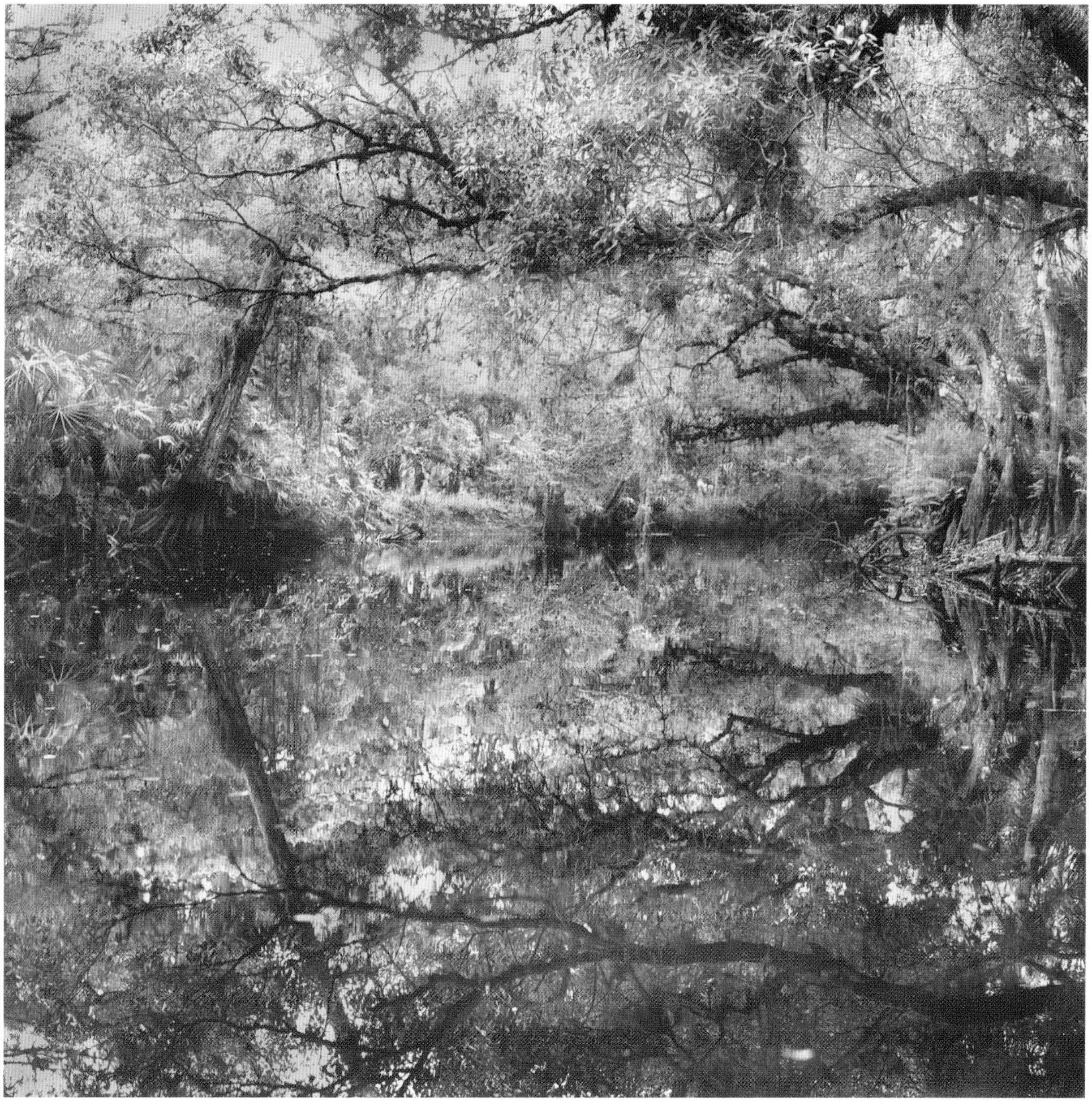

5

WORKSHOP 3 **ENHANCING INFRARED PHOTOS**
RIO GRANDE VALLEY TRAIL, LA JUNTA

Photoshop's tools are a great aid when you want to enhance and optimize your black-and-white infrared photography. Because it is often a chancy exposure, many people get dense negatives that look quite flat when prints are made. The effect is there (glowing trees, ethereal light), but it is often difficult to optimize the image through conventional methods. Using a high-contrast paper brightens tones but loses detail, and highlights can look mottled and gray. Burning and dodging is the best approach, yet knowing how much to burn through a dense negative can be a real trial-and-error effort.

The approach to tonal control taken here with this scanned 35mm negative is to first attain the proper base contrast and then apply selective addition and reduction of tonal areas. Use a Selection tool here to help enhance this image.

IMAGE 1
This image has all the common characteristics of infrared, with dense highlights and fairly large grain; the scan helped even out some of the tonality. I didn't want to lose the character but instead to enhance the differences.

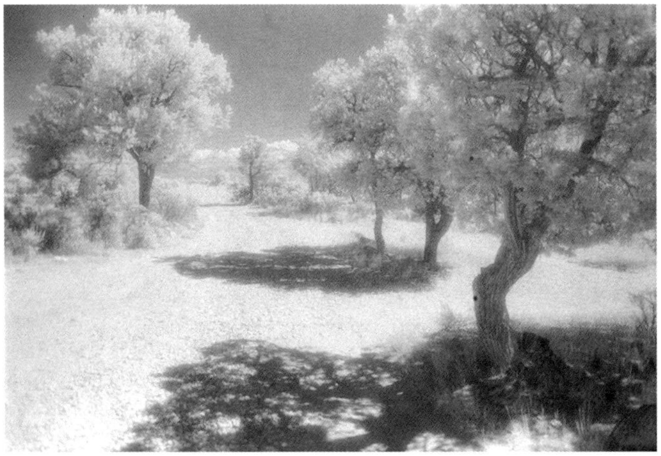

1

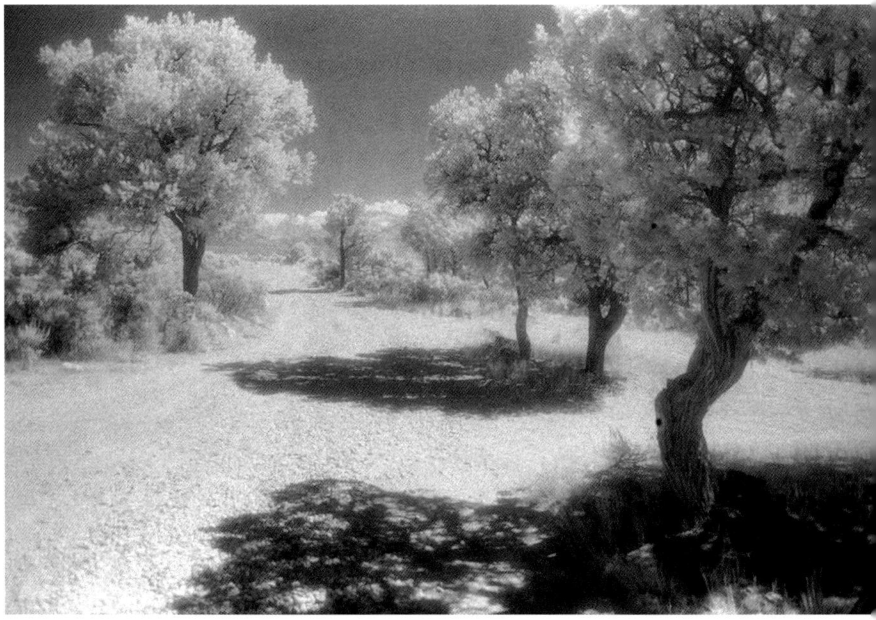

2

IMAGE 2
One way to create those differences is to make the image darker overall and then bring back certain areas with dodging. If I were to lighten the whole image and create the differences with burning, I might have lost highlight detail in some spots. Because this loss in detail was about to happen to the image here, I started with an overall darkening by going to Layers >New Adjustment Layer. From Layer Blending mode menu, I chose Multiply, which has the effect of darkening the entire image. Multiply is great when you have a thin negative or need more overall density in the scene without increasing contrast.

TIP
When you burn and dodge, don't expect to accomplish everything with one stroke. Go over areas a few times with a low Exposure setting on the tool. The effect is cumulative, and this technique gives you much more control.

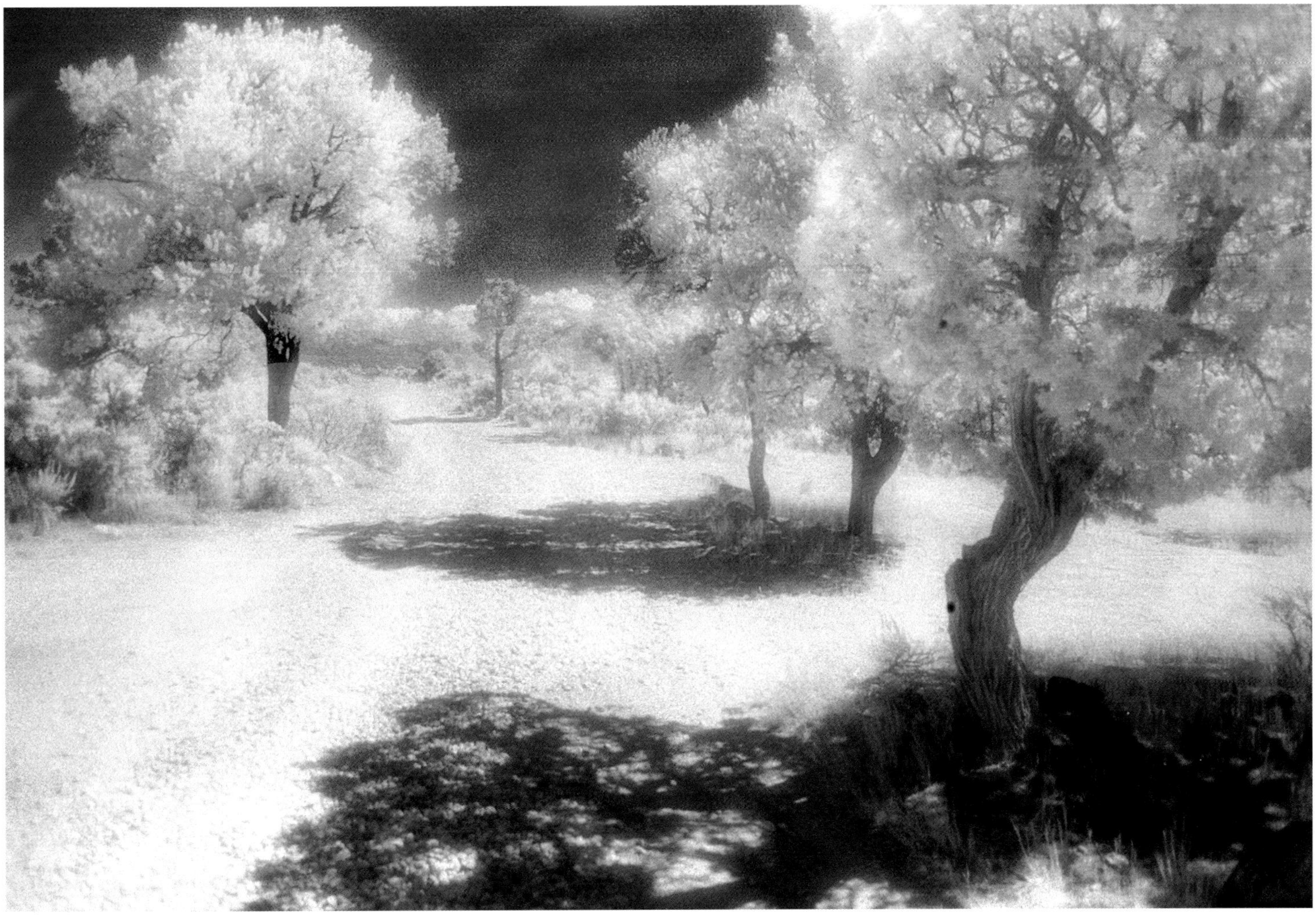

3

IMAGE 3

This image involved a series of burning and dodging steps—a matter of taste, play, and experimentation. Here, I created a pathway and divided certain tonal areas using burns and dodges; texture and tonal borders were the goal. Note how the darker trees have been given variety through dodging. You can use the History palette to check your steps or create a layer for this work to help you to toggle between versions as you go. You can create numerous layers to help check out each stage of the work.

TIP

You cannot burn and dodge on a new adjustment layer, so use another layer on a copy of the background image, or work on the background image itself by clicking on it in the Layers palette.

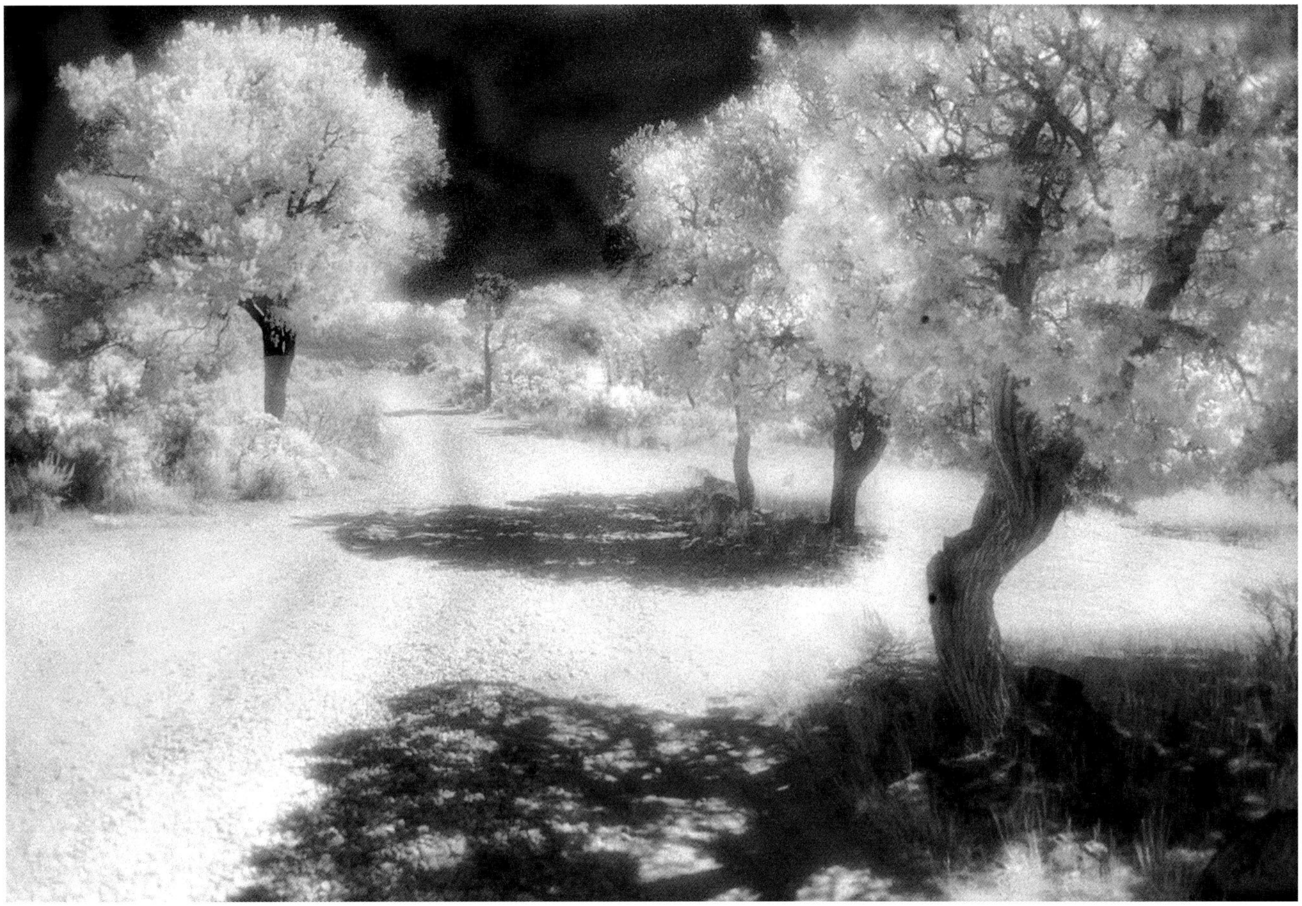

4

IMAGE 4

Everything worked fine except for the sky, so here I selected the sky and applied a gradient. In the toolbar, I chose the Magic Wand. I also chose Contiguous in the Modification menu and a Tolerance of 5; clicking on Contiguous ensured that equivalent tones in other parts of the image would not be selected. I clicked in the sky area until it was surrounded by the Marquee. The Marquee gets in my way, though, so I unchecked Show Extras (or Hide Edges) in the View menu. I then chose the Gradient tool and clicked on Black to White. I dragged the Gradient tool line from the top of the print to where the horizon line sat in the center of the frame. The sky filled with a deep, luxurious black-to-gray fade.

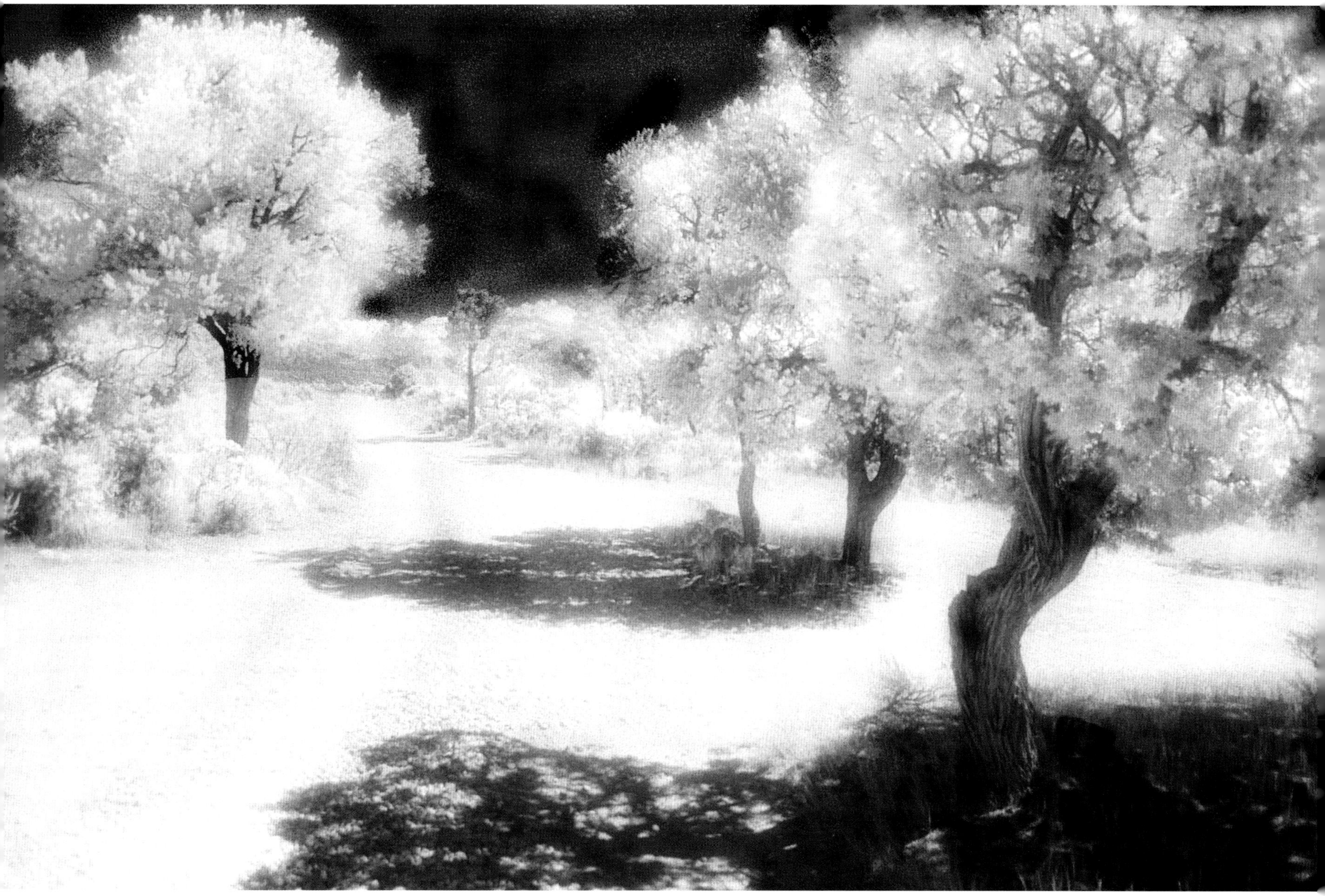

5

IMAGE 5
Finally I switched to Duotone mode. I chose Tritone and used a middle gray for the second ink and a light gray for the third.

WORKSHOP 4 **SELECTIVE TONAL CONTROL**

CLOUDS

I have always enjoyed making photographs of clouds, a pastime that can become a passion when I'm shooting in New Mexico in August. It seems that every afternoon is filled with an amazing display of gathering thunderheads that change every moment. One trouble commonly encountered with cloud photographs is highlight control. Made too harsh, the print will lose texture in the key areas that define and cap the tonal play; too weak, and the print will lack the drama that first inspired the photograph. For those who wish to study and master tonal control, clouds afford an excellent opportunity.

IMAGE 1

This photograph was made on black-and-white slide film and scanned. The tonal values are very deep, but from looking at the transparency on a light box I knew that more range resided in the image. I could have raised contrast in the scan, but that carries a danger of driving the highlights over the textural edge. In addition, when going from image to print, there was a strong possibility that the highlights wouldn't make the transition. All of these considerations make a challenging image.

IMAGE 2

To open up the tones, I chose Layers > New Adjustment Layer, Levels. I worked mainly with the darker areas (by sliding the middle gray slider), keeping the whites where they were and the blacks deep. If I had tried to lighten the image using the white-point slider, I would have compressed the values and gotten too much contrast. I did bring the white point in about 10 points using the Output Levels control slider; this added texture to the white without causing the highlights to go too gray.

In essence, the input sliders affect image contrast while the output sliders affect print contrast.

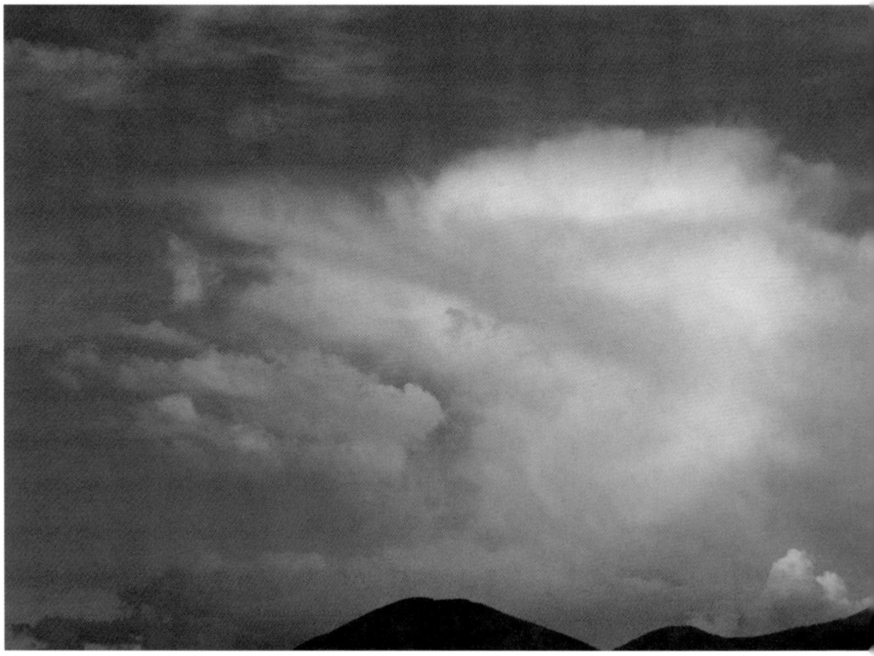

1

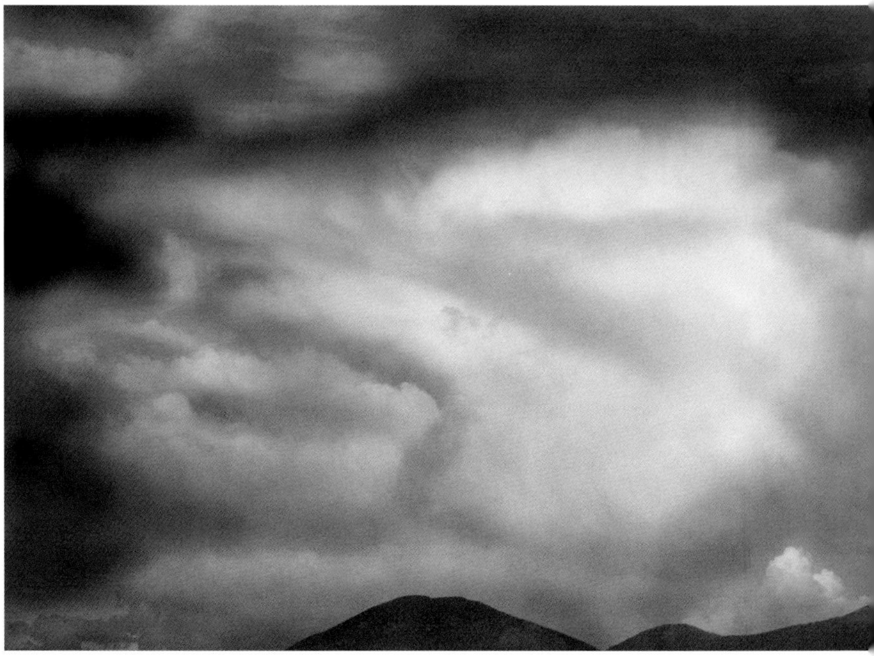

2

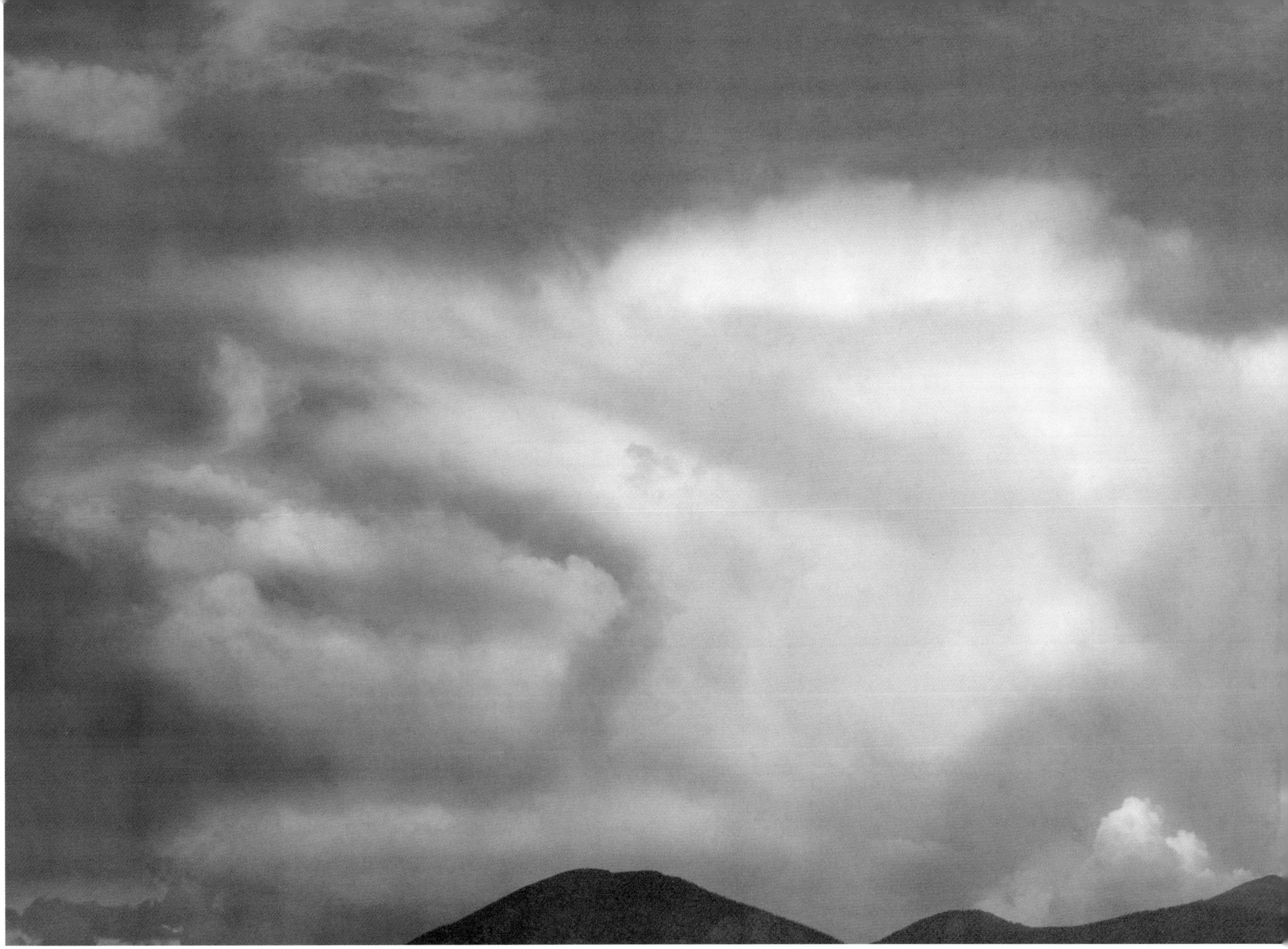

3

IMAGE 3

Once the overall variety and intensity of the tones were established, I got down to the real play of this image: the selective tonal reduction and intensification. I chose a large brush size because I wanted broader effects. I placed a History Brush into the first state of the image. I then used the Screen Blending mode to lighten areas and the Multiply Blending mode to darken. I used a low Opacity on each stroke for control.

TIP

When working with any Painting tool, such as Burning, Dodging, or the History Brush with different Blending modes, use a low Opacity or Exposure setting for more control.

Selection Tools

When you make a selection in Photoshop, you are defining areas in which you want to perform work to the exclusion of other areas. Photoshop has many refined tools that help you do this; you can even extract very detailed elements within a scene for use with image composites. Your aim here is to work with selection tools that help you define areas for tonal control or change to either enhance contrast or blend disparate densities. In conventional printing, there is a technique known as split contrast, in which one area (such as the sky) gets a different contrast-grade treatment from another (such as the ground). This is an established but difficult technique, one that overcomes exposure problems in many negatives. It and other tonal blending techniques are made easy when working with Selection tools.

The basic way of making a selection is with the freehand Lasso tool, then using the Quick Mask mode and Airbrush/Eraser tools to modify the selection (see the first volume of this series, *The Digital Darkroom: Black-and-White Techniques Using Photoshop*). Basically, you draw or create a selection, choose Quick Mask mode from the toolbar, and get a red (or any color) mask over the selection. You can then add to the selection by using the Airbrush and subtract from it by using the Eraser. I have used this method to good effect for many prints.

Other ways to make selections that use Photoshop's ability to differentiate between tonal values include the Color Range, Magic Wand, and various masks. Each provides an easy way to create selections.

The Shift key is another good selection tool. You can add to a selection by making the first selection and then holding down the Shift key when you make your subsequent selections. In Photoshop 6, you can do the same by clicking on the Add to Selection box on the Selection Tool modification screen. You can also use this modification area to subtract from a selection.

Selections can be modified in many ways. One option is feathering the selection, which means modifying the way the selection blends from one defined space or tonal area to another. In the conventional darkroom, you produce feathering as you move your hands or the Burning and Dodging tools as you work. In the digital darkroom, the Feathering setting is made from the Select>Feather dialog box (and with the Selection tool modifier box in Photoshop 6).

When working with selections, become familiar with the various ways to hide, invert, and restore them. When you hide a selection, the area stays selected, but the bothersome (to me) marquee disappears. This is a great way to preview changes as you work your way through them. If you deselect an area and then decide you want to work on it again, open up the Select menu to reveal keyboard shortcuts for these commands (such as Command D on a Mac to delete a Selection).

WORKSHOP 1 **COLOR RANGE SELECTIONS**

HONG KONG TEMPLE

One of the most versatile selection tools is Color Range. Although it sounds like it's just for those who work in color, it's also great for black and white. Color Range allows you to make finite Selections even with raggedy edges (like trees) and discontinuous horizon lines. You can preview the selection right in the dialog box. Black-and-white printers can select highlights, midtones, and shadows. Color printers can actually pick out specific colors.

IMAGE 1

I scanned this image from a 35mm Kodak Tri-X film negative. The scan holds all the image information and awaits some work to bring out detail in the background. The main trouble with the image has always been keeping the burn from spilling over into the shadow areas. For a conventional print, I would have printed the background area first and then burned in the foreground and edges. Color Range selection was used to first pick out the shadow areas, and then to open them up. I picked the background by using Select > Color Range, Shadows. A marquee appeared that selected the shadow areas (1-A). I used View > Show Extras (unchecked) to get a good look at what was selected (or Hide Edges in versions of Photoshop previous to 6.0).

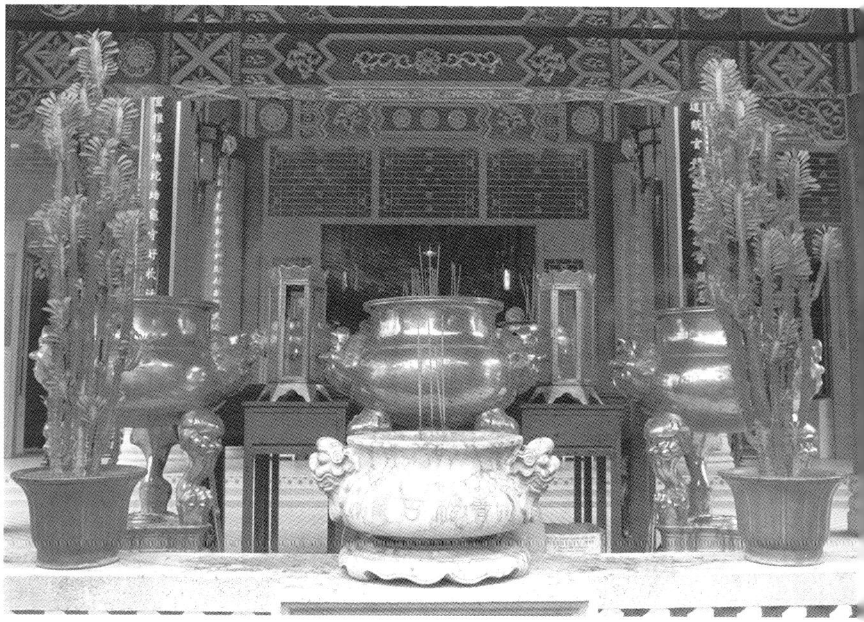

1

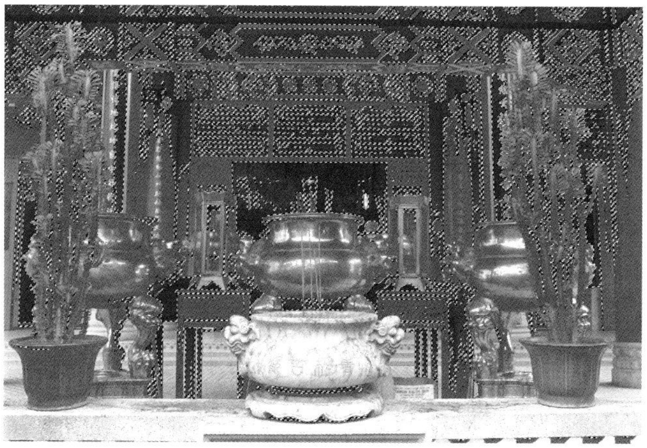

1-A

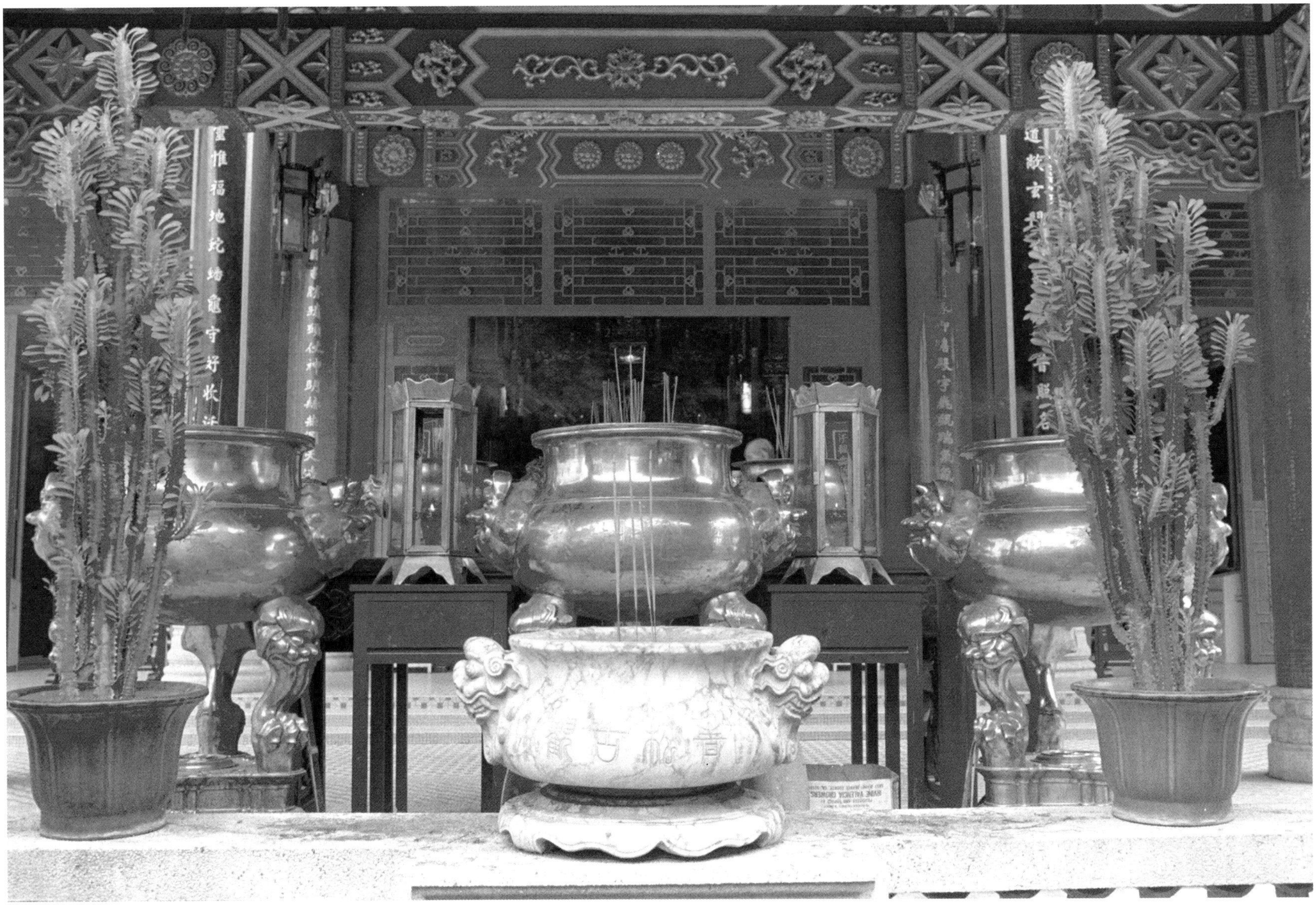

2

IMAGE 2

I used Image > Adjust > Levels to open up the background detail. I then went to Select > Inverse to work on the rest of the image.

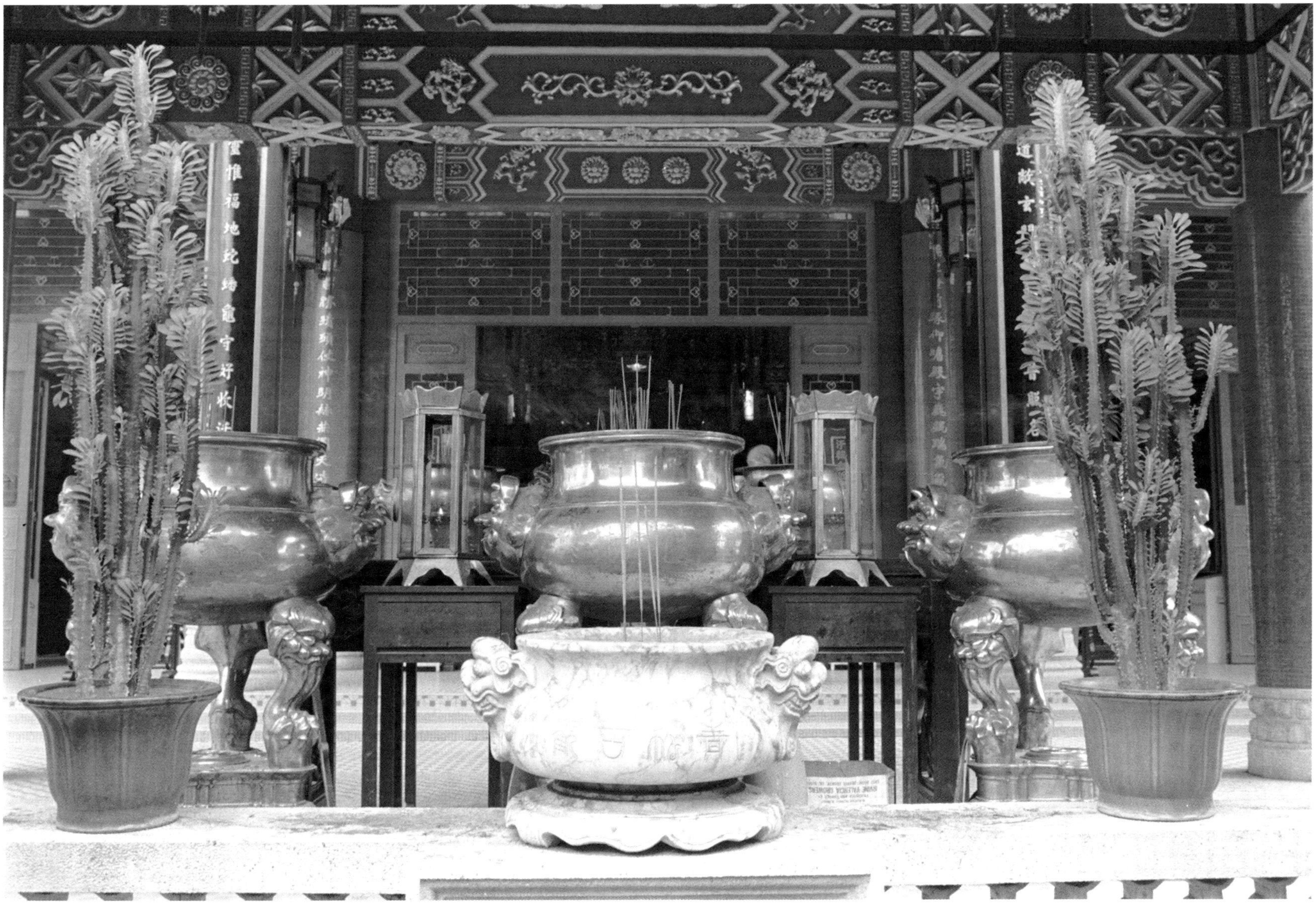

3

IMAGE 3
The final image, after I used Levels and Burn and Dodge to work all tonal areas to my satisfaction.

WORKSHOP 2 **MAGIC WAND**
TRAILER

I often use the Magic Wand tool for selection because it can identify either a very finite tonal range or a wider range, depending on how it is set up. The ability to refine the Selection makes it a versatile tool that can be used for colorization, tonal control, and manipulation. In Photoshop 6, set the Tolerance of the Magic Wand in the toolbar settings. (If you have Photoshop 5.0 or 5.5, set the Tolerance by double-clicking on the tool itself.) Set a low number for a lower range of tones and a higher number for a broader range. In Photoshop 6, you can have the Magic Wand select continuous or non-continuous pixels. In non-continuous, it selects all the pixels of a certain identity throughout the image; the continuous setting stops the selection when it hits a tonal border different from the area selected when it is higher than the Tolerance setting.

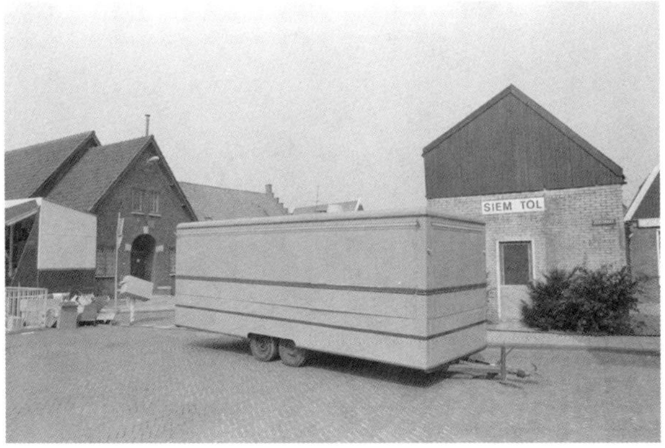

1

IMAGE 1
I scanned this image from a 35mm black-and-white negative. I had exposed the photograph for the ground on a hazy, backlit day so the sky went blank. The result is fairly flat, although there is a good range of tonal information sitting under the veil. My aim here is to enliven the image without making it too contrasty and to do something with the blank sky.

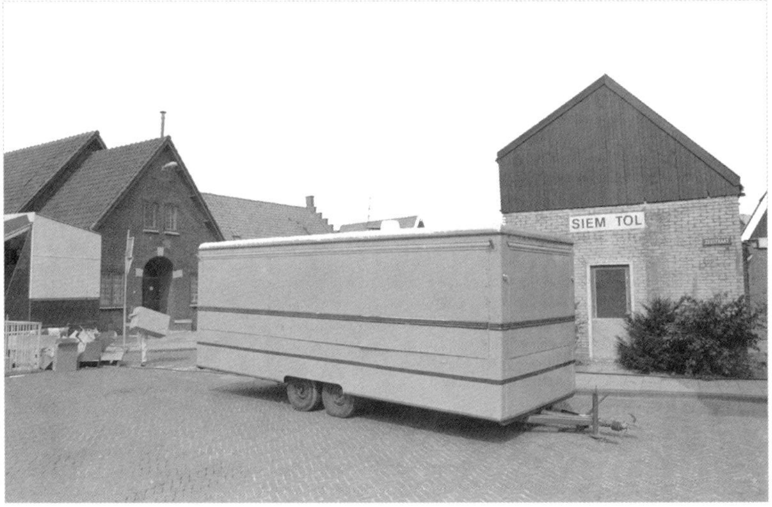

2

IMAGE 2
I created a layer via Duplication by dragging the Background (foundation) image in the Layers palette to the copy icon. I then chose the Magic Wand and entered a Tolerance of 16. I used this tolerance because I wanted to get all the sky and its slight variations selected while avoiding selecting any parts of the foreground scene. I clicked the Magic Wand in the sky, and the sky was selected. I then used Levels to make the sky brighter. The next step was inverting the selection (inverting takes what has not been selected and selects it while deselecting the previously selected area). I then used Levels to tighten and brighten the tonal values in the foreground. The change this produced was slight, but enough to yield some snap, about half a grade in variable-contrast terms. Now I had a blank sky and a well-defined foreground.

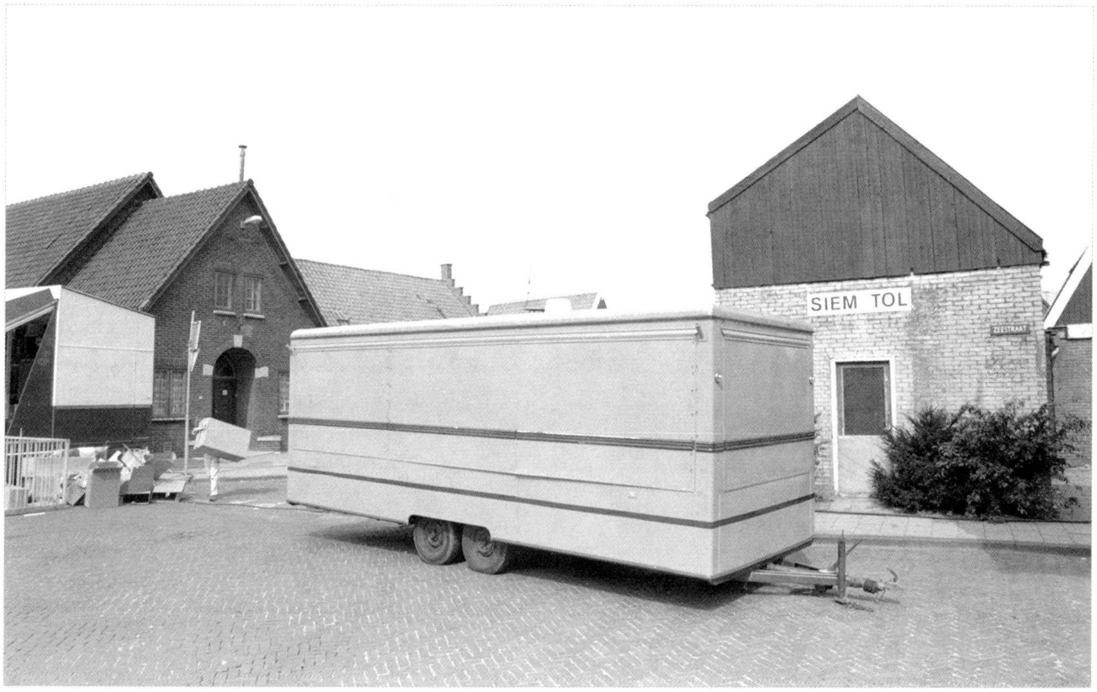

3

IMAGE 3

I inverted the selection again, because after working on the foreground I wanted to achieve something else with the sky. This often happens when you change one tonal area: you begin to recognize where other areas need to be worked, and getting a blend is the point in most printmaking. Once the sky was selected, I opened up Filter > Blur > Gaussian Blur and set it for 10 pixels. My aim was to clean up the sky by blurring it.

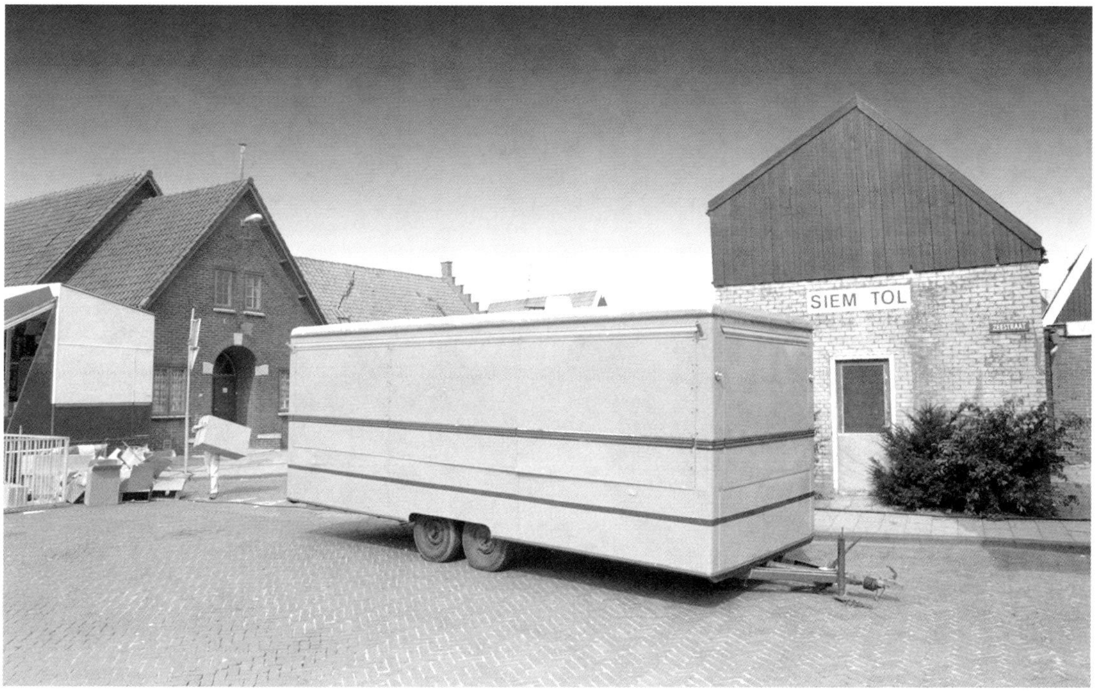

4

IMAGE 4

I then decided that I wanted to get a bit surreal by working with a Gradient tool. Gradients can be edited and changed easily, but I wanted a straightforward deep to light-gray motion from the zenith down. I clicked on the Gradient tool (Black to White) and drew it from the top to the horizon line.

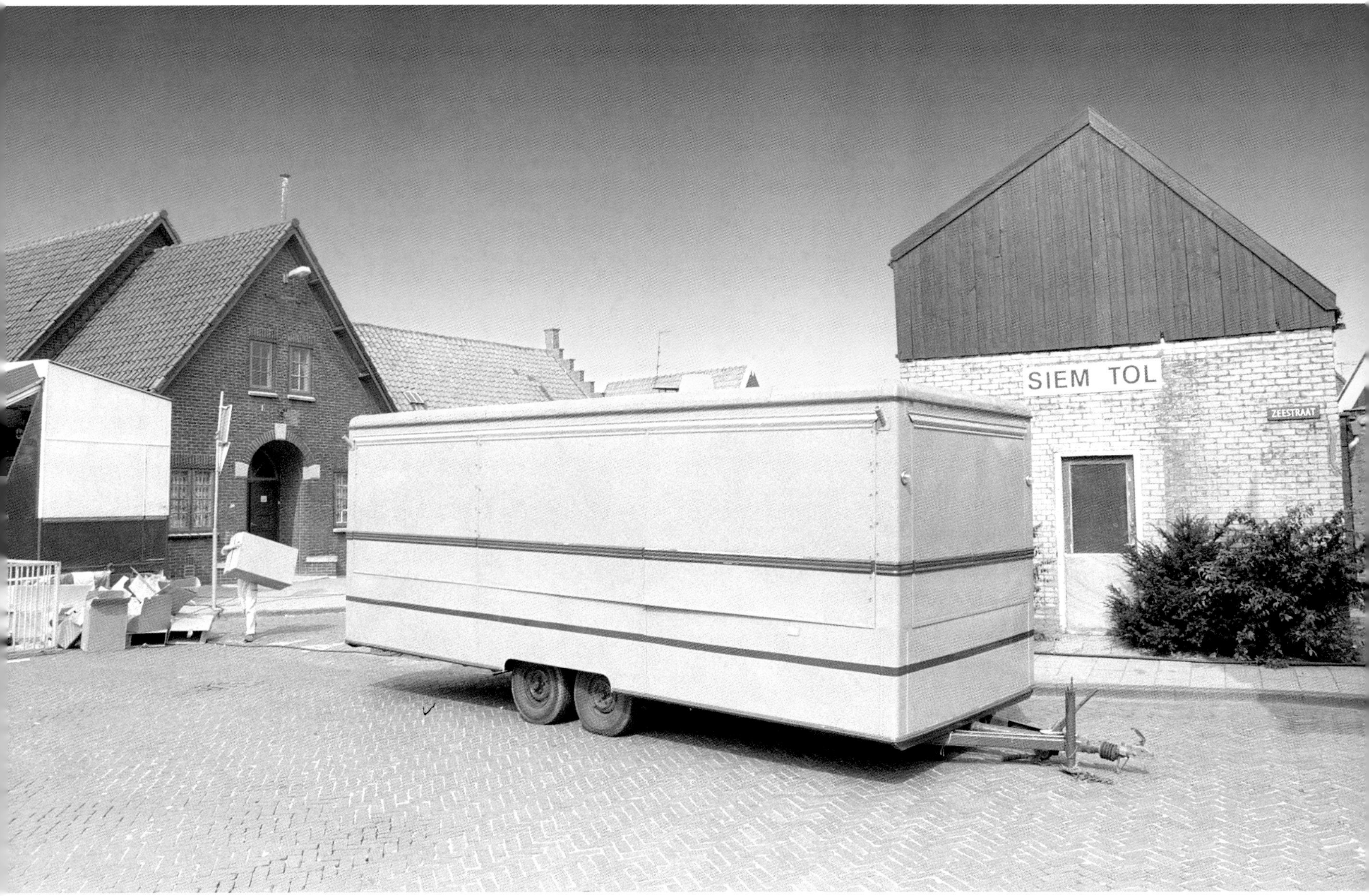

5

IMAGE 5

The effect now was fine, except the Gradient tool felt a bit harsh. I decreased the effect by fading it.

WORKSHOP 3 **MAGNETIC LASSO**
FLOWER

The Magnetic Lasso tool is designed to grab tonal edges as you draw the selection. You can set a number of parameters for when and how often the edge is grabbed, including edge contrast (the degree of difference required), frequency (how often it grabs an edge; more complex images should be set at a greater frequency), and lasso width (the number of pixels it defines).

There are a number of ways you can use the Magnetic Lasso tool to make selections, ranging from the straightforward to those requiring a degree of dexterity. The Lasso does take some getting used to, however, as it sometimes seems to have a mind of its own. The freehand draw, for example, can be fun, but it takes time to learn and requires some facility with the mouse or stylus. You also must be sure to end where you started, and to get a marquee moving before you move the mouse or stylus again. No question, though, that the tool is a time saver, especially for those of us raised on pre-Magnetic Lasso Photoshop.

IMAGE 1

I scanned this image as grayscale from a 35mm color slide made on the late, lamented Scotch Chrome 1000 film, a very grainy but exciting material. The lighting was flat, although there is a good deal of potential for tonal play.

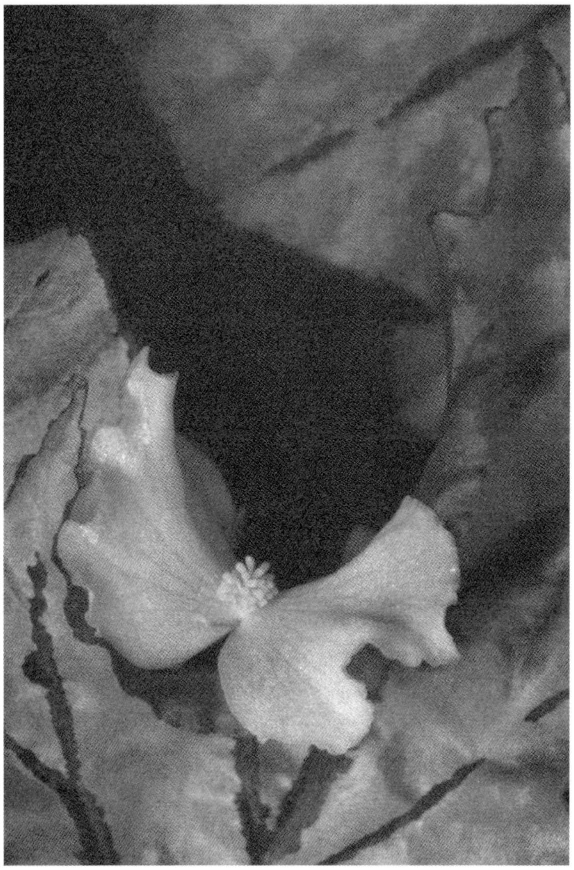

1

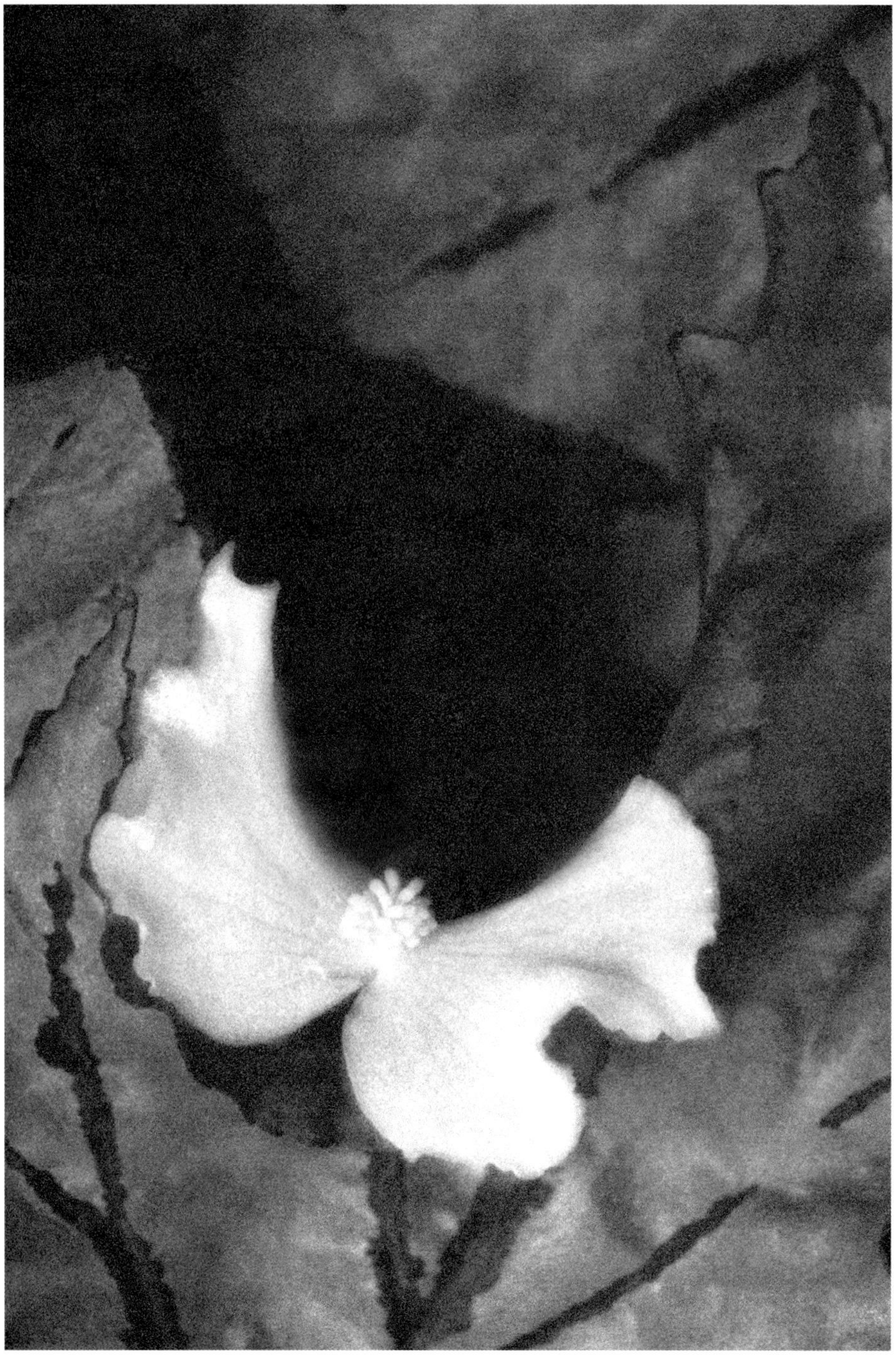

2

IMAGE 2

I chose the Magnetic Lasso tool and made the settings Lasso Width 2, Frequency 22, and Edge Contrast 22. I slowly dragged the Magnetic Lasso around the flower petal. If the edges wandered, I moved the Lasso back to where I needed it to sit and clicked to set another anchor. I brought the tool to where it started and double clicked to create a selection marquee (2-A). I then opened Layer > New Adjustment Layer and chose Screen in the Blending mode to lighten the flower.

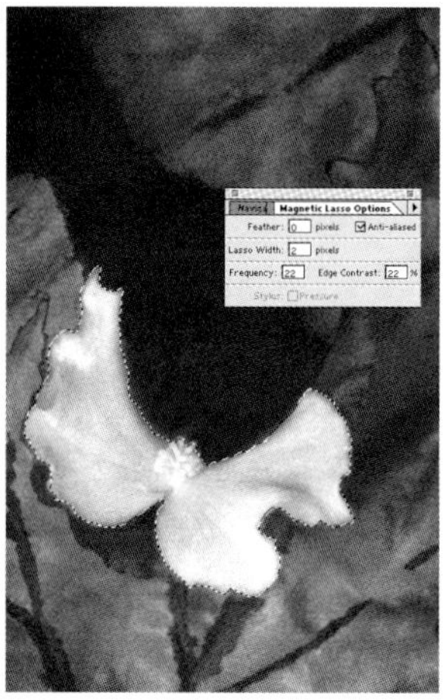

2-A

IMAGE 3

I then deselected (Select > Deselect) the area and created a dupe layer. I opened Image >Adjust > Levels and lightened the overall image for a bit better tonal blend. For a final print, I chose a Tritone mode with black, Pantone 1345CVC, and Pantone 413CVC.

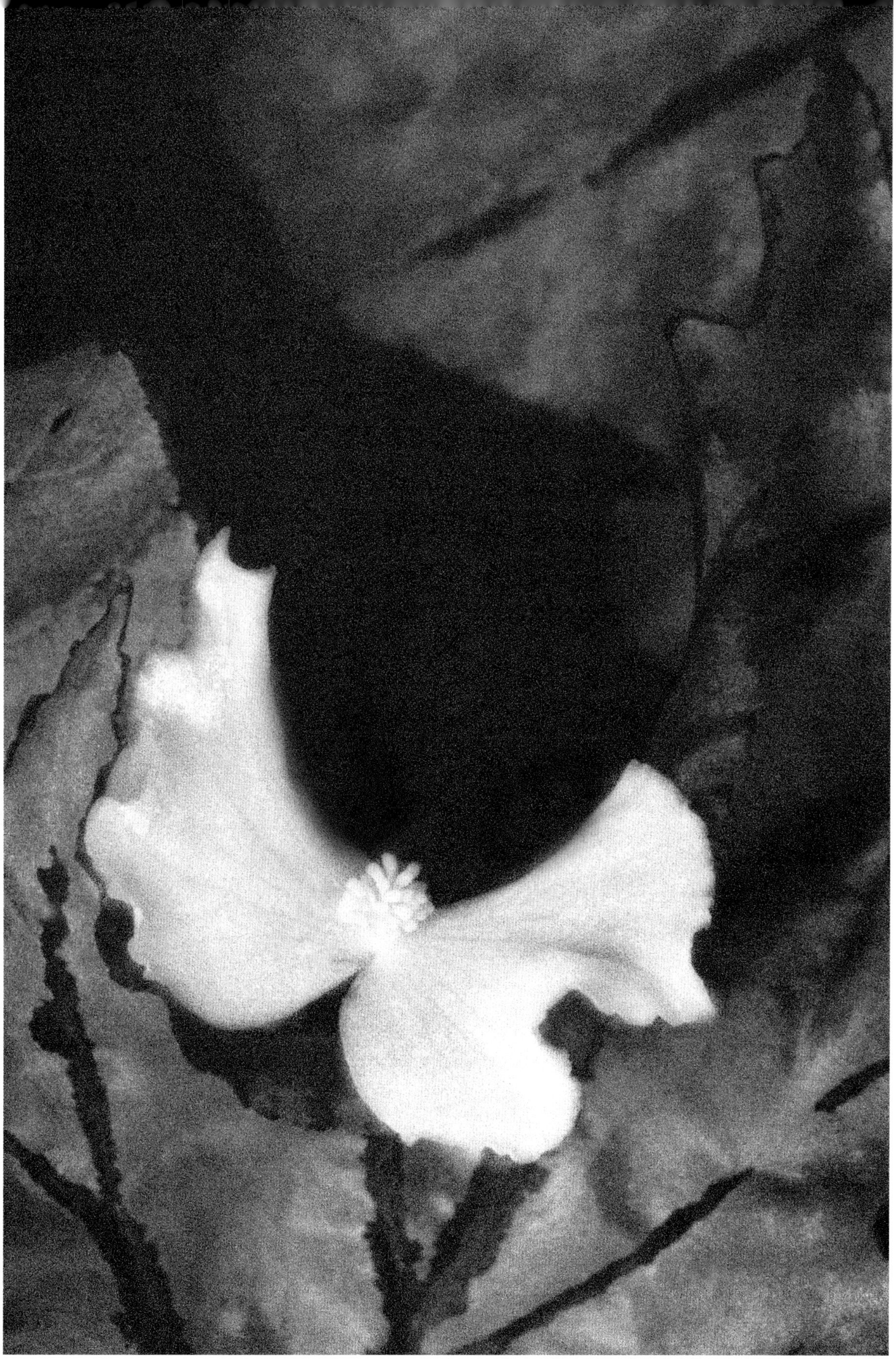

3

WORKSHOP 4 **ELLIPTICAL MARQUEE**

FIGURES IN STONE

Edge burning, a time-honored tradition among printers, is often used to create a subtle center of light in a print. It can be more evident when used as a vignette, a popular technique in portraits to make the face more dimensional and brighter than the surround. Edges are usually burnt with lots of feathering to create a gradual transition of tones from center to edge. I often edge burn in the digital darkroom for the same reason I did in the conventional one.

Edges can be burnt with the Burn tool, but I often find it's easier and more consistent using the Elliptical Marquee tool. When you activate the Elliptical Marquee, you get a cross hair that you click and drag to create a shape. This shape can be moved around the image and then placed by releasing the mouse or stylus pressure. It does take some time to get the right shape and size of the oval, but soon enough it becomes easy to do.

When doing edge burning with an Elliptical Marquee, use the Feather command to modify the tonal blend, and check anti-aliasing to smooth the edges. To see a good representation of what the mask will look like, create it on a layer of its own and deactivate all the other layers. Then, modify the blend as required.

IMAGE 1

I scanned this image from a 6 x 6 cm black-and-white negative. These shapes were under a rock ledge that threw a shadow over the entire scene, resulting in very little tonal variety. The exposure is good, but the light is flat. You'll see how I used the Elliptical Marquee to select the central figure, painted around it to identify some other interesting shapes, and enlivened the image with tonal variation.

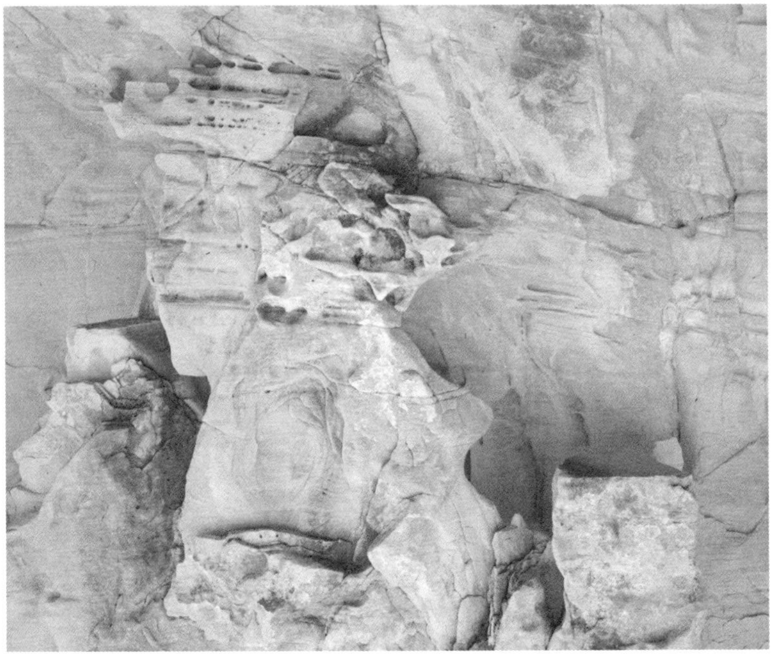

1

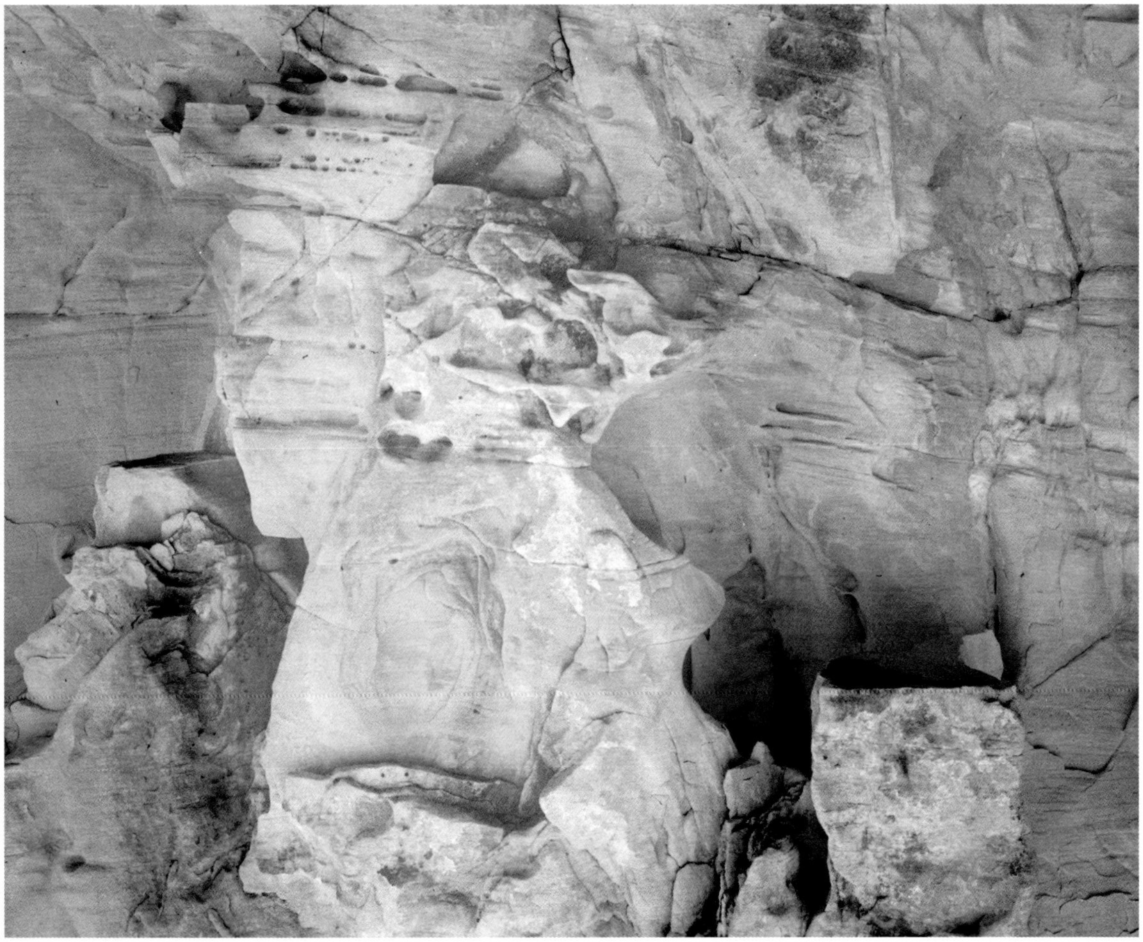

2

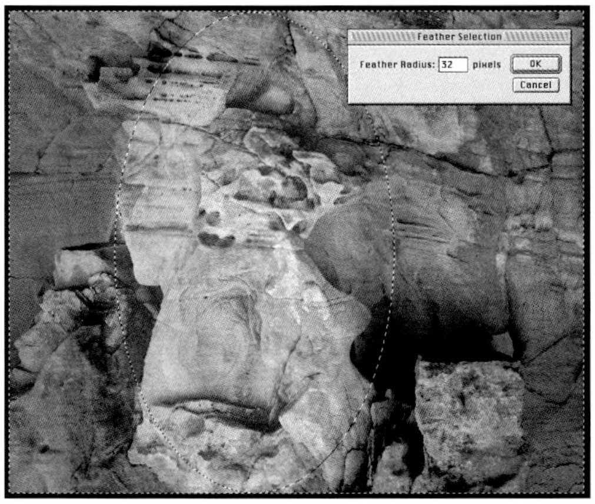

2-A

IMAGE 2

I used the Elliptical Marquee to surround the central portion of the image with a selection, and inverted the selection (Select > Invert) so that every area except that defined by the oval was active. I then darkened this area using Layer >New Adjustment Layer, Levels, and worked the sliders until I got the effect I wanted. The mask had been set at a Feather of 32 so that it blended from light at the inner edge to darker at the outer edge (2-A). I then removed the selection using Select >Deselect.

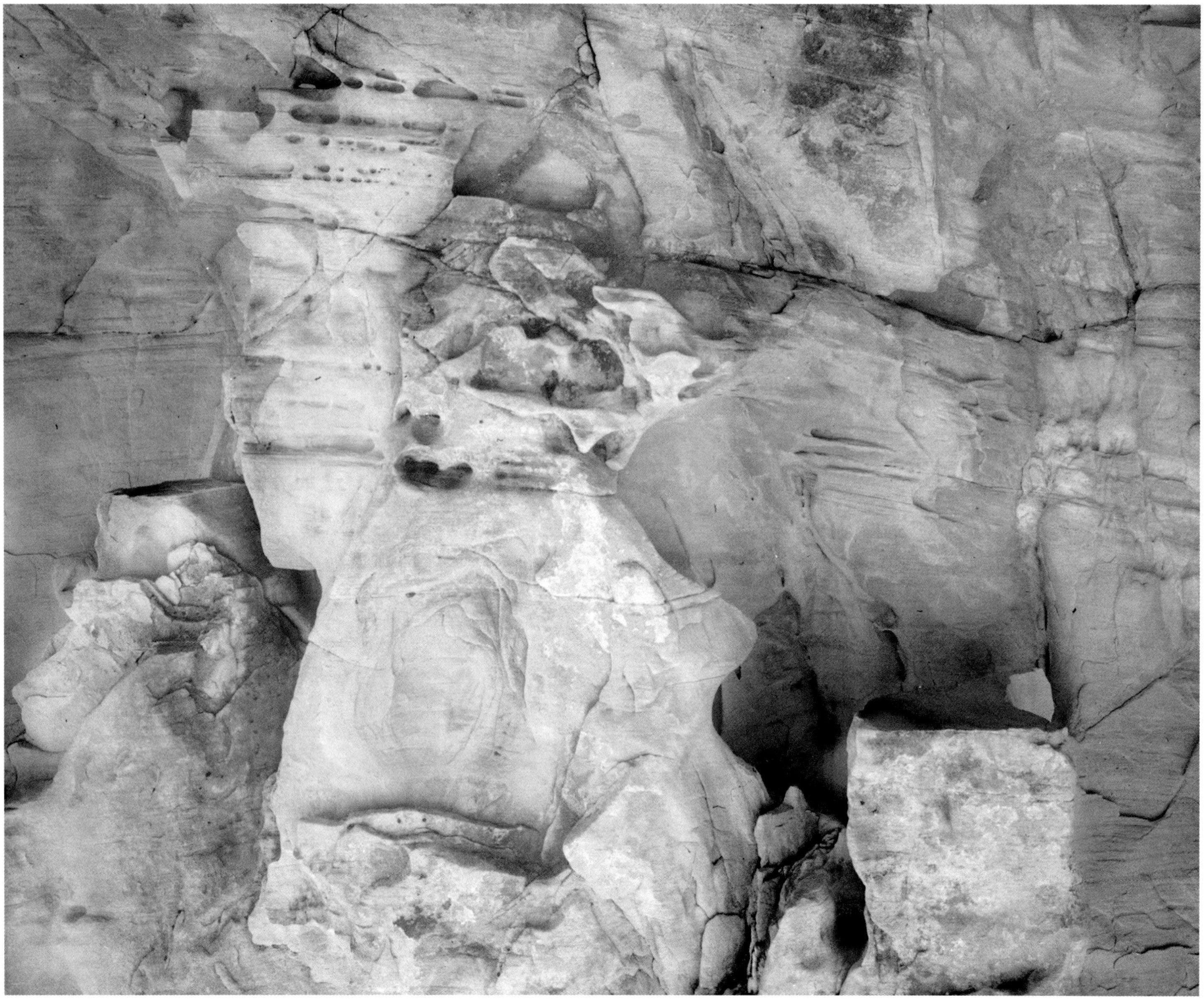

3

IMAGE 3

I then did the following: chose the History Brush, placed at the opening state; set the Blending mode to Screen to lighten the areas on which work was done; set the Opacity at 30% to make for a gradual decrease of density; and chose the brush size and enlarged the image to make careful strokes. The image became defined as density was painted back in certain areas.

WORKSHOP 5 **POLYGONAL LASSO**

BODIE WALL

The Polygonal Lasso is one of the best tools for those doing still life or architectural work, as it creates a freehand straight edge for you—something not easily done otherwise. To use it, just click on the start and end point of the line it selects, remembering to enclose the whole area with the marquee.

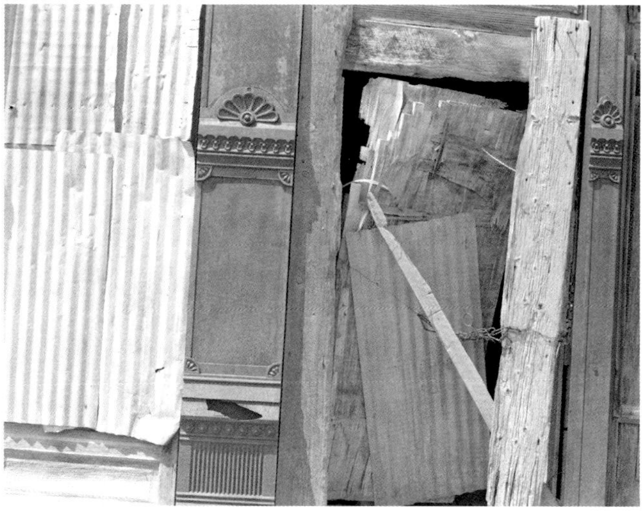

1

IMAGE 1

I scanned this image from a 35mm black-and-white negative. It has a very good variety of tones but is burned up on the left side. If I were to attempt to fix this with an overall contrast adjustment (Levels or Curves), I would be sacrificing tonal value on the right side. The answer is to select the left side and work on that individually, leaving the right side alone. I chose the Polygonal Lasso and created a box around the left side of the image.

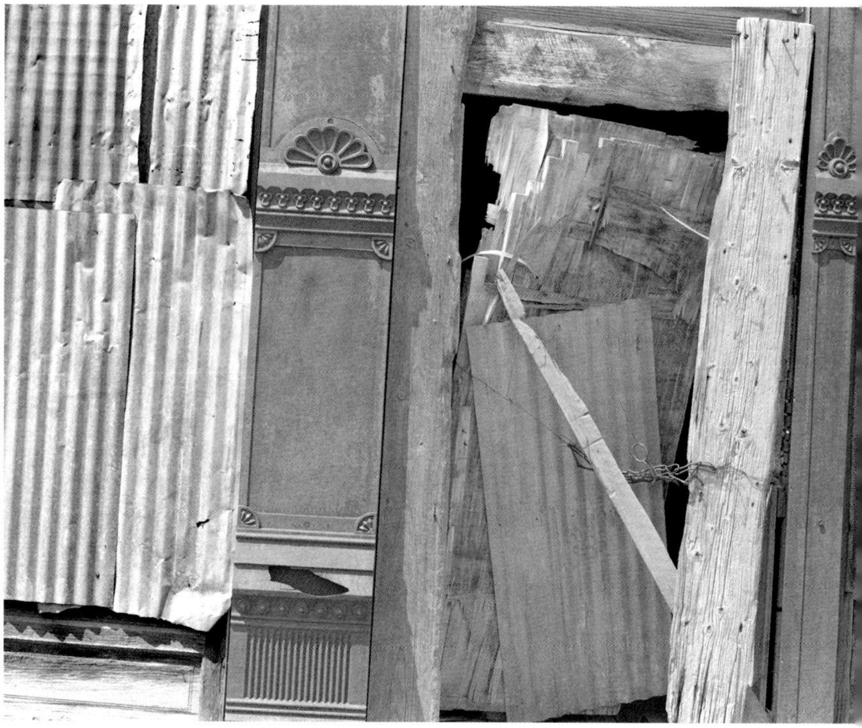

2

IMAGE 2

I adjusted the tin sheeting first with Image > Adjust > Levels, input 87/78/255. This was fine for that area, but the bottom portion was still overexposed. There was no way to deepen the tin area further, so I needed another approach to controlling the burned-up highlights.

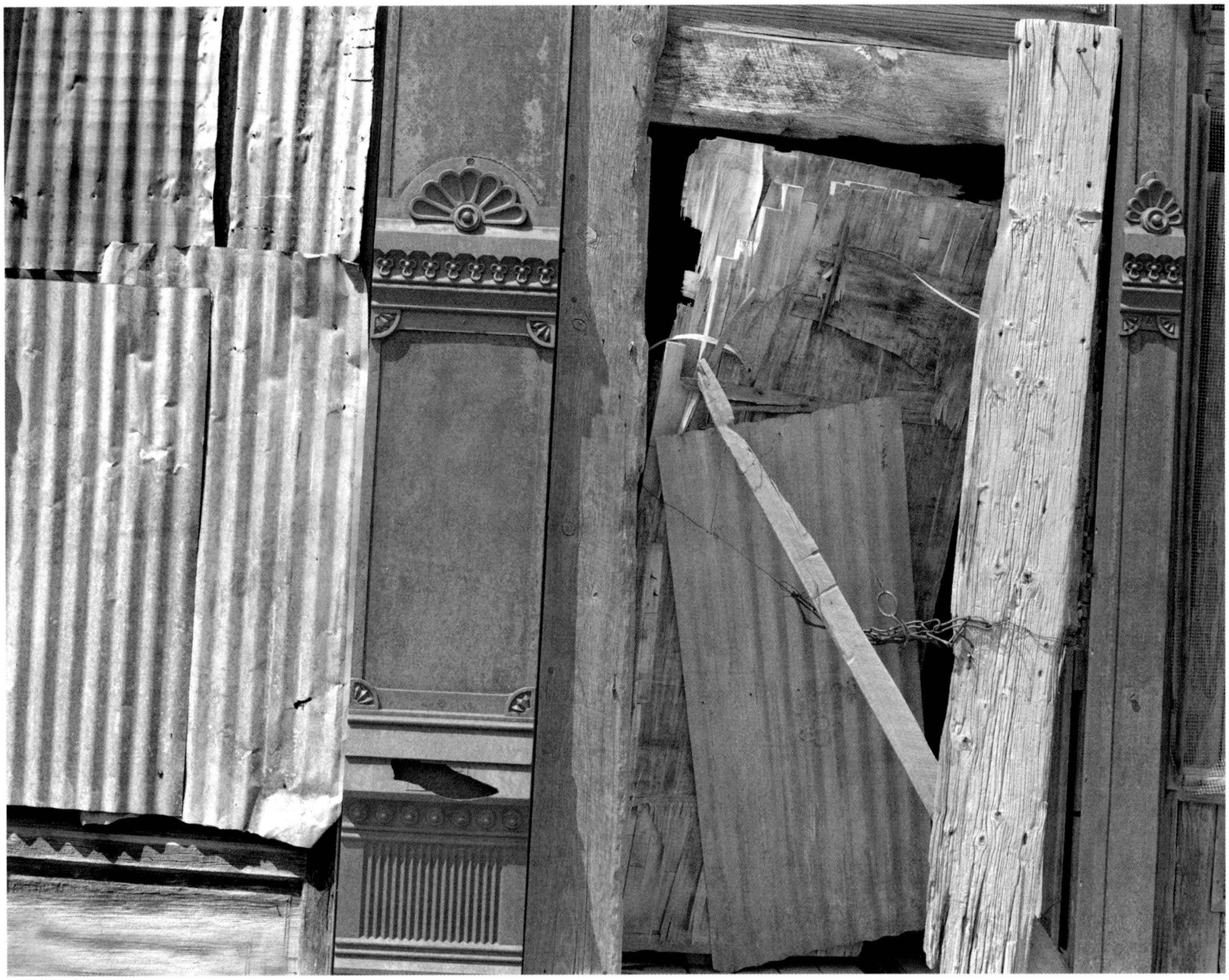

3

IMAGE 3

I did this with the Clone (Rubber Stamp) tool, using it to clone an area with the same texture but more density, and deposit it over the burned-up highlight part of the image. The Rubber Stamp is one of the most useful tools in Photoshop, particularly in retouching or restoration work; it is the tool that takes the place of the spotting brush as well. When you click on the Rubber Stamp, you get a brush size (if you have chosen it in the Displays and Cursors Preferences) that acts as a guide. Place the tool size over the area you want to clone and hit Alt/Option click. This will pick up that area according to what you've defined. Now move the Rubber Stamp over the area to paint with the cloned pixels and click. This lays down the pixels in those areas.

Retouching and Restoration

I have the greatest respect for airbrushers, retouchers, and restoration artists. The work requires infinite patience, attention to detail, and a masterful eye and stroke. As with much in imaging, though, the photo restoration arts are becoming digitized. The scanner is replacing the copy camera, and the digital darkroom has made the use of inks, airbrush pens, and friskets (a vellum mask) obsolete. The reason for this change is the relative ease of doing retouch work digitally.

The availability of inexpensive, image-ready computers and image manipulation software has combined with equally affordable scanners and printers to make retouching an art that, while still requiring discipline and training, is more accessible than ever before.

To get a sense of how digital retouching has changed the game, let's look at how restoration work is done using film and silver paper techniques. Let's say someone has a worn photo from an old family album. He brings it into a photo studio or lab.

At the studio or lab:

- The photographer puts the image on a copy stand and photographs the picture.
- The negative is developed and a work print is made.
- The work print goes to the airbrusher and is fixed.
- The airbrushed work print is rephotographed, the negative developed, and the final print made.
- The final print may be sepia-toned.

Digital work flow on the same image:

- The image is scanned; the original is returned to the customer.
- The operator works the digitized image, using a digital copy that has no generational loss from copy negative/print cycles. When done, she applies a tone to the image without setting up chemical baths. The customer gets the new prints, a floppy disk, a CD, and perhaps an e-mail posting where the images can be shared with family and friends.

Retouching—whether in the home or studio—relies on the same controls used in fine printing, but often starts with a damaged original or one that needs more cosmetic fixes than a well-stored negative or slide would require. Though there are a number of things that can be done in the scanning stage, such as sharpening, cropping, and even some contrast control, most of the retouching work will be done in the image-processing and manipulation software.

Restoration is a bit more complex. It may mean cleaning up images, colorizing them, adding density, fixing tears, eliminating revisionist or recidivist relatives, bringing missing aunts back to family picnics, making old wedding albums look new, and converting treasured backyard snapshots to fine-art images.

Those with standard darkroom experience or those who have done conventional retouching and restoration work have a leg up on those with little or no experience in the craft, but an understanding of all the techniques and tools of a software program does not necessarily prepare you to know what to do with the image once it's on the screen. In addition, retouching and restoration are not just about special effects or tricks. Although the results can seem like magic, the work requires a lot of zooming in and out, tonal matching, and an eye for what will work.

There are a number of tools that are consistently used in the retouching arena, including the Dust and Scratches filter and the Rubber Stamp, and using Layers to add density to an image. If you go back into your own family album or collect old photographs from flea markets and antique shops, you'll see a huge need for restoration and retouching. If you have the patience and are willing to put in the time, it can be absorbing, satisfying work—and perhaps even a source of income.

WORKSHOP 1 **MINOR RESTORATION**
LES AMERICAINS

This image was among a packet of postcards I purchased at a flea market about 20 years ago. It is in good shape for an image printed in 1917, but has begun to fade and show the usual signs of age. I decided that it would make a good study print for retouching.

IMAGE 1
The unmanipulated scan is an excellent representation of the original postcard. It's grainy but can be repaired. There are no major cracks or flaws.

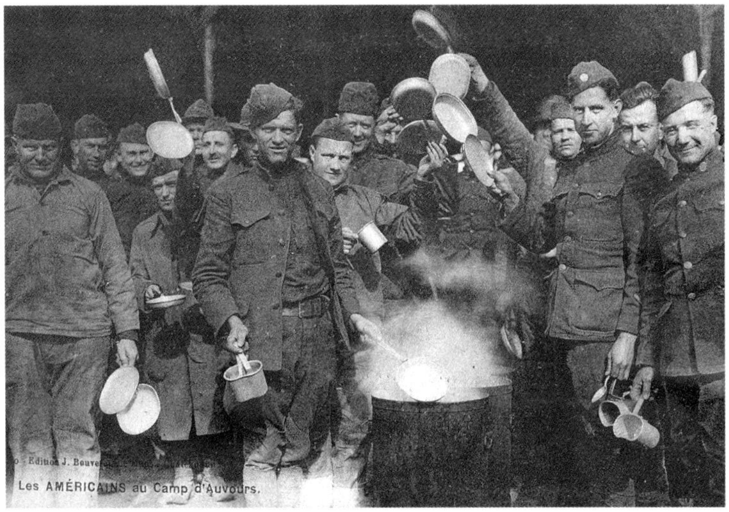

1

IMAGE 2
To start work on the image, I made a duplicate layer and then selected a brush from the Brushes palette. For the blending mode, I selected Lighten. I then used the Eyedropper tool to take a sample from a darker area of the print, the shadow behind the soldier's heads. (The sample you choose in this way shows up in the foreground color box at the bottom of the Tools palette.) I then painted with the Paint Brush tool. This affected only those areas that were darker than the tone in the foreground color box.

IMAGE 3
I then changed the option to Darken and continued to paint the image. This brought some snap back to the image without raising contrast too much.

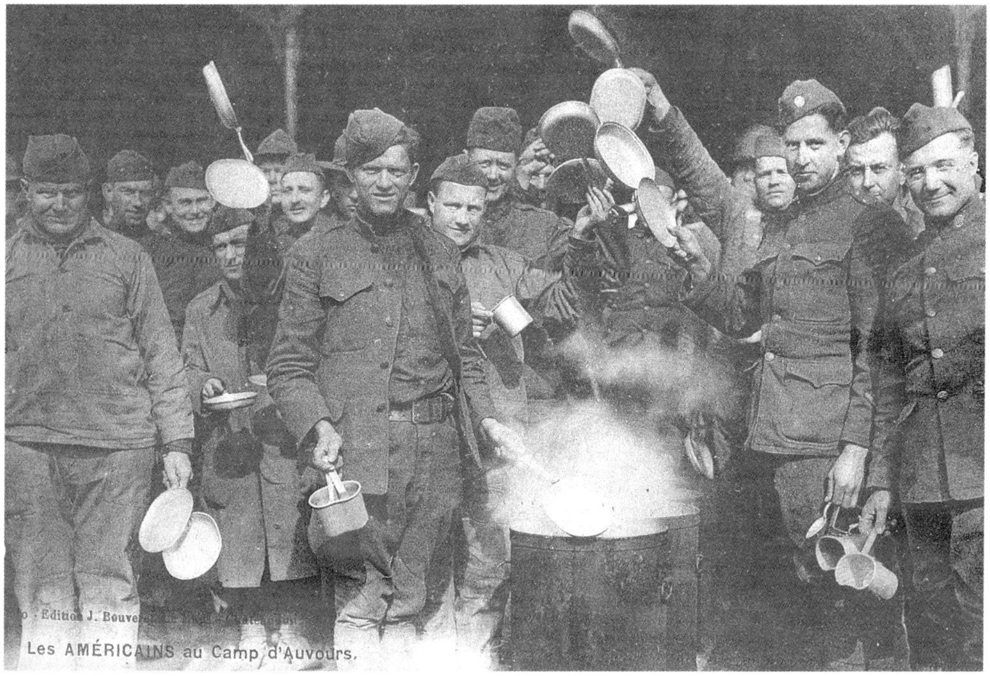
Les AMÉRICAINS au Camp d'Auvours.

2

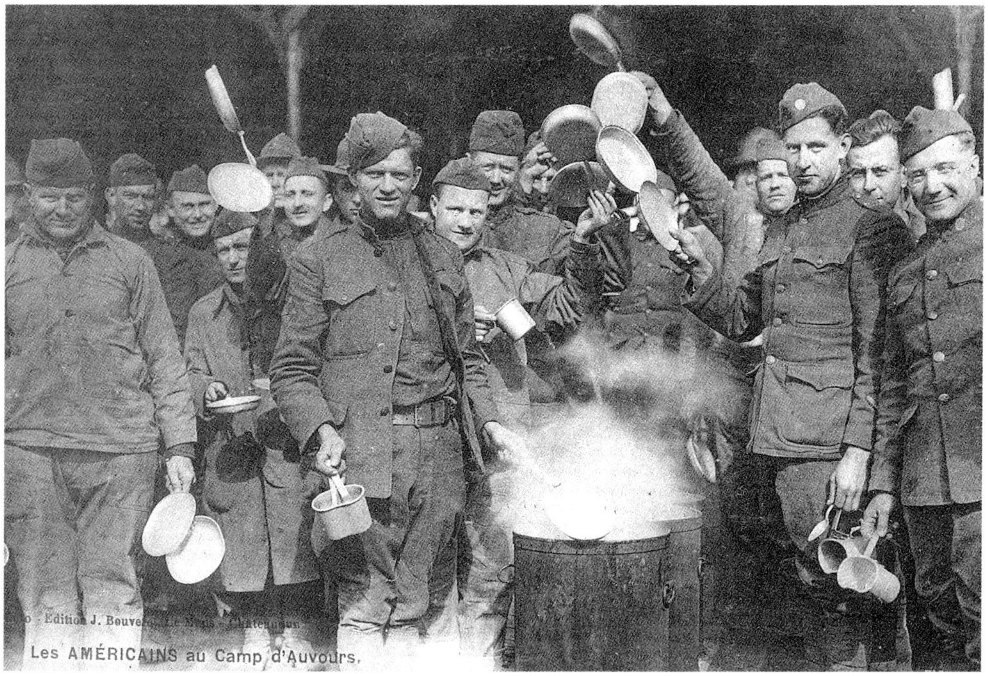
Les AMÉRICAINS au Camp d'Auvours.

3

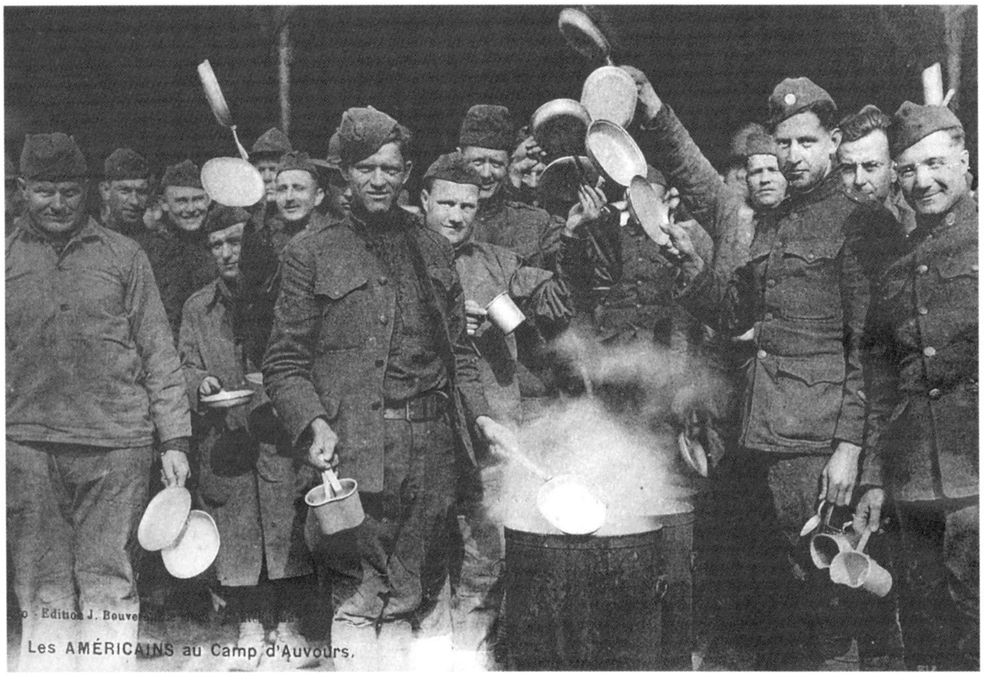

4

IMAGE 4

To help get rid of some of the excessive grain, I made a duplicate layer and used the Median Filter by going to Filter>Noise>Median. I tried different settings until I got rid of the grain without getting too blurry. The Median filter blends the brightness of pixels and discards those that differ too much from one another. I often use it to reduce grain.

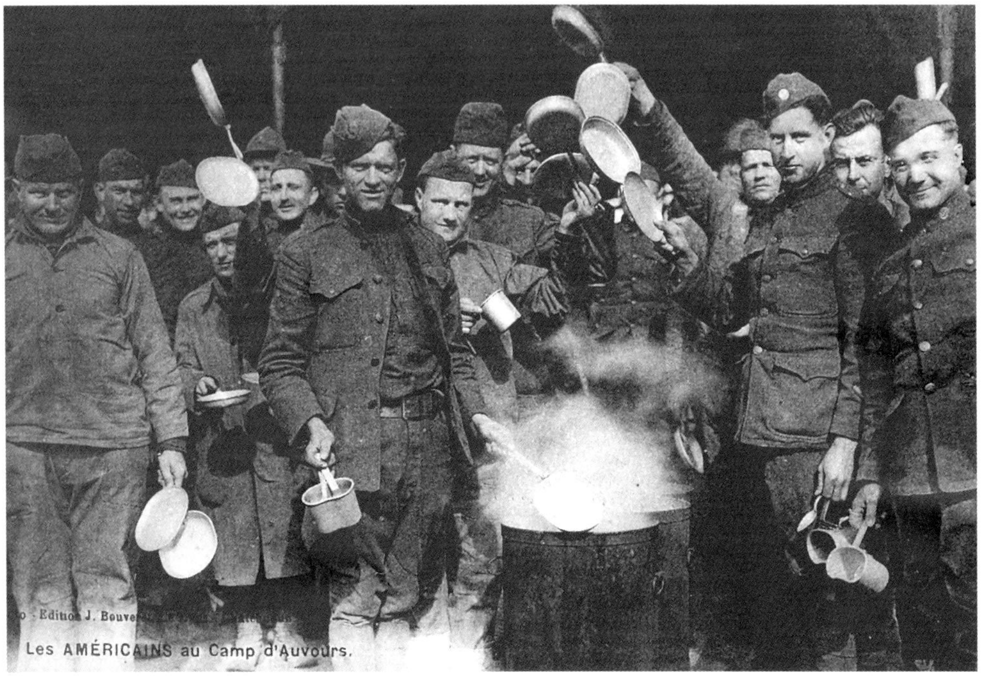

5

IMAGE 5

For a final touchup, I tightened up the image using Levels and worked with the Rubber Stamp (Clone) tool to patch any tears and discontinuity. To work with it you hold down Alt/Option and click on the area that you want cloned. You can change the coverage by expanding or contracting the Brush size with the bracket keys. I find it is better to click and clone often rather than work in very broad strokes when retouching. Watch for the cross hairs as you work, as they set the source for the cloning and application strokes.

WORKSHOP 2 **GLASS PLATE NEGATIVES**

THE HAT

On a recent trip to visit photographer Dave Wade in Maine, we stopped by a row of antique stores in the town of Bath. Dave was known to the shopkeepers as having an interest in old glass plate negatives, so when we walked in, the storekeeper already had a box of them on the counter. Because I have handled this type of negative in the conventional darkroom, I know what a problem they can be; most have at least one major or minor glitch. In addition, getting them to sit in an enlarger without using a glass carrier can be tough, and if you use a glass carrier you always run the risk of Newton's rings (irregular patterns of colored fringes). Nevertheless, glass plates hold an amazing legacy of images for our families and our society. Many have a real beauty in their tonality and a richness that is a joy to print.

The flatbed scanner is a wonderful tool for working with glass plates. When scanning, back the plate with a plain white piece of paper with no surface texture. Unless you want the backing paper's texture to show up in the scan, make sure there is no weave or watermark that can be read.

IMAGE 1

The original scan of the negative shows both a pretty good tonal scale and a fair amount of wear and tear. By the clothes and mustache, I judge this image to be from about 1890.

IMAGE 2

To get from a negative to a positive image, I used Image>Adjust>Invert.

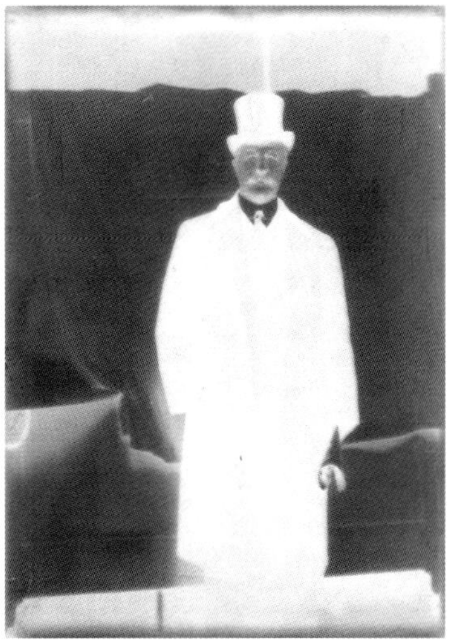

1

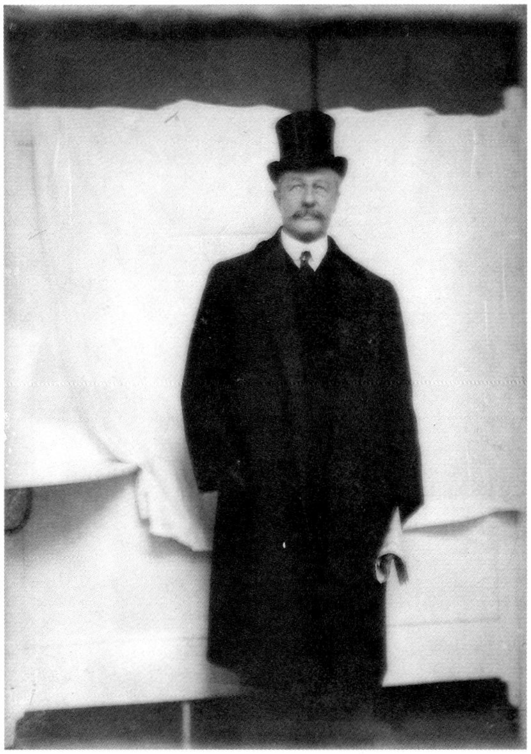

2

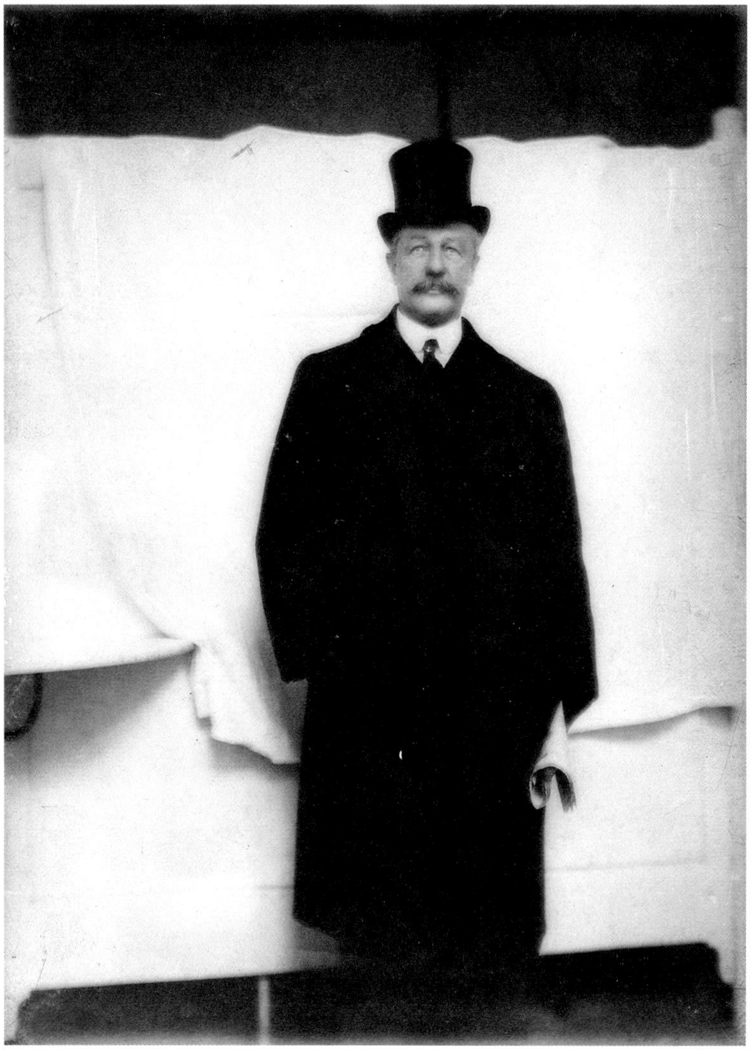

3

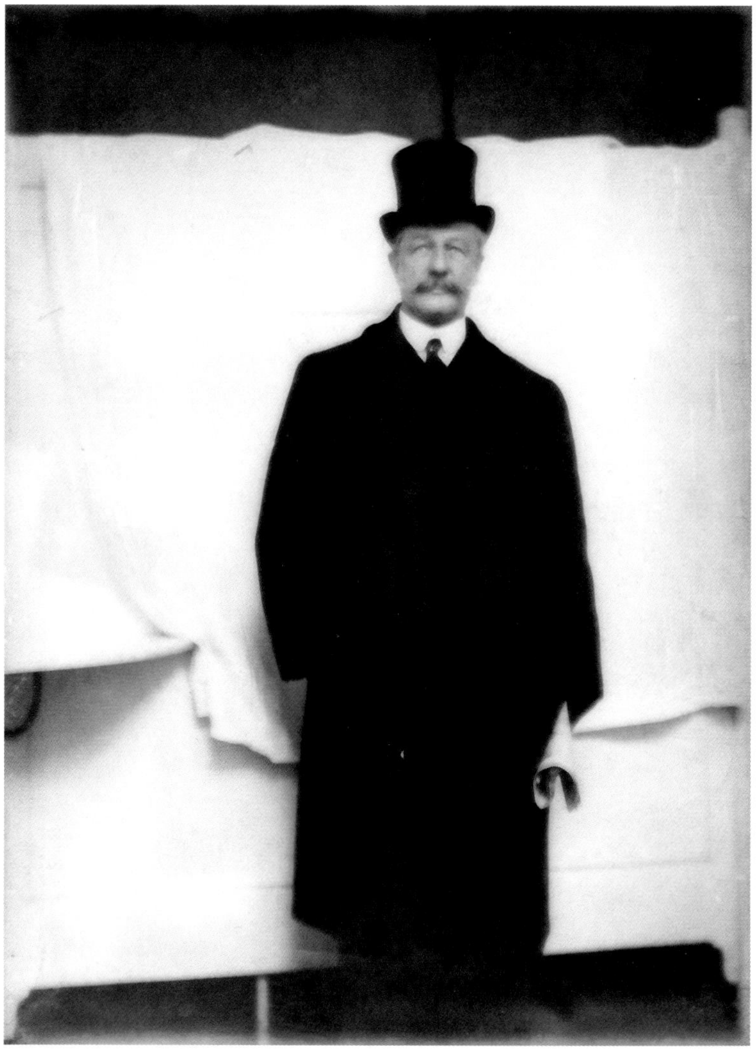

4

IMAGE 3

The first stage of working on this image was getting the right tonal scale and contrast. I made a duplicate layer by dragging the background (foundation) image in the Layers palette to the copy icon. I then set the Blending mode on Soft Light.

IMAGE 4

I made another copy via Layer and used the Dust and Scratches filter set at a Radius of 4 and a Threshold of 5 to balance the blur with the grain. This filter is found at Filter>Noise>Dust and Scratches.

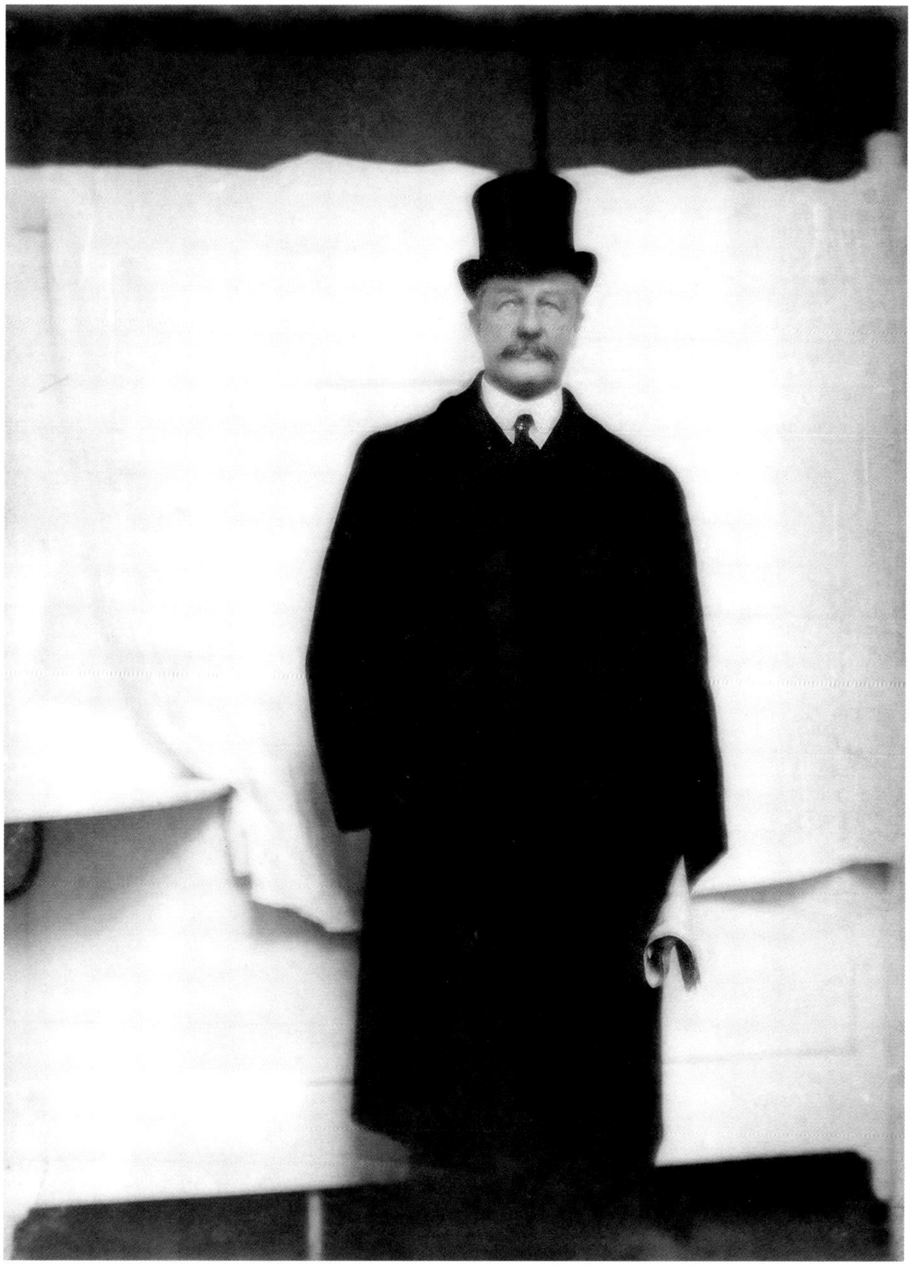

5

IMAGE 5

For the final stage, I used the History Brush and placed it in the History palette just before using the Dust and Scratches filter. I then painted back the face and cravat area so that the loss of sharpness in those key areas was minimal, yet the filter could do its job on the overall image.

WORKSHOP 3 RESTORING FADED PHOTOGRAPHS
REUNION

It is heartbreaking to realize how many images have been lost to the ravages of age and time. These visual legacies are subject to so many deteriorating forces that it's a wonder any survive. Color photographs made in the 1960s and 1970s have begun to go magenta. Many black-and-white images have begun to fade, due in part to poor processing but in the main to poor storage conditions. If you are the keeper of your family's photographic legacy or are considering using your restoration as an income provider, you will encounter many types of image deterioration.

I chose this image because it is one of the worst I have ever seen. It was among the images in an old album I picked up in an antique store. The reproduction here is no exaggeration, as the image had literally faded away. The memory of the people in the photo and the moment they were all together was almost entirely lost.

I had little hope for this image. If I had been doing the restoration by photomechanical means I would have made a copy negative and printed it on a very hard (high-contrast) paper. This would have helped, but I would have also lost most of the image details and the faces would have resembled line drawings. Although the final image I show here is still not a complete restoration, it does bring the image back to life.

Sometimes, as I work on an old image, I realize that it may be the only memory or remnant that remains of a life, especially when the albums and pictures have been left to flea markets and antique stores. When I work on such an image, I begin to feel that I somehow maintain that memory for a bit longer and begin to connect to the person or group in the image. It's an odd but satisfying feeling.

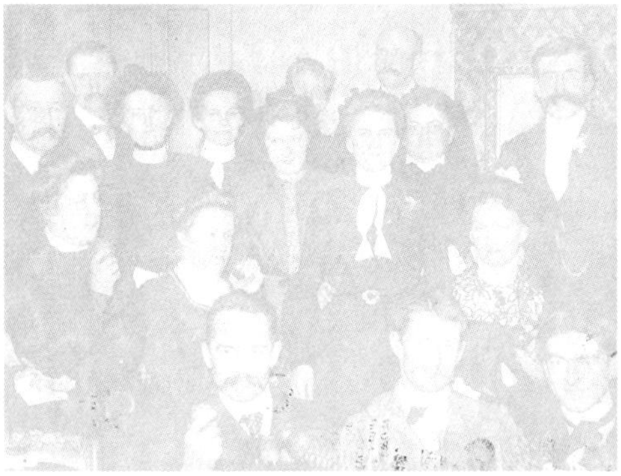

1

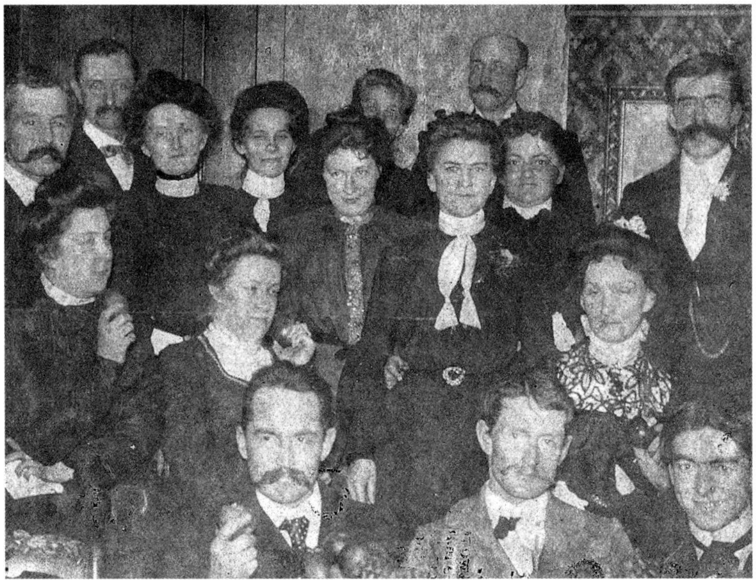

2

IMAGE 1
Impossible! How can I expect to get anything from this image? This is no exaggeration of how badly faded the image was.

IMAGE 2
After I scanned the print and opened the image, I used Layer>New Adjustment Layer, with the Blending mode set at Multiply. This added density to the image and yielded more information than I ever imagined could be available. After another Multiply layer, I created a Layer>New Adjustment Layer, Levels to kick up the contrast a little.

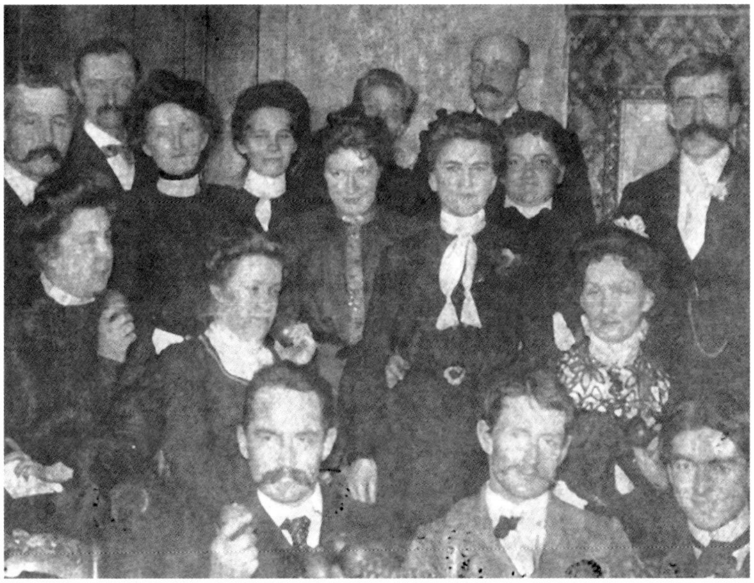

3

IMAGE 3

My next stage was to soften the grain. I went to Filter >Noise >Median and set it at 2%. This helped modify the difference in pixels and reduced the appearance of grain.

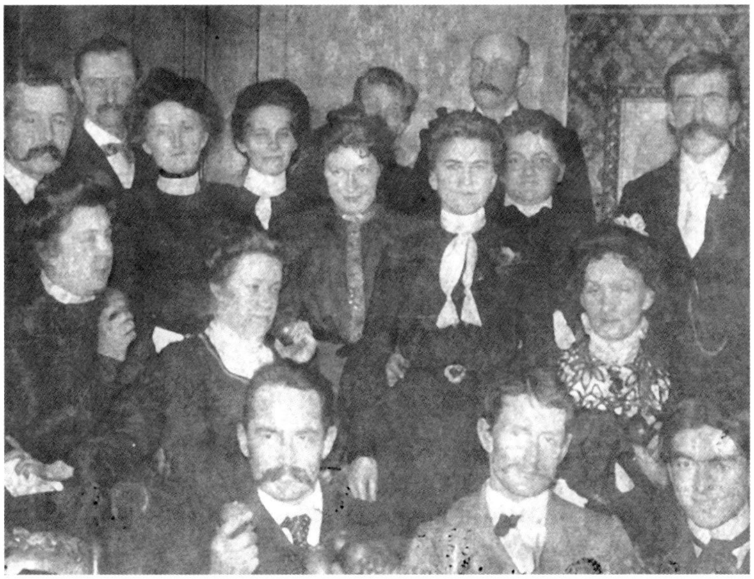

4

IMAGE 4

I then set the History Brush in the Duplicate layer and painted back the faces so they were a bit sharper.

WORKSHOP 5 **RETOUCHING SCRATCHED SLIDES**
FIGURES

I scanned this image from a slide that had been through the wars. Scratches and glitches existed on both sides of the film. It is a modern image made about ten years ago, and I include it in this group because I've learned that not only old images need retouching help.

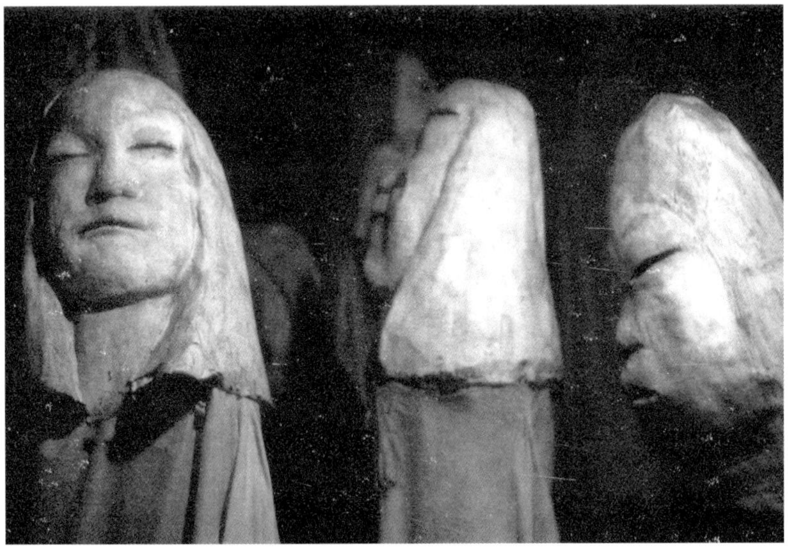

1

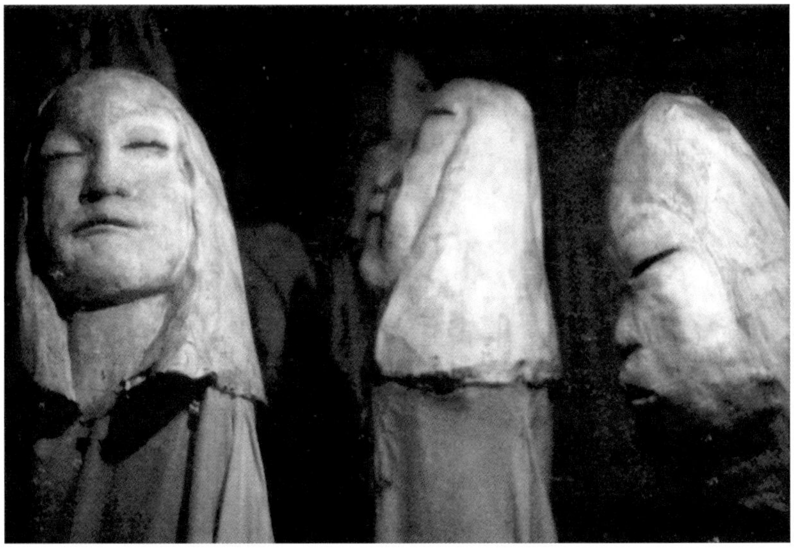

2

IMAGE 1
This image is what the image looked like after the first stage of work. I used a new adjustment layer set on Levels/Screen mode to add some contrast and open up the image. I now had the tonal balance where I wanted, but I still had to take care of the dings and scratches.

IMAGE 2
I opened the Dust and Scratches filter via Filter >Noise >Dust and Scratches and set the dialog box up at a Radius of 5 and a Threshold of 20. This struck a good compromise between sharpness and cleanup.

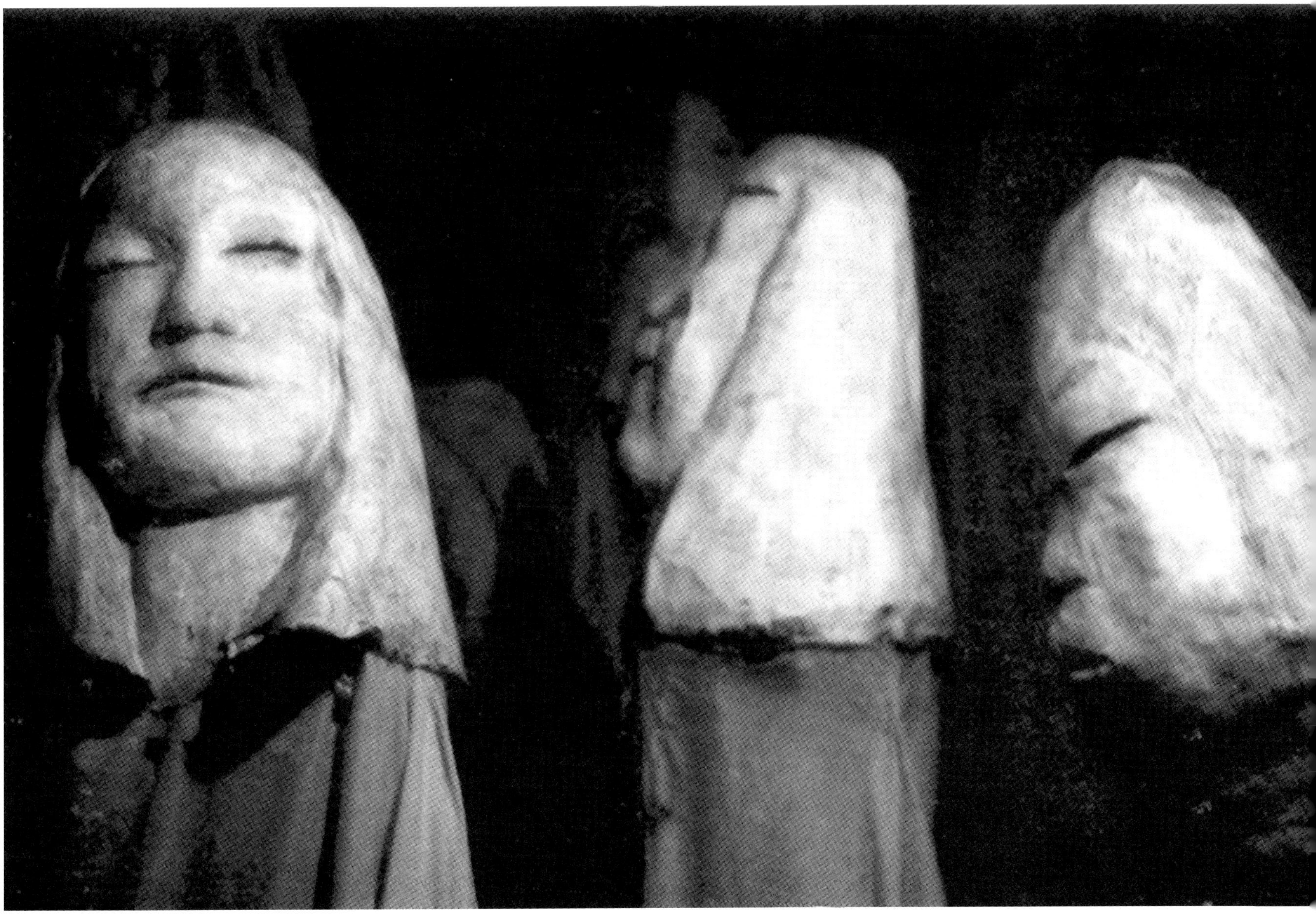

3

IMAGE 3

To finish up, I used the Rubber Stamp tool to clean up any remaining glitches. I then used the History Brush, placed at the Duplicate layer and set on Screen. As I painted back the faces, I worked with their contours to bring back some sharpness and contrast.

WORKSHOP 1 **DUOTONE AND TRITONE**

RIVER BANK

I made this image from an RGB scan of a 6 x 6 cm black-and-white negative. The sky was quite overcast, although there was some variety in the moving clouds and fog. I like shooting square format because I can crop horizontally or vertically later. The negative is somewhat flat, although some extra developing time gave it a bit more kick than the lighting values imply. My aim with this image was to maintain the New England feel and lighting, a mood I associated with the somber sky and tonal values. I also wanted to give the image some color value to aid the subject matter.

IMAGE 1

My first step was to decide on cropping. Following the subject matter, I decided to make it a panoramic crop, yet maintain some approximation of the rule of thirds within the frame. Above all, I knew I had to keep the reflection whole. After I cropped the image, I switched the mode from RGB to Grayscale via Image >Mode >Grayscale and used Filter>Sharpen>Unsharp Mask, 150/.1/12. I played the Threshold off against the Sharpening to get a smooth transition.

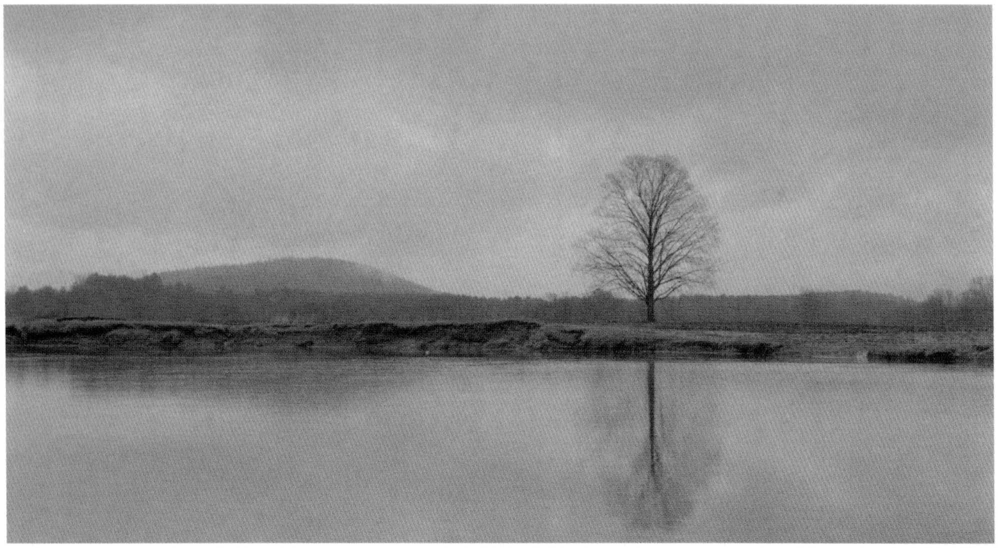

1

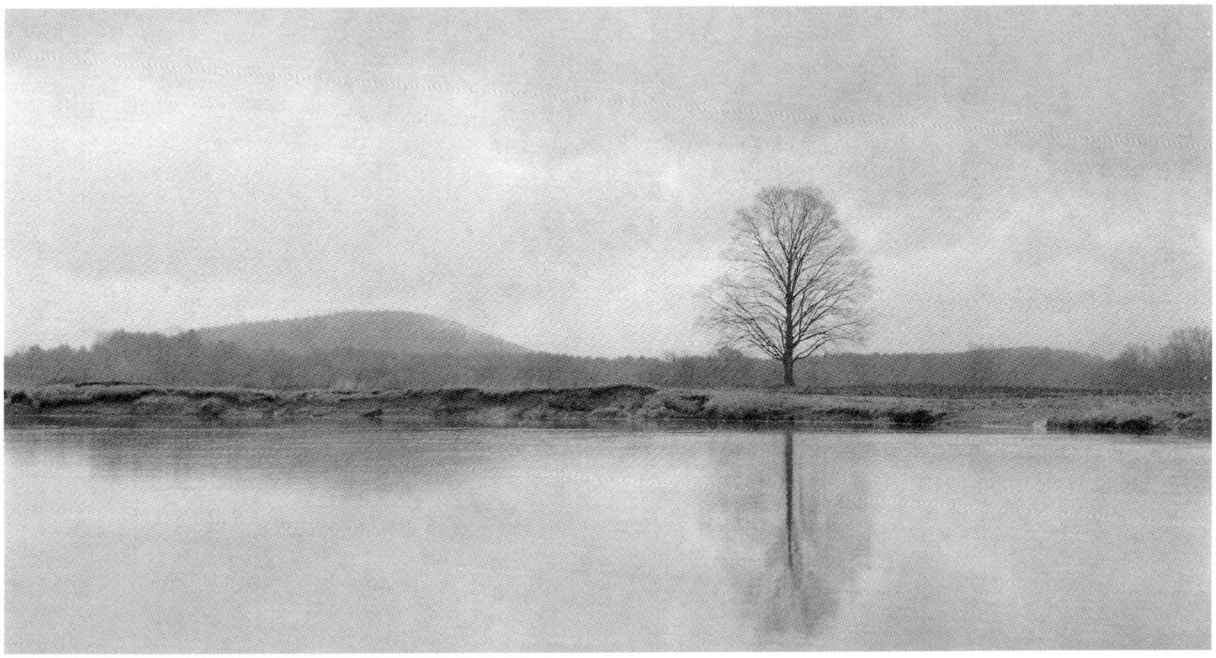

2

IMAGE 2

When I looked at the image I knew that I wanted a bit more snap, but I didn't want to lose highlight detail in the breaks in the sky. The compromise was keeping the flat look but accentuating detail and showing some tonal separation in the river bank. I opened an adjustment layer through Layer >New Adjustment Layer and picked Levels, Normal. I slid the markers to 18/85/208 Input and 15-251 Output. This somewhat odd approach looked right on the screen. It kept the mood while providing some tonal separation, and pointed out the need for monitor calibration. If you are finessing values, you must be able to see an accurate representation on the screen.

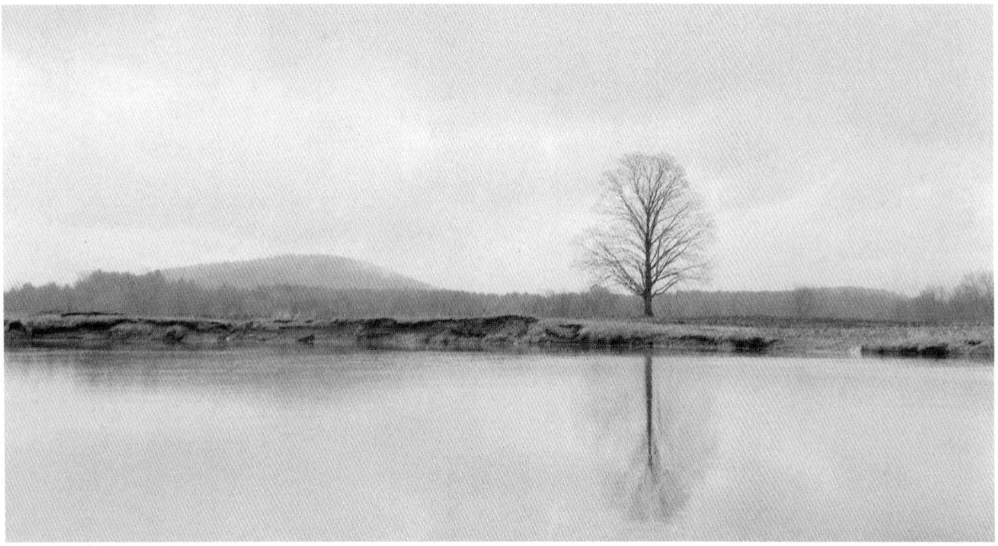

3

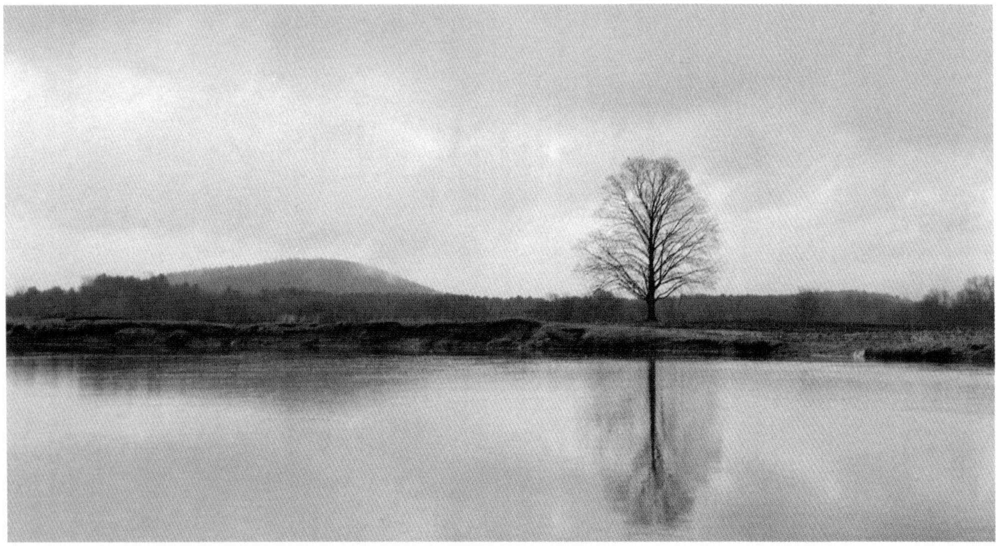

4

IMAGE 3

The grayscale version was a nice slate gray, but I kept seeing 19th-century prints in my head; the ghost of Coburn led me toward duotones. I decided to try a Photoshop preset, so first I opened the Duotone dialog box by using the route Image > Mode > Grayscale > Duotone.

When the Duotone box opened, I clicked on Load and the finder popped up on the screen. I clicked and scrolled my way through Photoshop to the Duotones Presets folder. You can also save and name your own sets, great for when you are making an edition of images and want to have the same effect throughout.

I picked one of the presets, dubbed Aqua Gold in the Tritone option, that gave me black (always the first ink), Pantone 313CVC, and Pantone 127CVC. This preset lightened the image due to the nature of the curves of each ink. You can change the curves to change the effect of each set, but I don't recommend changing the presets. Instead, make your own and save and name them for later use.

IMAGE 4

I wanted to bring the image back to a darker mood, and did so using a new adjustment layer set at the Multiply Blending mode. This created the mood without raising relative contrast, and worked well for me as the final image.

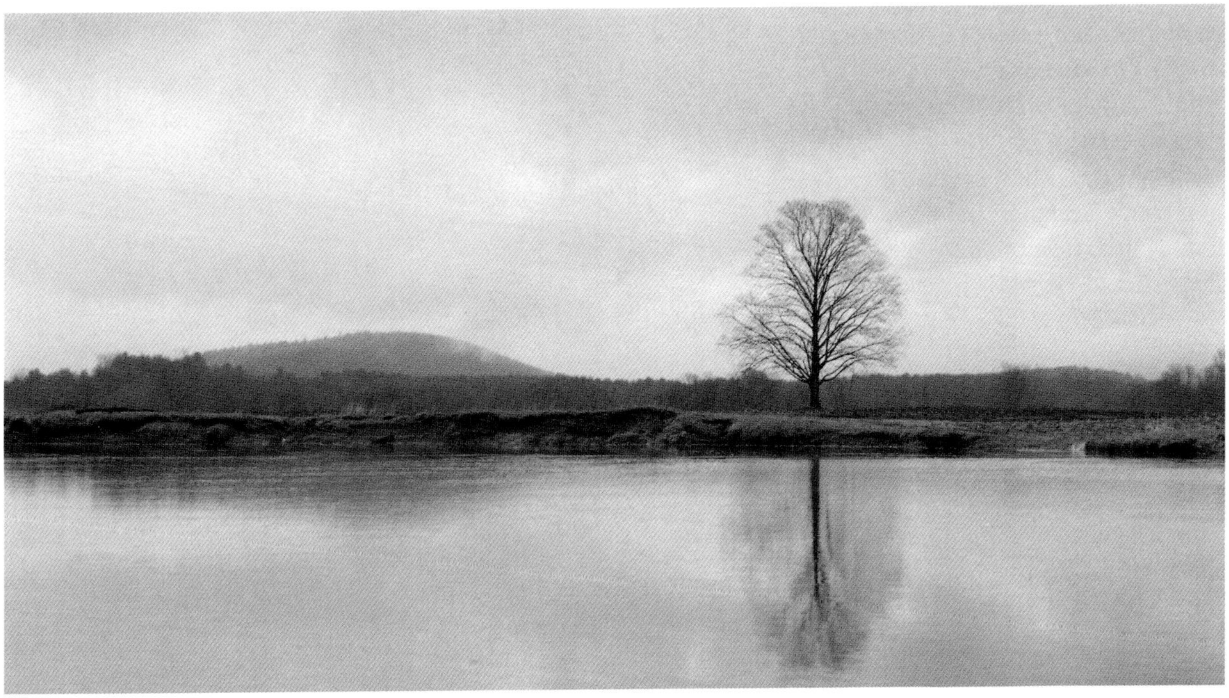

5

IMAGE 5

To try out another option, I saved the previous image by doing File > Save a Copy. I then went back to the Image 2 state by opening up the History palette and highlighting the step where I created the new adjustment layer. I copied the state by using File >Save a Copy and naming it. (In Photoshop 6, you can also do this by dragging the state into the Snapshot box.) I then opened that file and chose Grayscale > Duotone, then chose Tritone and used the Custom Color Picker to pick my three inks. I scrolled the Picker and clicked on different color combinations. Whenever I highlighted a color, the Preview would change. I chose black, Pantone 437CVC (burgundy), and Pantone 127CVC (yellow), a nice combination for a selenium-tone look. I finished off the image by applying Layers >New Adjustment Layer, Levels, Multiply.

TIP

If you want to see the individual colors in your duotones, tritones, and quadtones, go to Image > Mode > Multichannel and take a look. Be sure to switch back to Duotone when you're finished, easily done by using Edit > Undo.

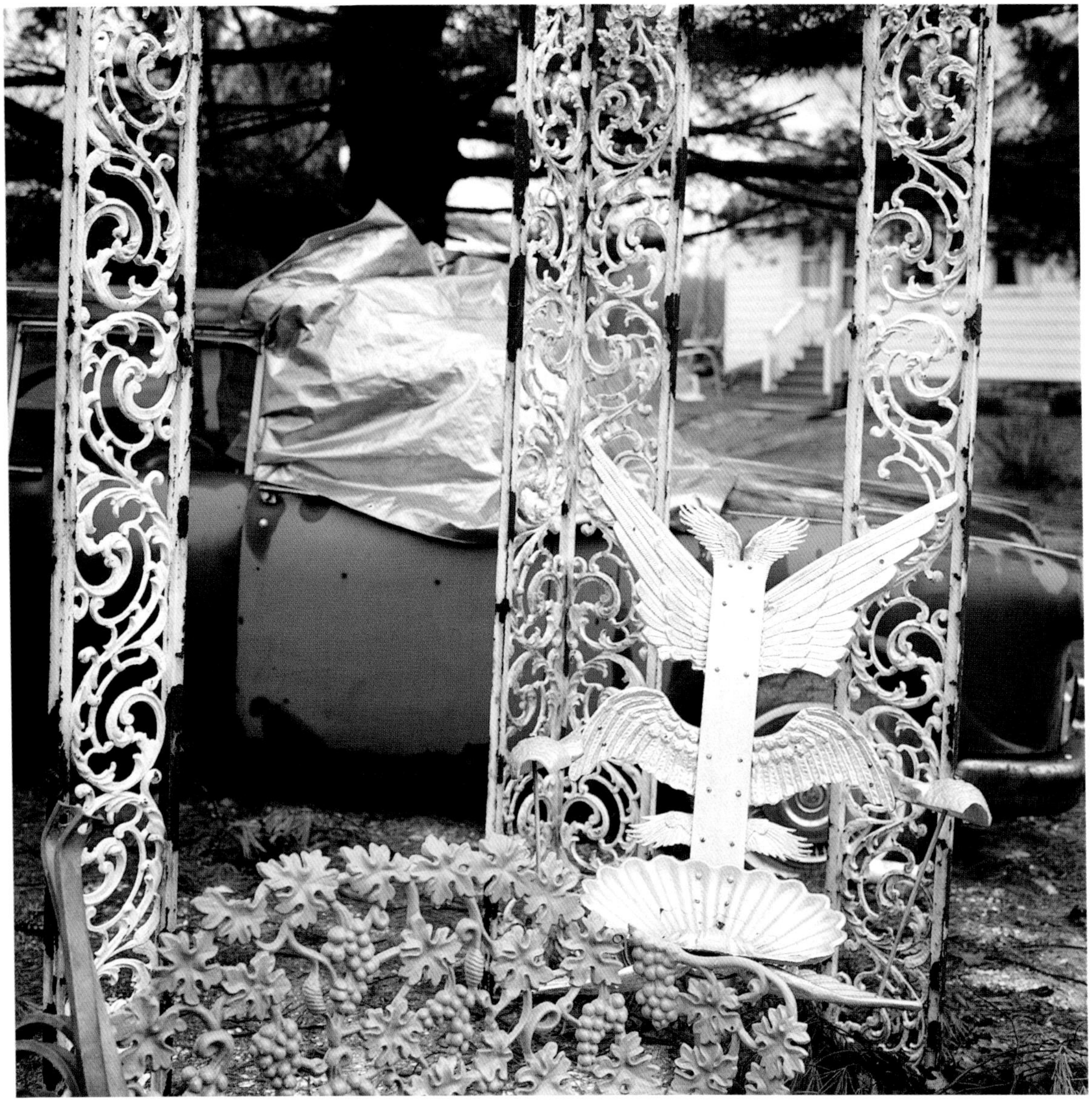

4

IMAGE 4

To finish off the image for printing, I chose a cool gray Tritone preset from the Photoshop offerings—black, CG9, and CG2.

WORKSHOP 3 **BLENDING WITH SOFT LIGHT**

LEAF

There are some images that are a pleasure to work on in both the traditional and digital darkrooms. Exposure, distribution of tonality, lighting, and subject matter all seem in harmony. It's as if you exposed the image ready to print. (If only all images were so easy!) Such ease continues through the scan. Everything goes butter smooth, and the image that shows up on your screen is a perfect match to the image on film. It's a Hollywood ending.

That's the case with this image. It was made from Agfa Scala black-and-white slide film, which I often choose when doing black and white with digital imaging in mind. When exposing slide film, you think differently from when you're using negative film. You have to, because otherwise you could lose precious shadow and/or highlight detail. And once that detail is gone with slide film, it's gone, even though you can clone and graft it in some cases. This makes exposure more critical but also yields images that are much easier to work with in the digital darkroom. I now, in fact, choose color slide film to make later black-and-white prints for the same reason.

IMAGE 1

This image has a very good tonal range and could pass just as is. Here I sharpened the image by 150% in Filter>Sharpen>Unsharp Mask. I placed the Radius at 1 and the Threshold at 0.

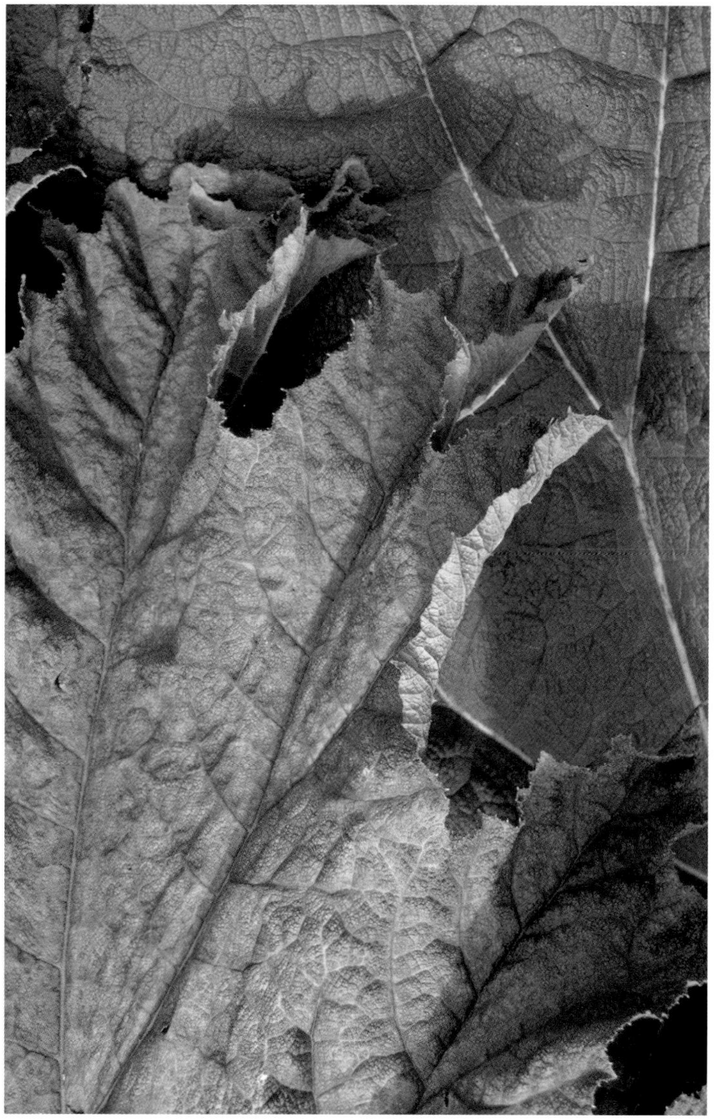

1

WORKSHOP 4 **CONVERTING COLOR PHOTOGRAPHS TO BLACK AND WHITE**

MEN'S CLUB

There are a number of ways to convert from color to black and white (grayscale) images. The simplest way is to work with Image > Mode > Grayscale from an RGB scan or to do Image > Adjust > Desaturate. Choose one or the other depending on what you might want to do with the image later. Image > Mode > Grayscale eliminates the color channels and is a good way to go for duotone printing; Image > Adjust > Desaturate keeps the image in RGB color mode (yielding a file three times the size of the grayscale file with the same resolution) and can be used for subsequent colorization or toning options.

Another excellent choice for conversion is Channel Mixing, located under Image > Adjust > Channel Mixer. When you open this option, a dialog box appears that allows you to custom blend the transition using separate color channels or by checking the Monochrome box and working the sliders in the different channels. I find that red and blue affect contrast, and green changes brightness and tonal details, or luminance. You can use the colors in the different channels by selecting the channel at the top, or you can work on them in only one channel. I work with Monochrome checked; you should try both. What you'll find is that you can do an amazing job and create many different options with this control. Channel mixing would be an ideal feature to have on the software for studio and home scanners.

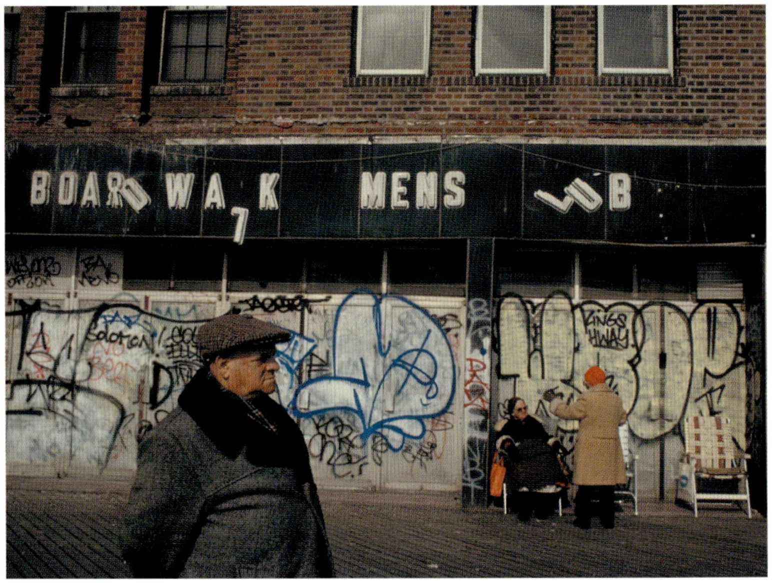

1

Photographed by Grace Schaub on Kodachrome 64 film.

IMAGE 1

Here is the original color scan. Kodachrome is a fairly warm film and the values are a bit pink, but this is no problem for Photoshop to balance. This photograph works well in both black and white and color. The graffiti and graphics that serve as the background provide a very effective context for this candid portrait, especially when converted to black and white.

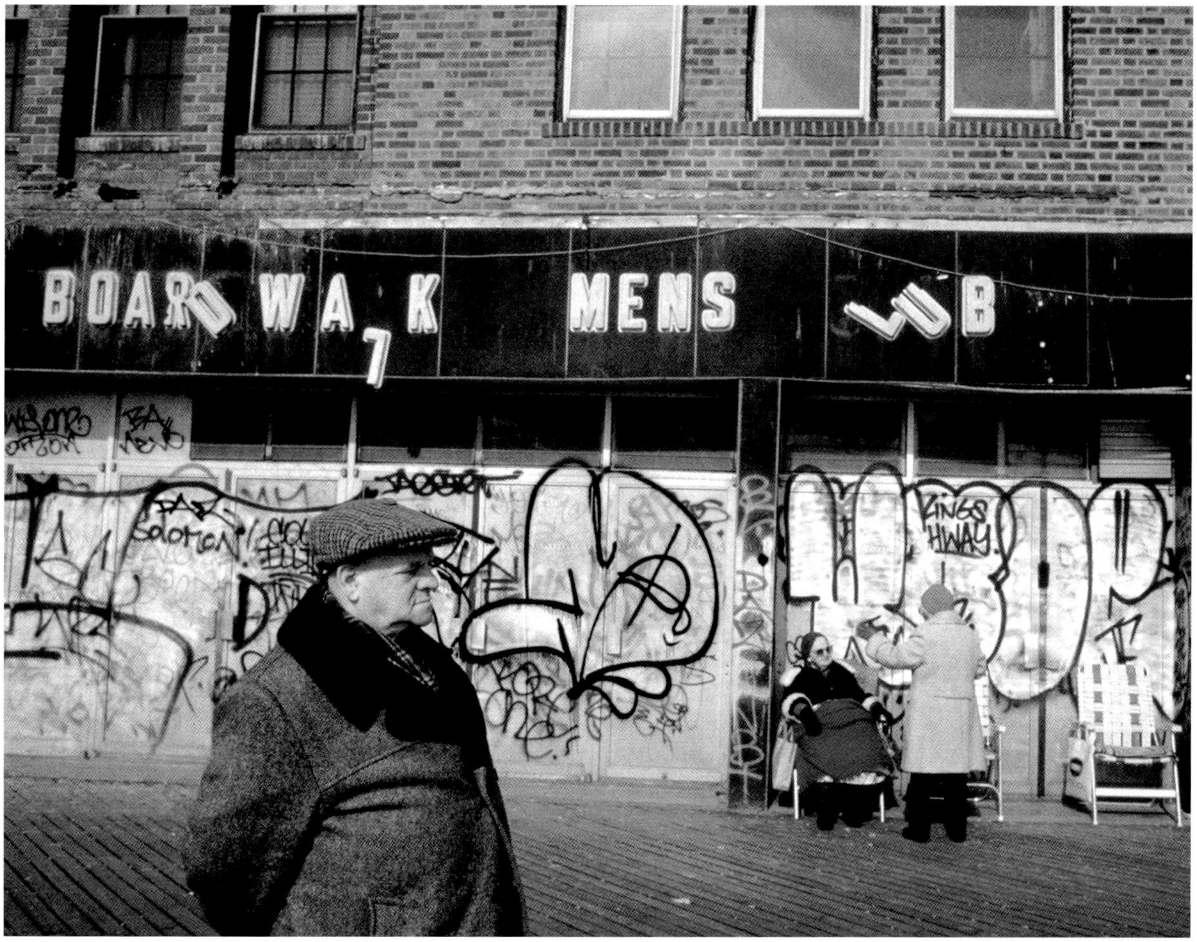

2

IMAGE 2

I made the conversion to monochrome using the Channel Mixer. The selection was Red +90, Green +133, and Blue –114, and Constant set to 0. When you get an image into Channel Mixer, play with the different settings until you get a feel for how each affects the final rendition. This will provide you with many hours of interesting play.

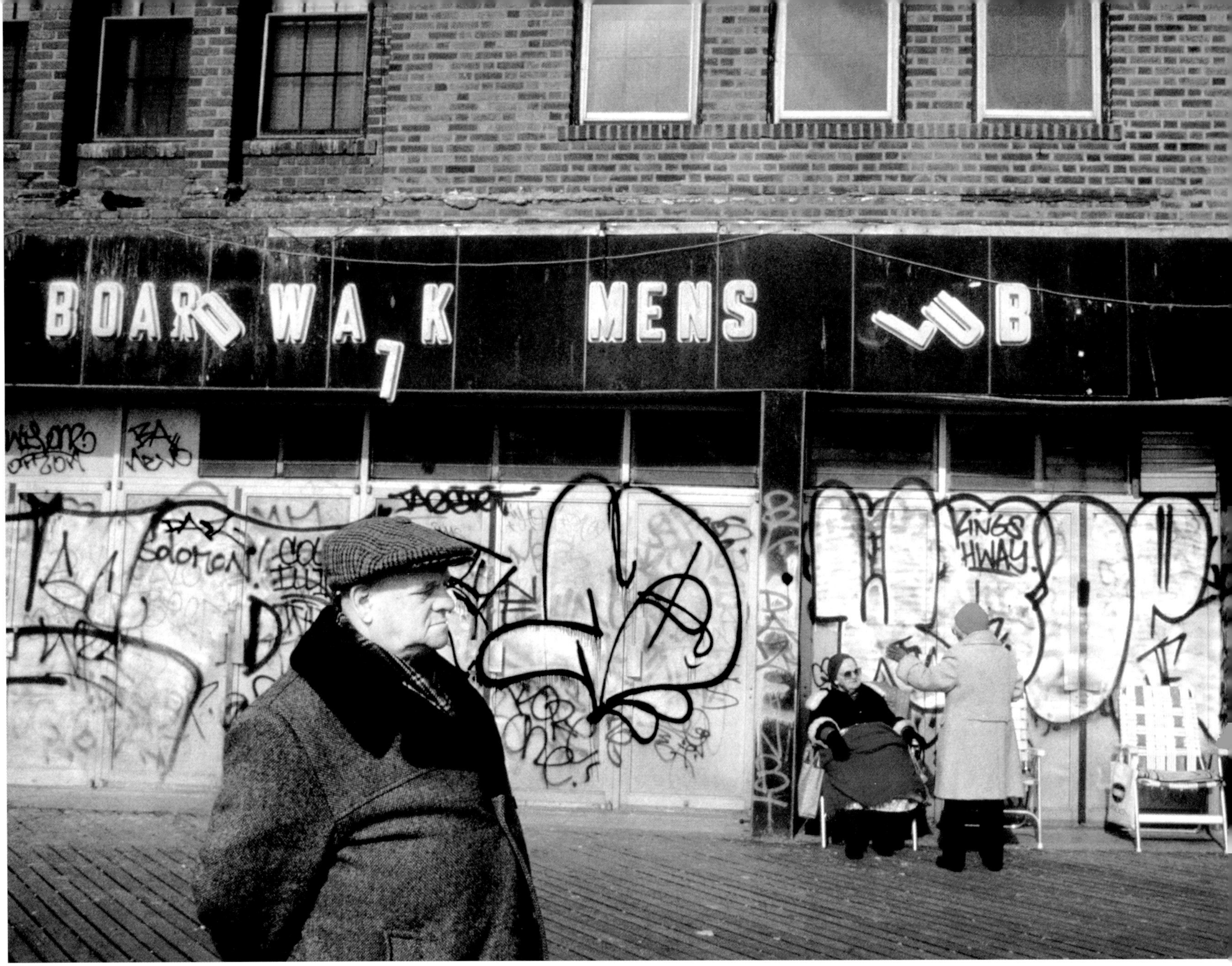

3

IMAGE 3

After I made the conversion, I did some touchup work. I chose the History Brush and set it at Screen Blending mode, Opacity 34%. I chose a fairly large hard-edged brush and placed it at the former state and lightened the letters on the background sign and graffiti. I did some opening up on the foreground figure's face and clothing and the rest of the image. Screen mode lightens the area over which the brush paints.

WORKSHOP 5 **TONAL CONTROLS**

TAOS OVERLOOK

This is the view of Taos as you come around the big horseshoe bend up and out of the Rio Grande Gorge. It's a view that tells us we're home, and a welcome sight each time. We have come up that road a hundred times and each time the light and what it reveals is different. I made this photograph late one afternoon with the sun angling from the west (left of the camera). The light kicked off the late August sunflowers and skimmed the top of the distant hills. When I made the photograph I had no black-and-white film with me, but I knew I would do just fine if I worked with color and converted it later.

IMAGE 1

Here's the color photo made on Kodak Ektachrome 100 VS film in 35mm format. I read the exposure directly from the sky and locked in, then changed the framing to include the foreground light skim on the sunflowers. A 24mm lens gave me big sky and a good diagonal sweep.

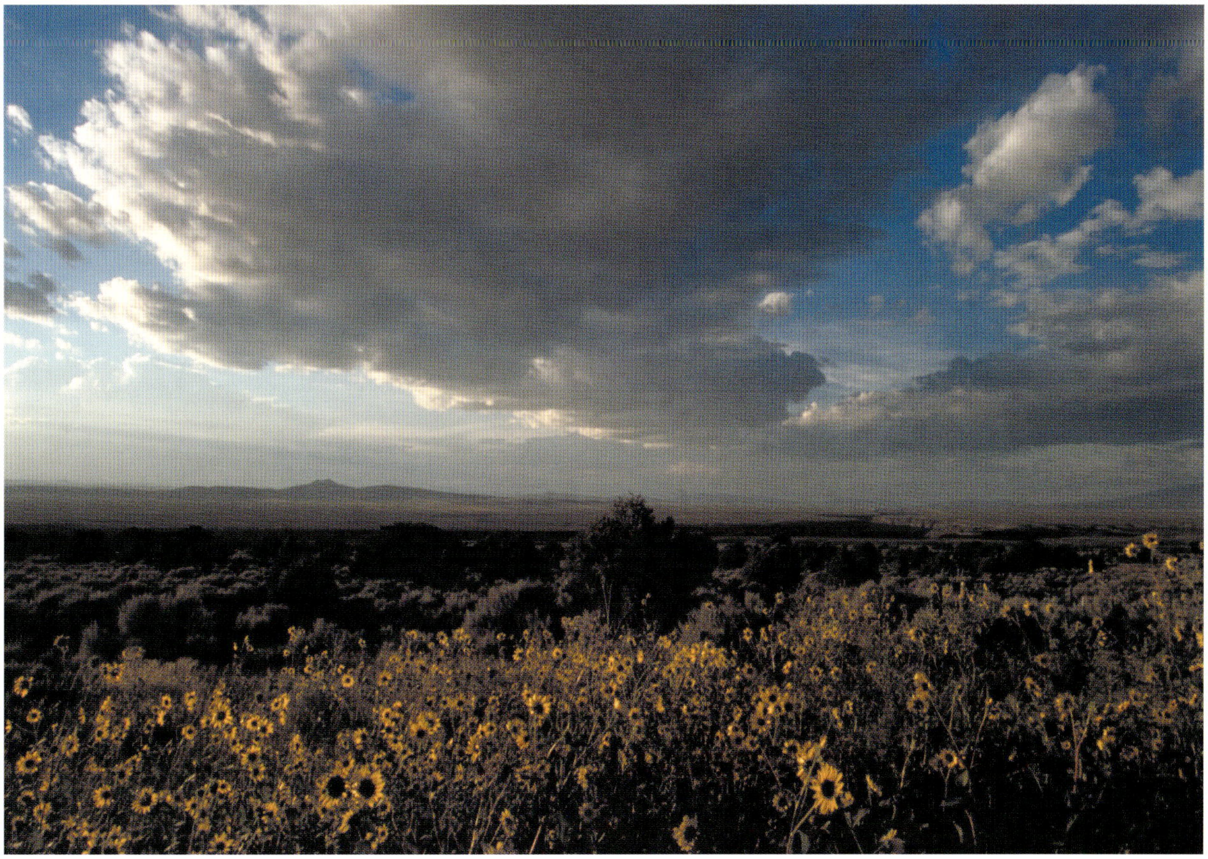

1

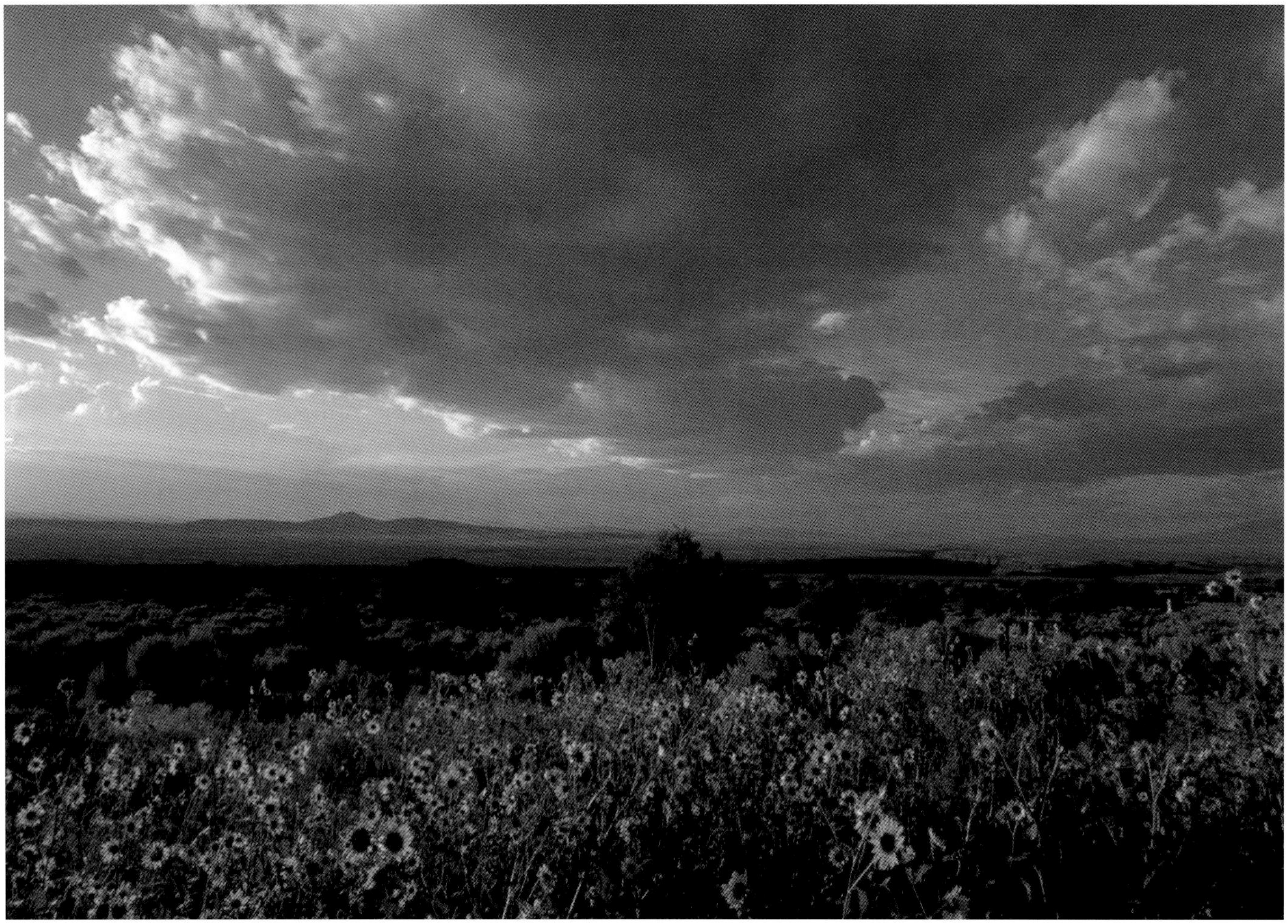

2

IMAGE 2

I converted the image to black and white using Image > Mode > Grayscale. I tried out the Channel Mixer, but the straight Grayscale conversion worked just fine. The image is a bit dark overall, but the tonal values are all there. The main trouble is the bright sky in the upper left portion of the image. In this and other instances, it is a good idea to let the image go dark to see how those bright tones record, and then to work back and lighten where needed.

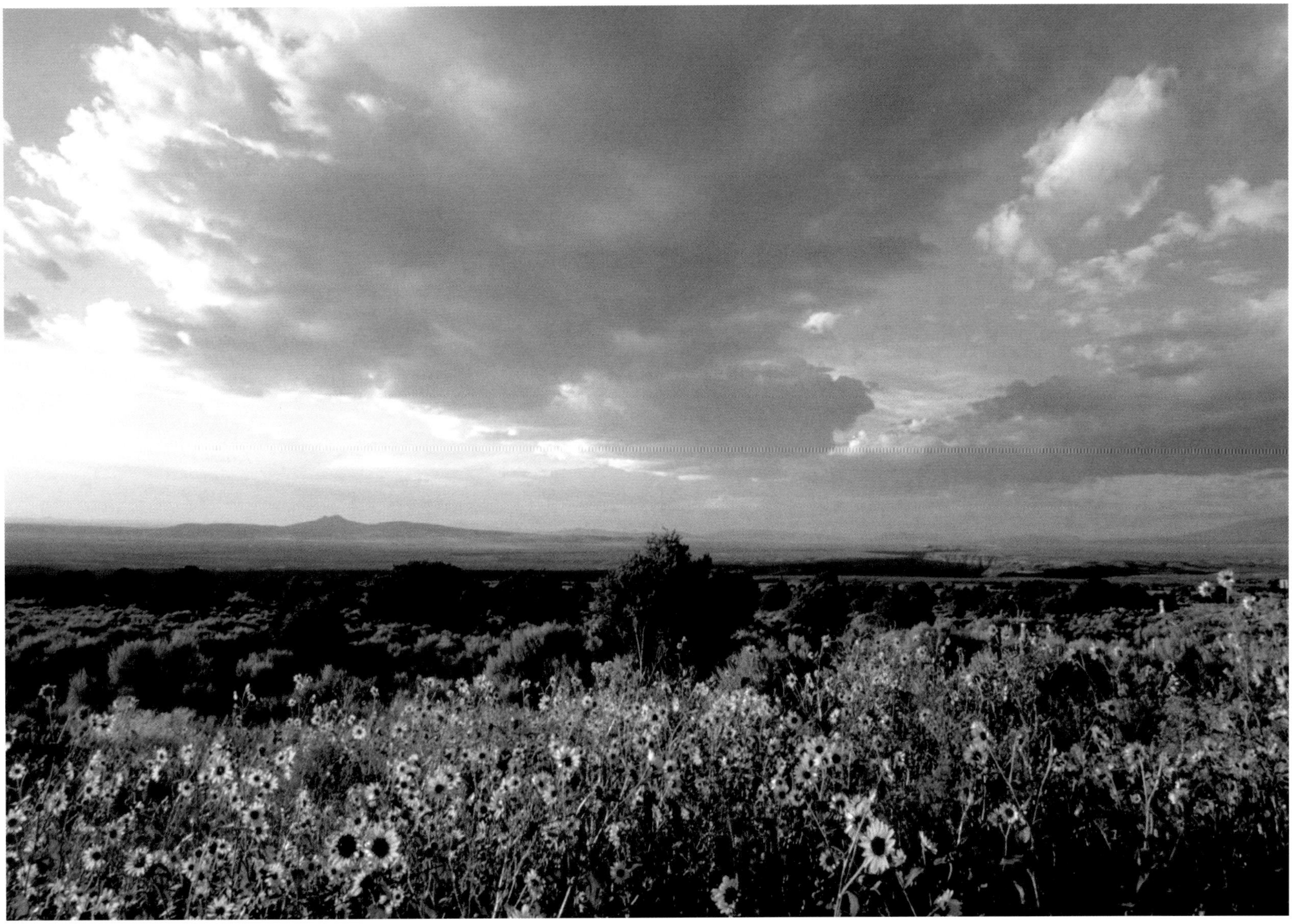

3

IMAGE 3

To open up the image, I used a new adjustment layer set on Screen Blending mode. This mode automatically cuts the density of the image, and here it kept most of the values in the sky.

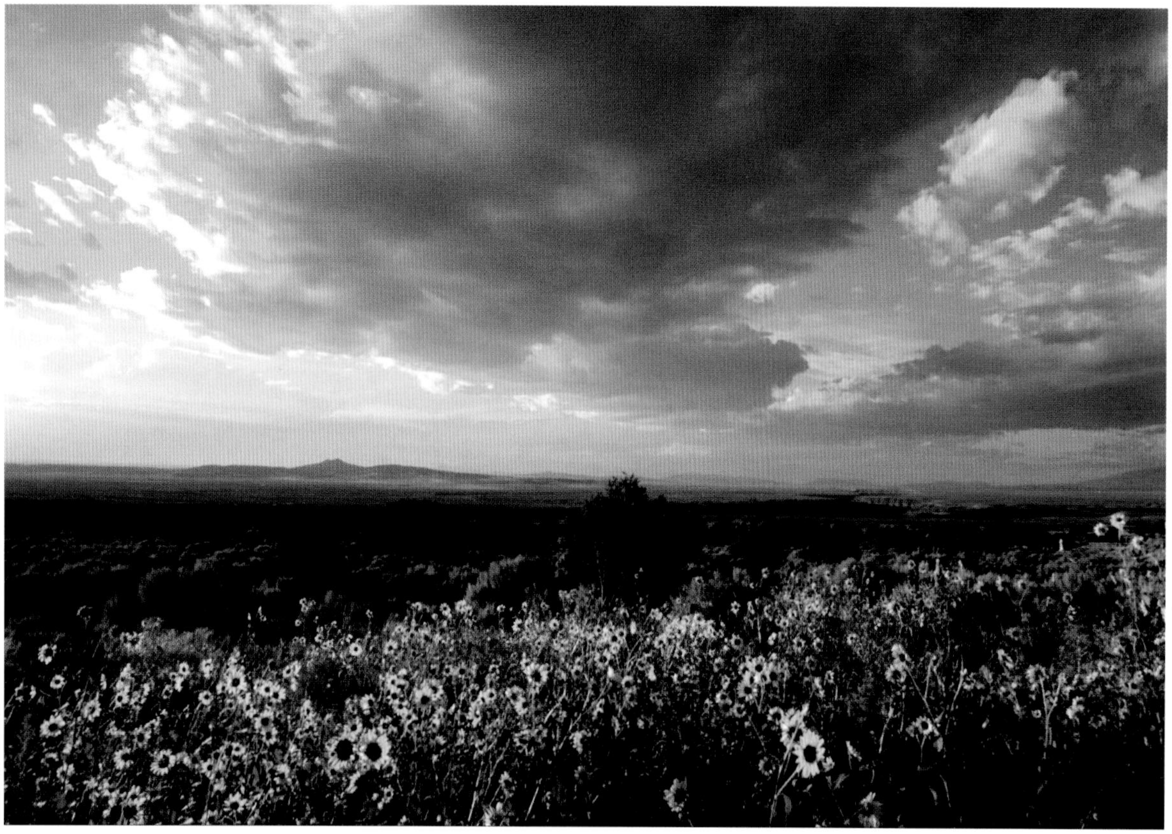

4

IMAGE 4

I wanted to add color to the image, so I converted it to Duotone in the Image >Mode menu. I chose a Photoshop Tritone preset, Aqua Gold, composed of black, Pantone 313CVC, and Pantone 127CVC.

IMAGE 5

The final steps refined some of the values on the screen. In an image such as this, it is important to keep the highlight levels slightly below paper white. Avoid using the white input values, as this can cause crossovers and exaggerated tonal edges; instead, use the Levels output indicators in the white or highlight areas. This mutes the highlights without making those scattered tonal edges. To do that here, I opened up a new adjustment layer with levels and set the Output to 221. I moved the gray Input slider slightly; it would begin to cause posterization if I went too far. I then used a Dodge tool to open up some flowers in the foreground.

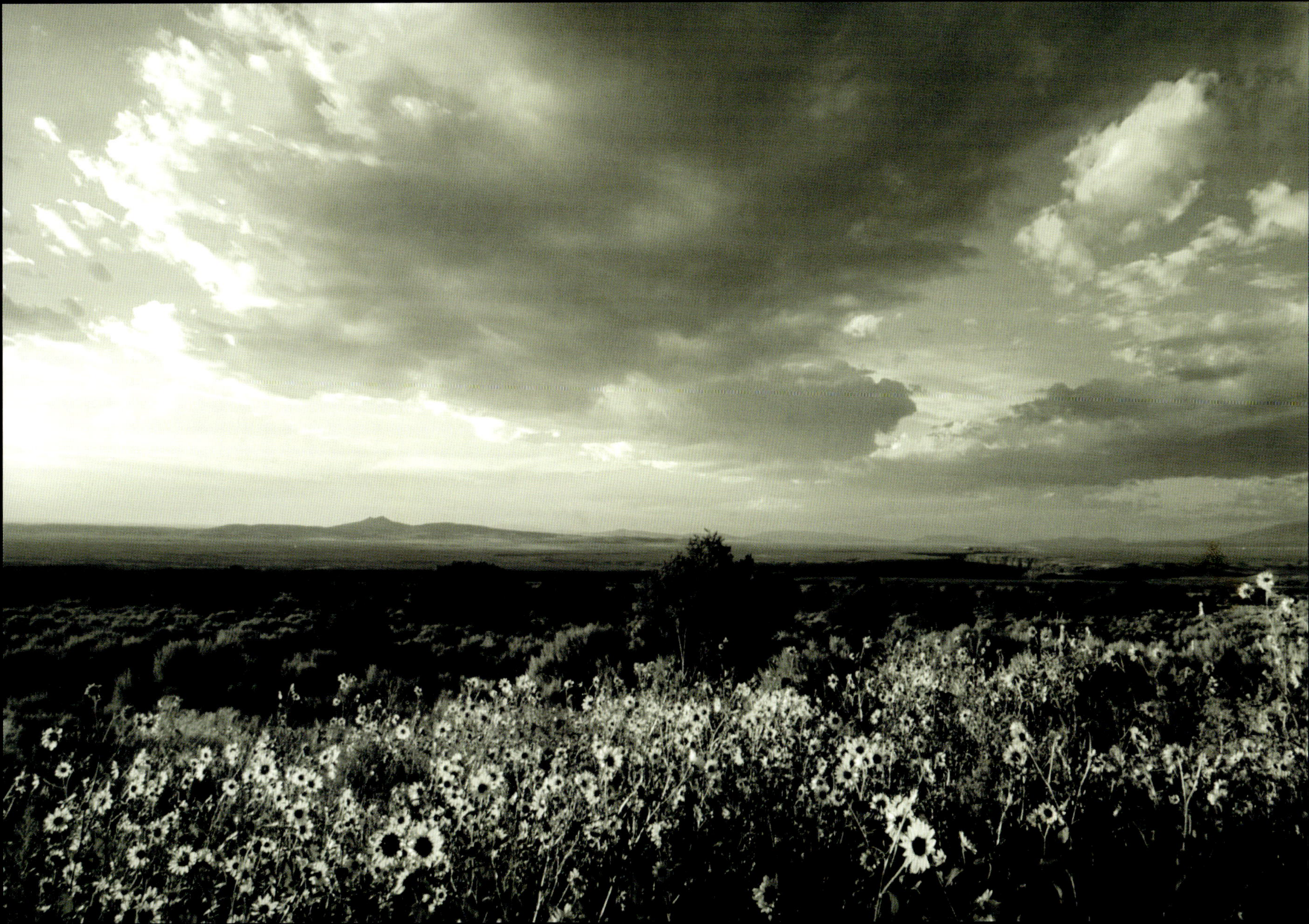

WORKSHOP 6 **INFRARED SIMULATION**
ADOBE HOMES

Many people are fascinated by the effects of infrared black-and-white film, yet find that handling this film is difficult and that its cost is quite high. Infrared must be loaded and unloaded in complete darkness and exposed through a deep red filter on the lens. Most field shooters carry a changing bag for film handling, although I've seen one or two photographers climb into their car trunk to do it—not a recommended course of action. The job of the assistant in those cases was to help the photographer get out of the trunk.

I have worked with infrared and find it an exciting medium, although paying three times the price of conventional black and white is not a thrill. Developing and printing the film is always a challenge, as contrast is generally high, as is density. Just for fun, I decided to try to emulate the infrared effect using conventional film and the digital darkroom. The degree of contrast and tonal control is such that it would seem quite easy to do. My experiments showed me that it would work fine as long as the image lent itself to the conversion. Not every image has the necessary qualities, but then not every scene benefits from an infrared point of view. This scene worked because it already had a deep sky and fairly even tones on the main subject matter. Contrast is strong but not excessive.

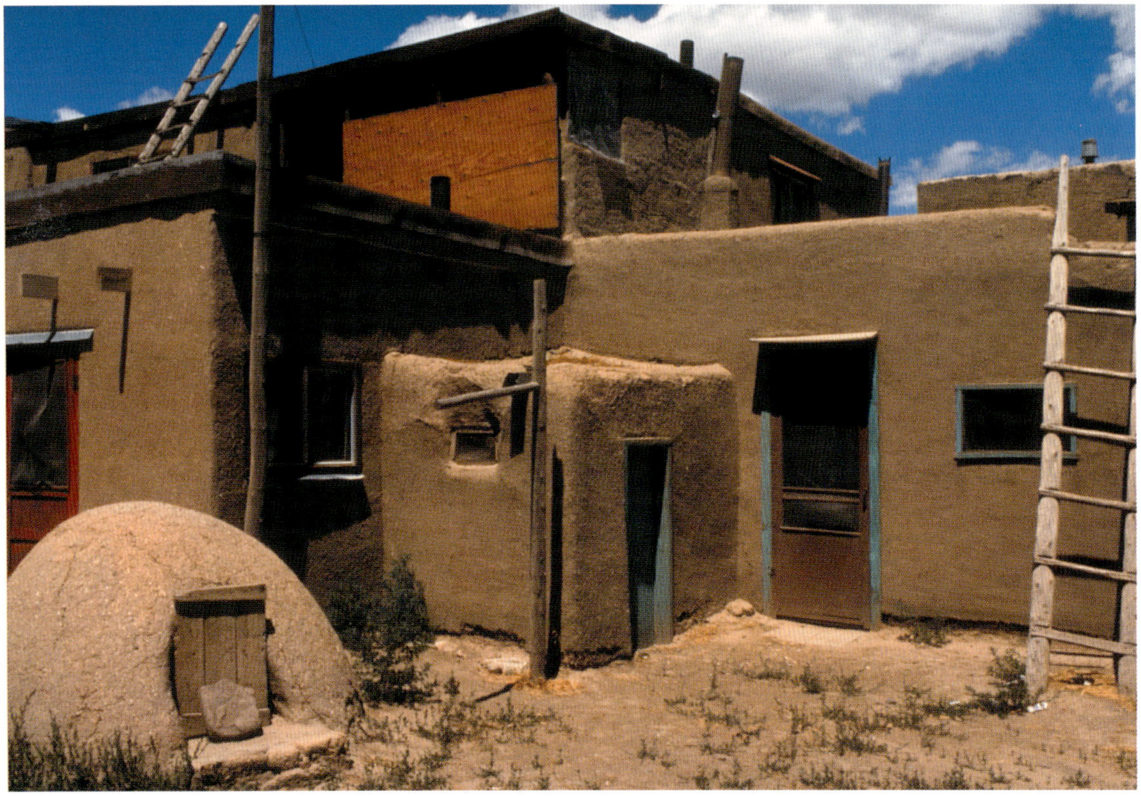

1

IMAGE 1
I made this image on Fujichrome Velvia 35mm film, a very rich and saturated film. The sun was coming over my shoulder, so no exposure compensation was necessary.

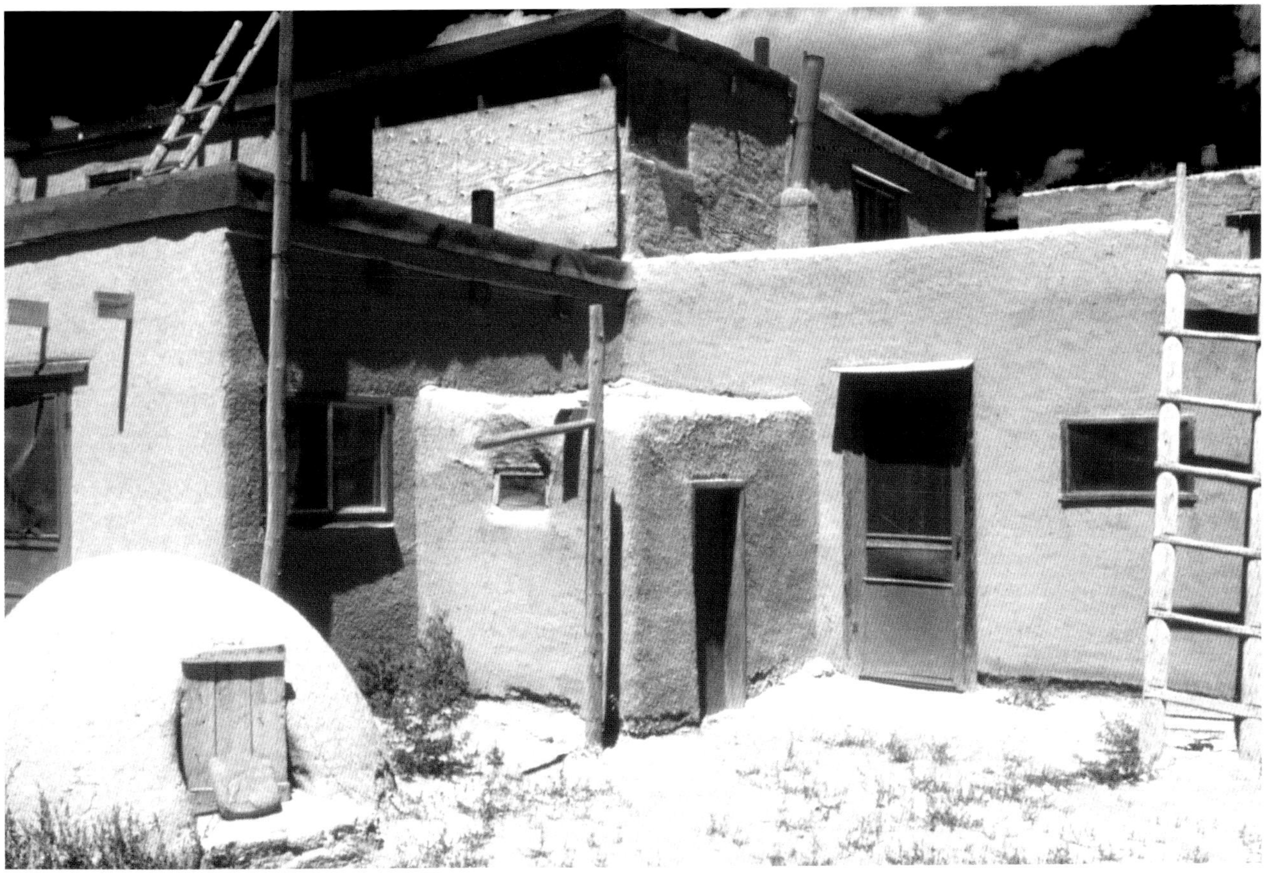

2

IMAGE 2

The most control you have in any conversion of color to black and white is through the use of Channel Mixer. Although this isn't necessary for every such conversion, it should definitely be used when aiming for a special effect. Infrared has a certain blown-out quality that produces an ethereal glow. Highlights are right on the edge and the sky always goes a deep black. In the Channel Mixer, you can move the values around to your heart's content. I have found that the Red and Blue channels work on contrast control, while the Green channel controls handle luminosity, or tonal values, themselves. The mix here is Red 114, Green 159, and Blue -106. The setting could have been a few points in either direction. I eyeballed this until I got it closest to what I considered "the infrared look."

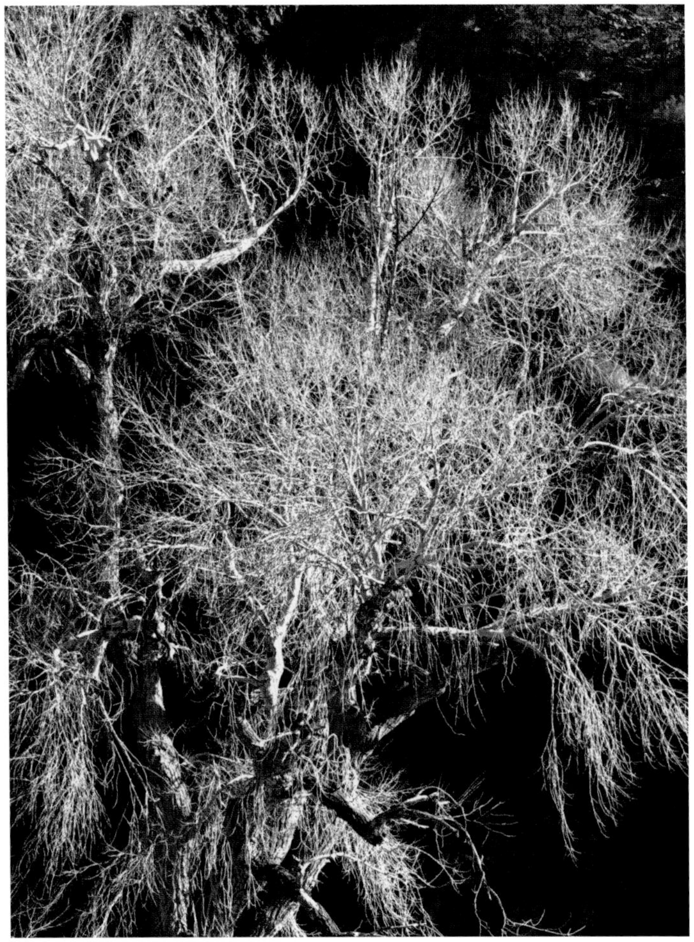

3

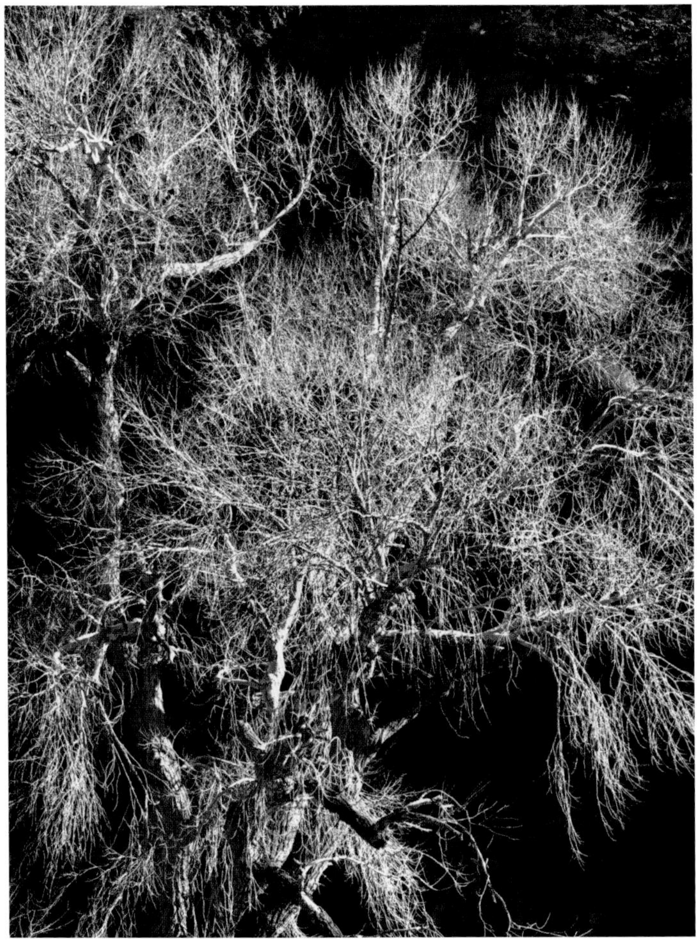

4

IMAGE 3

The conversion worked fine, but I wanted to get more of a graphic, edgy feel from the image, so I decided to darken the background. I could have done this with burning, but I decided to go an easier route using an adjustment layer. I chose Levels with a Multiply Blending mode. This took care of the background and added even more density to the tree.

IMAGE 4

The next stage is one of refinement. Whenever I have a continuous tonal area in an interpretive image, I try to break up the tonal constant with some judicious burning and/or dodging. This creates more visual interest by accentuating different forms; it also allows me to play with the form itself and mold it to my liking. Here I set the Burn tool to Midtones with an Exposure of 44%, and played in and around the branches.

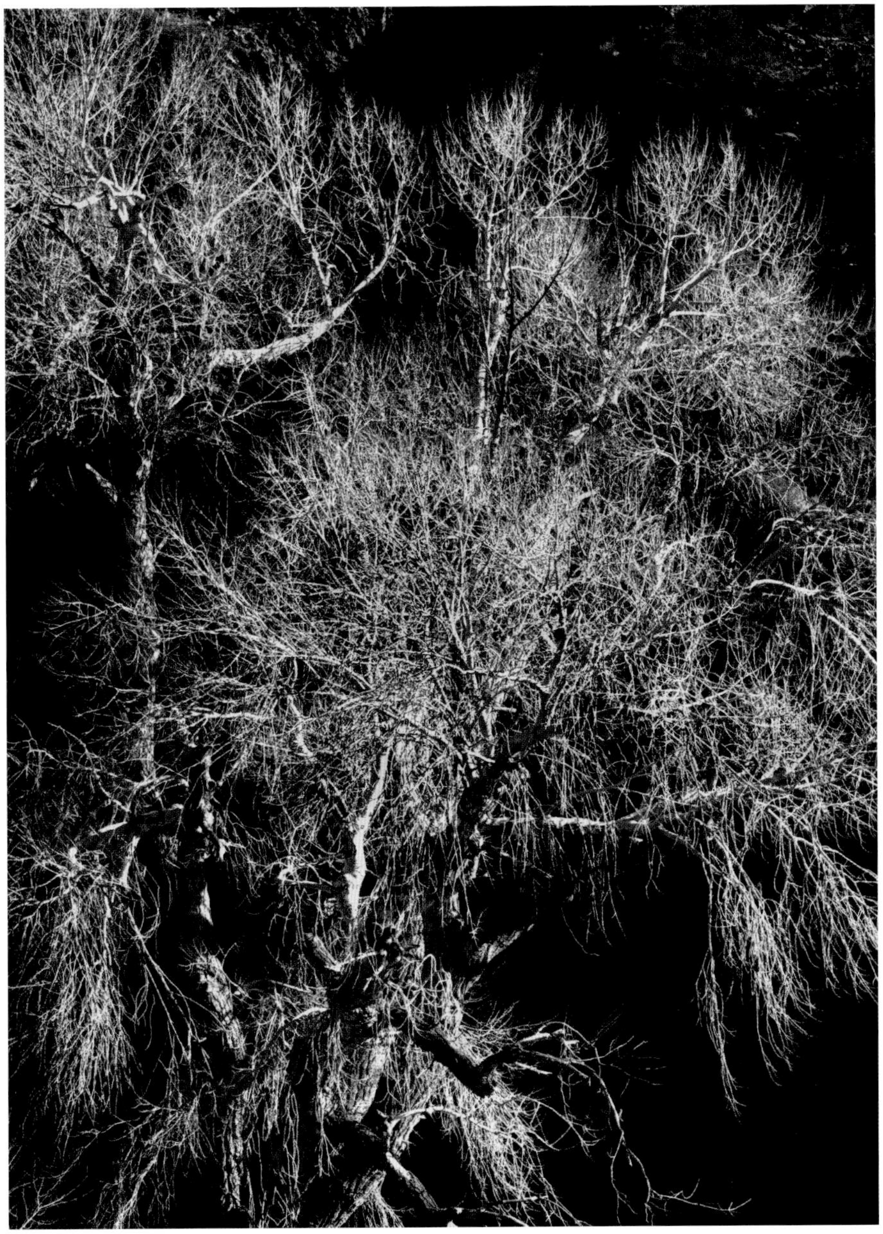

5

IMAGE 5

For the final touch, I decided to darken the image overall with the use of inks in Duotone. Some of the Duotone sets darken an image, while others lighten it. You can play with the ink curves to change how the sets affect the overall brightness or contrast of the image. Here, I chose a Tritone set of black, Pantone 5467CVC (a dark green), and Pantone 443CVC (a light gray). I played with the curves to create a more graphic effect.

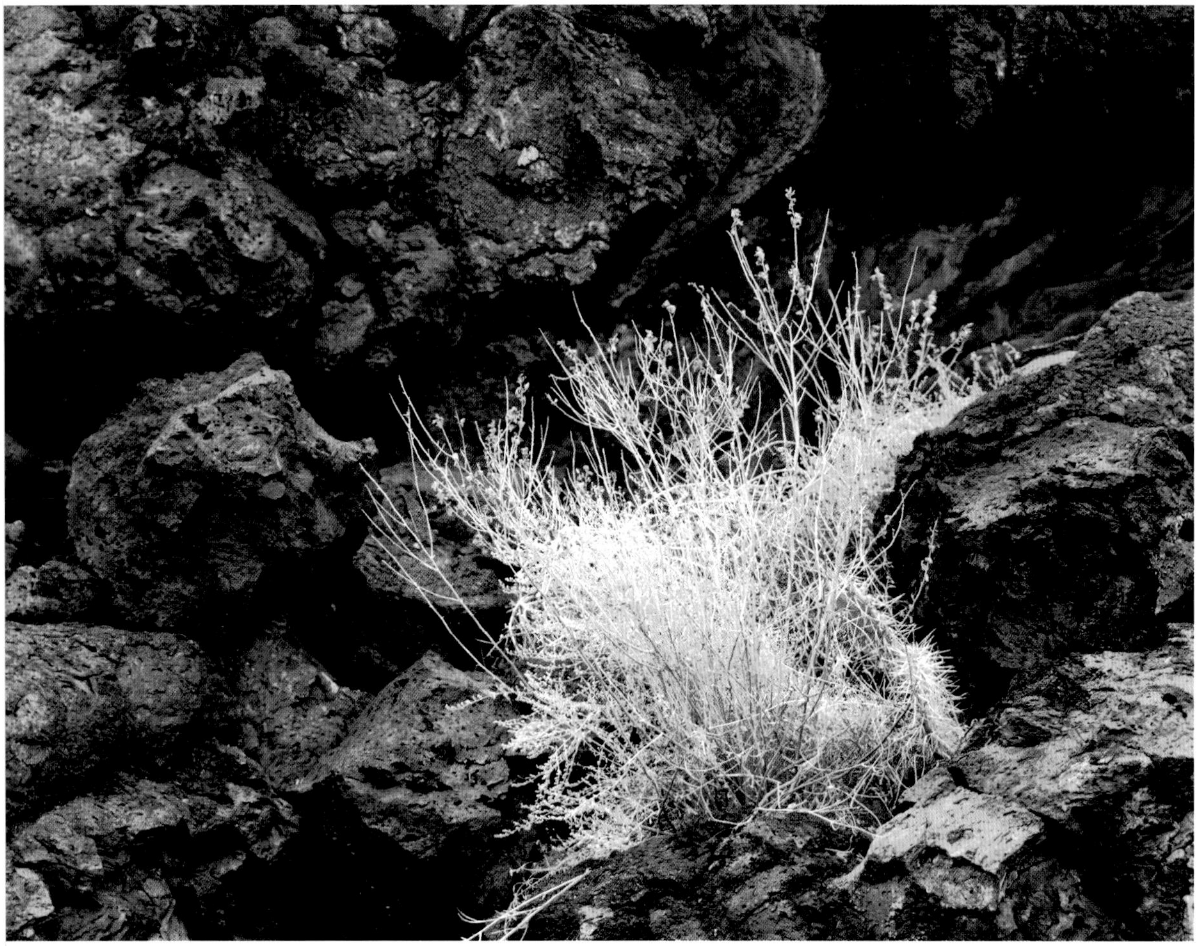

4

IMAGE 4

I inverted the selection with Select>Invert so I could work on the highlights and make them more tonally cohesive. I did this with Layer>New Adjustment Layer, Levels and opened the highlights with the middle (gray) slider. I did not use the white-point adjustment, as this would increase contrast too much. The image was then converted to a tritone with settings of black, Pantone Black 6CVC, and Pantone Cool Gray 8CVC.

WORKSHOP 4 **CONVERTING COLORIZATION USING THE CHANNEL MIXER**

LEAF POND

Images can be toned and colorized in many different ways. You can use Edit >Fill and choose opacity and color; you can digitally paint color onto images; you can use the Hue/Saturation or other global or selected area color commands. One way to quickly and easily colorize or tone images is with the Channel Mixer tool, which adds an infinite variety of color choices to an already dizzying array of options. To use this tool, you must have the image in RGB mode or make an RGB scan of a monochrome image.

In the chemical darkroom, you use toning to both add color to the image and make it of higher archival quality. The metallic toners bond with the silver to make a more stable compound. This is not the case with digital printing, where you emulate tone for a particular effect rather than for archival reasons.

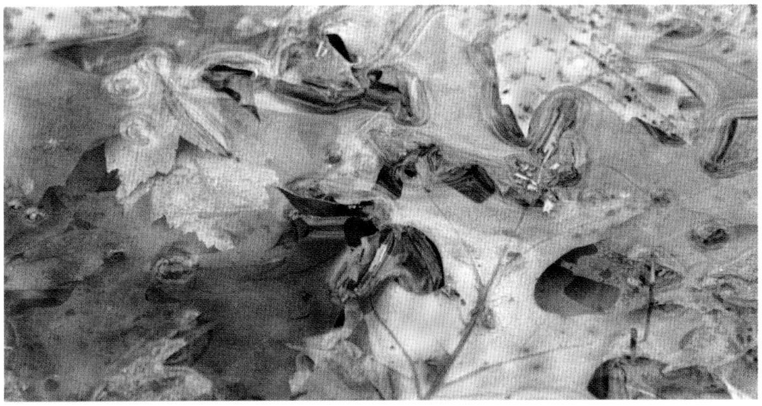

1

IMAGE 1

I made this image from a scan of 35mm black-and-white Kodak recording film, which I often used for abstract or pictorial subjects. It was rated at EI 1000, and the results were quite grainy. I made the scan in RGB mode so I could apply the toning effects from the Channel Mixer tool.

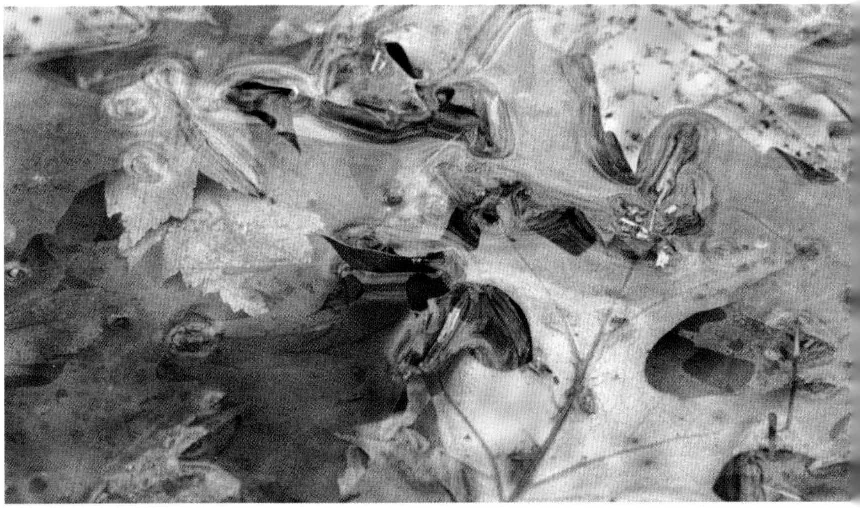

2

IMAGE 2

When you work with the Channel Mixer tool, you can check the Monochrome box or leave it unchecked, and work on all three channels or each channel separately; the range of choices is amazing. In this instance I worked off the Red channel and made the settings Red +122 and Green and Blue at 0, with Constant –24. The result is a cyan/green colorization.

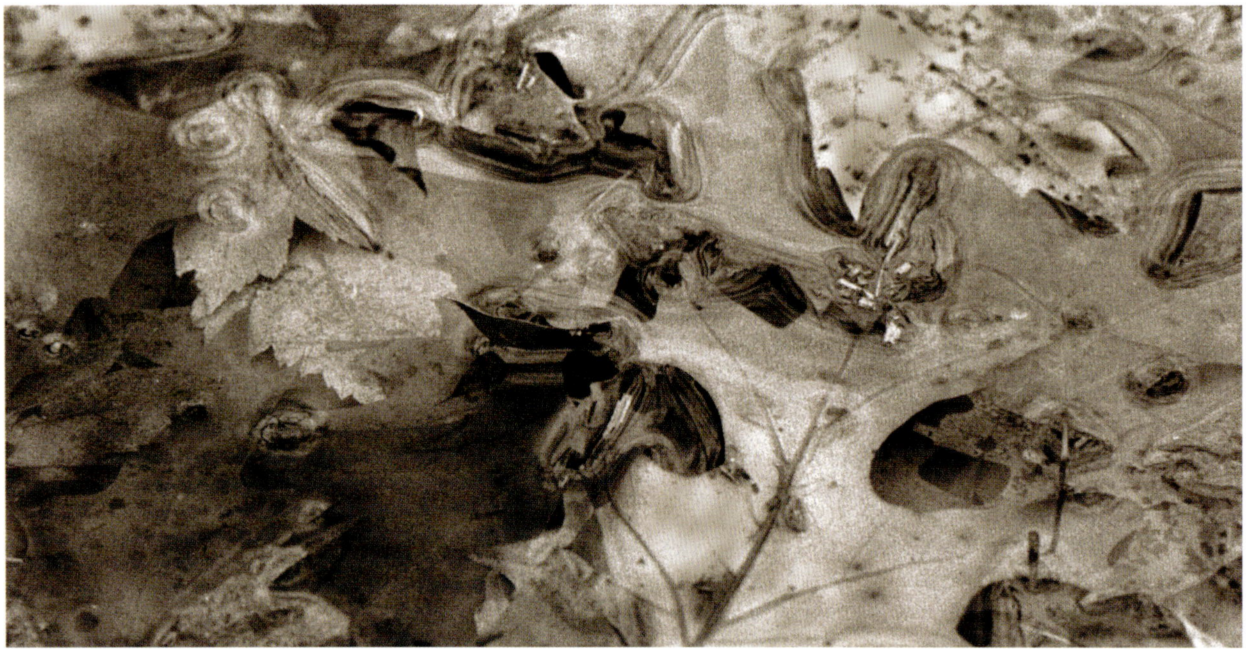

3

IMAGE 3

For this image, I worked on the Blue channel with the settings Red +27, Green +22, and Blue -37, with Constant -4. This is a very good sepia-tone emulation.

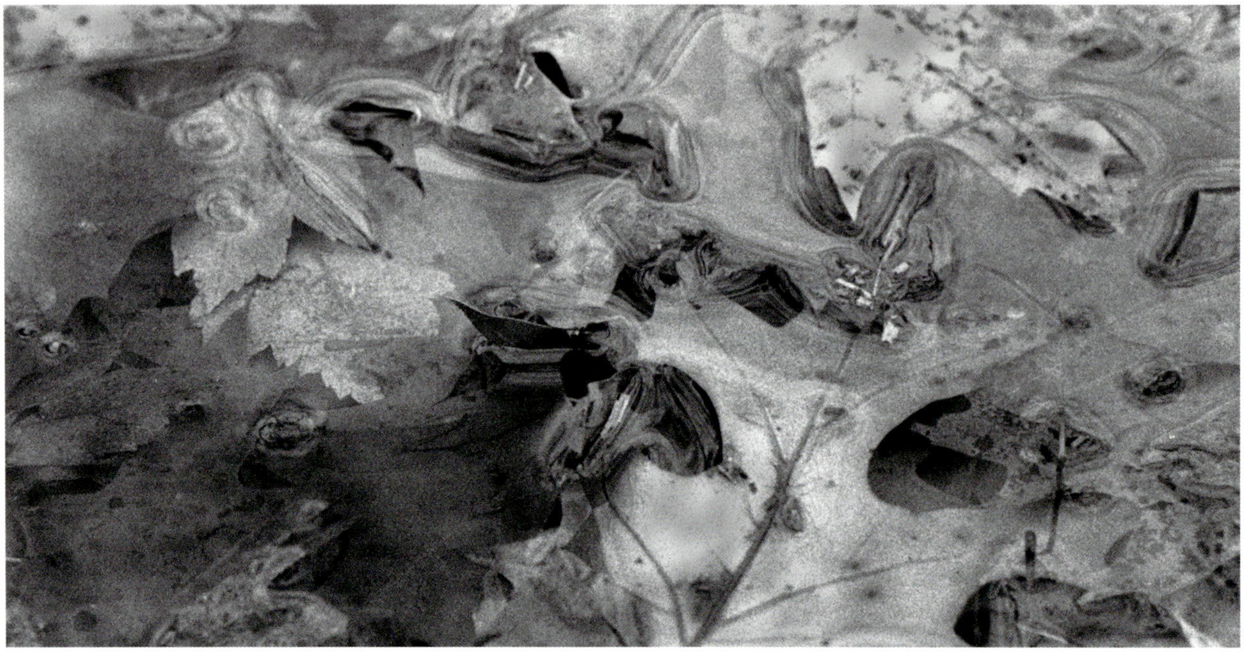

4

IMAGE 4

Channel Mixer is also an excellent way to convert to Grayscale, as it allows you to customize the image contrast and tone relationships. Here, I converted the image to Grayscale using the Monochrome check box.

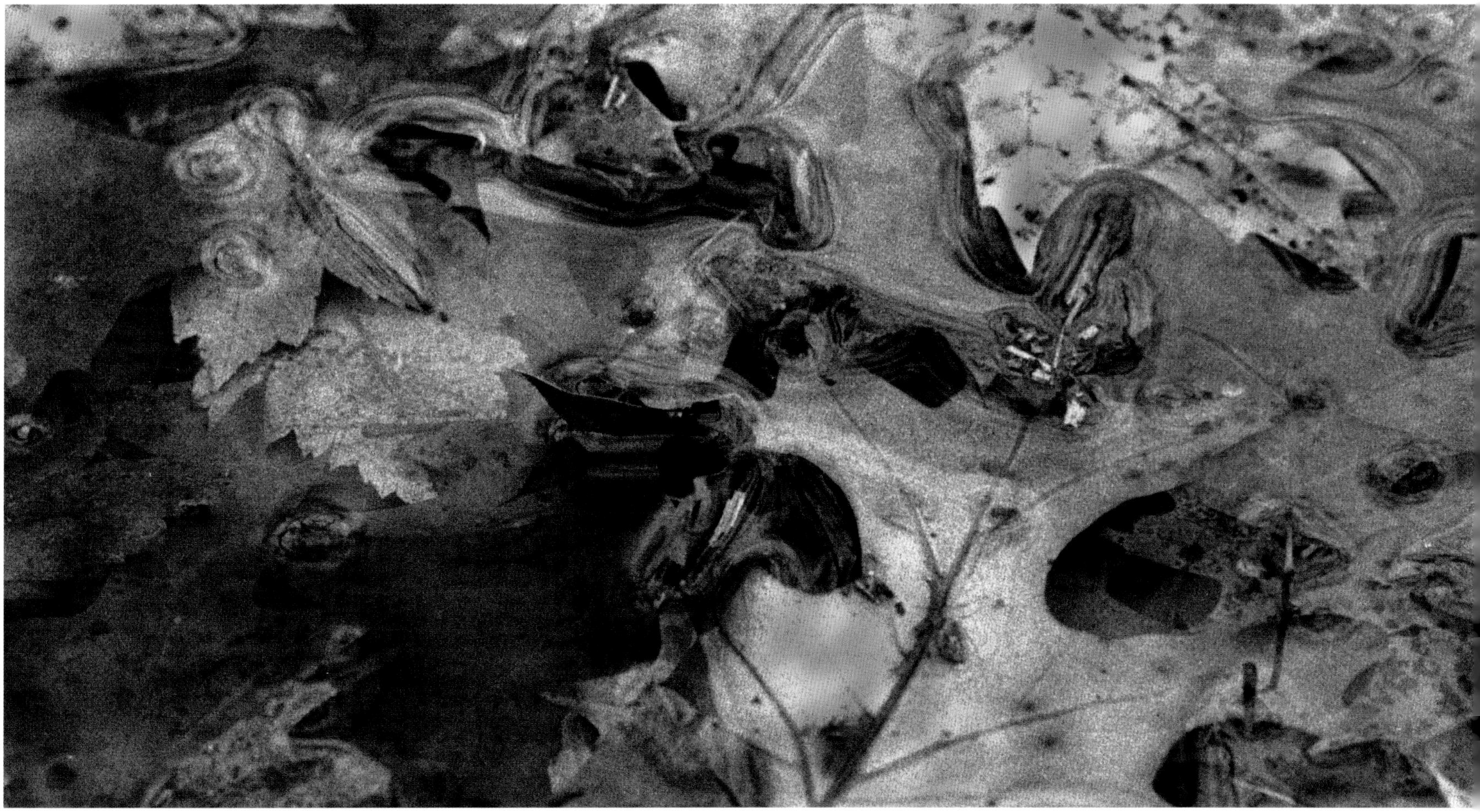

5

IMAGE 5

To show another option on this image, I converted it to Duotone and changed image color there. This is a fairly simple Duotone set of black and Pantone Black 6CVC.

WORKSHOP 6 **ADJUSTING CONTRAST**

TEMPLE

It's always interesting for me to return to images with which I've struggled in the past in the conventional darkroom and try them again in the digital arena. It always seems like less work in that realm, probably because I've gone around with them before and know their problems. Plus, the ability to preview changes as I go has many advantages in terms of both time and material.

I made this photograph in Hong Kong in the late 1970s and have printed it a few times on silver paper. The struggle here is the two burned-out areas—the roof and the courtyard. I could pretty much get the roof right, but getting a good burn and good contrast in the courtyard always meant going through more paper than I liked.

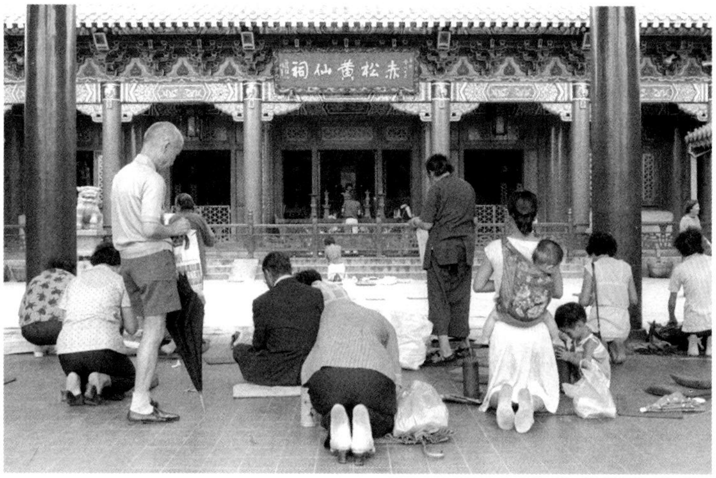

1

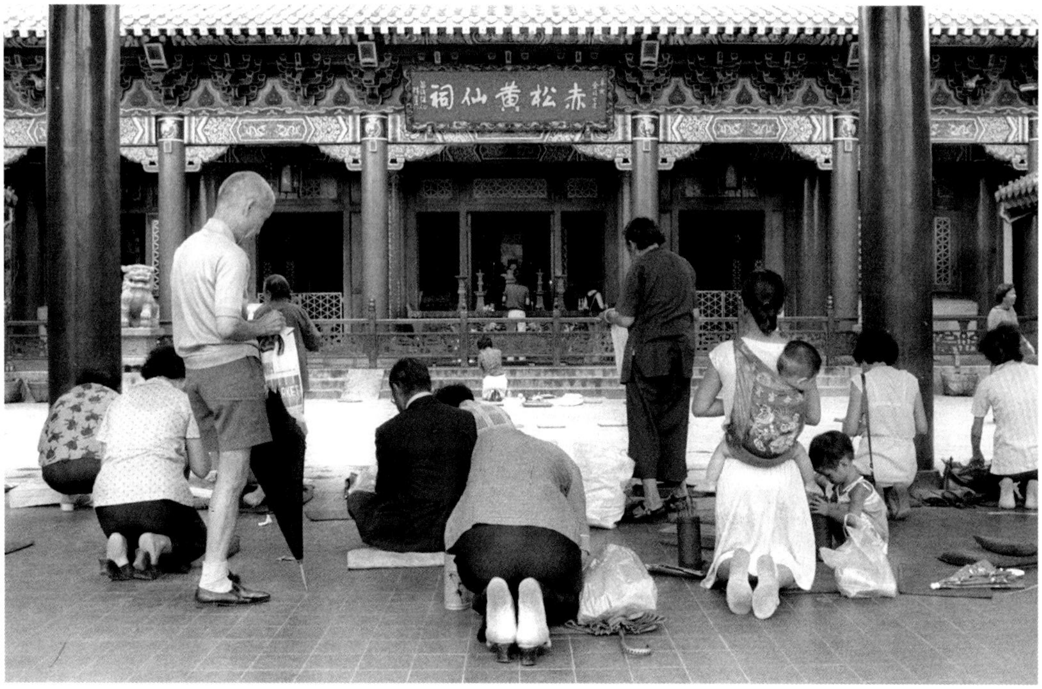

2

IMAGE 1

I made the scan from a 35mm Kodak Tri-X Pan negative. The scan is open, if a bit flat—a good starting point for a negative with some contrast problems.

IMAGE 2

To kick up the contrast a bit without affecting the white or highlight areas, I chose Layer>New Adjustment Layer, Levels, and worked with the gray-point slider. This brought richness to the scene.

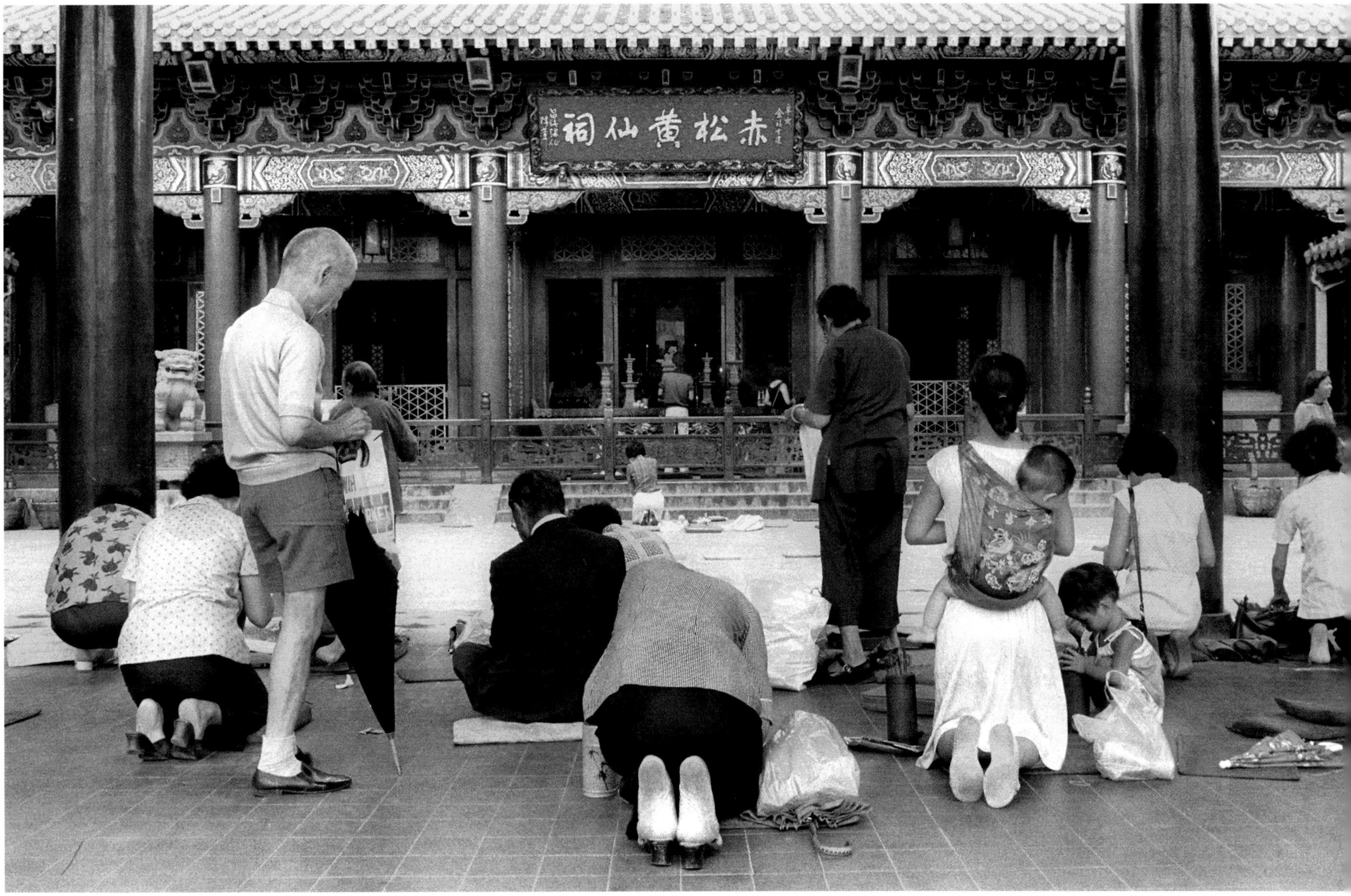

3

IMAGE 3

Now, I worked with the History Brush to affect the tonal areas selectively. I placed the brush at the first state and began to paint with a Multiply Blending mode to darken certain areas, then on Screen Blending mode to lighten others; for example, I used Screen to open up the shadows and Multiply to add tonal richness to the columns and woodwork. On some of the writing at the center of the image, I used Screen to whiten the letters and Multiply to deepen the tonal values next to them.

WORKSHOP 7 **HEIGHTENING EFFECTS**

RUNNERS

Although I usually don't get involved with special effects, the temptation is sometimes too great to ignore. Even when I give in, though, the work I do is fairly conservative compared to the amazing montages and odd images that some photographers produce. When the right image comes along, however, I try out different contrast renditions and sometimes play with the backgrounds. This book does not contain too much about special-effects filters. I don't have anything against them, but for the most part they play little part in my work.

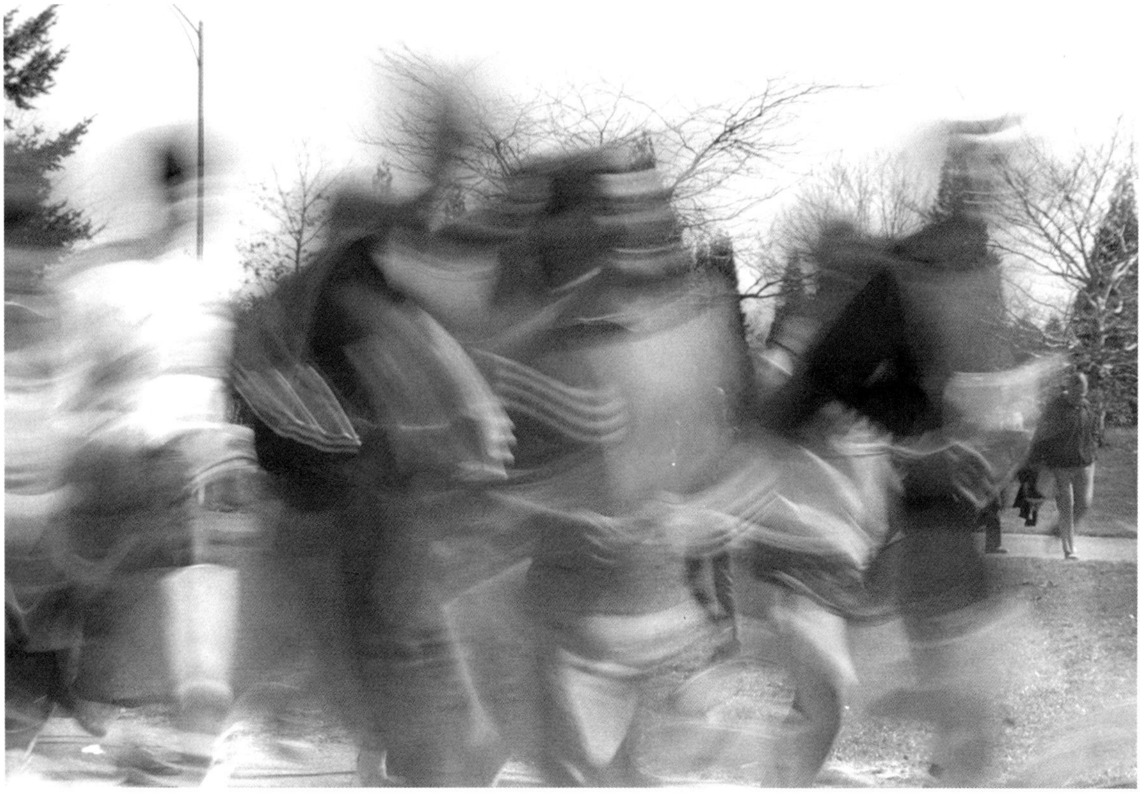

1

IMAGE 1

This photograph is part of an exploration of time and motion warps that continues to fascinate me. I took it at a marathon race just as the runners started. The camera was on a tripod and the shutter speed was 1/4 second. The image was scanned in Grayscale; the tone shown here represents the negative quite well.

WORKSHOI
TORREY BEACH

The ability to c
main benefit c
ventional or digita
light, but not nece
graph in the field,
which the subject
enhance what existe

I photographed
under flat, overcast s
white negative. The
judicious overdevelo
interpretive approach

IMAGE 1
I raised the contrast usi
deepened shadows and

IMAGE 2
I decided to play with tl
rocks and the beach sa
Blending mode and Opac

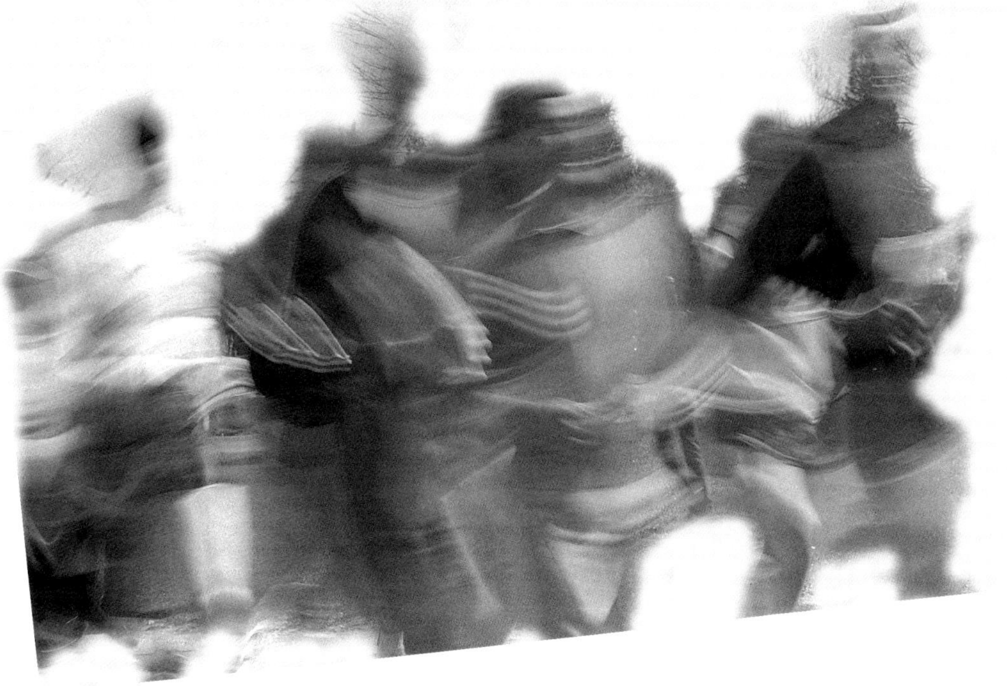

2

IMAGE 2
I selected the Airbrush tool, choosing a fairly hard brush edge and medium size. I moved the cursor to the foreground/background color selection and chose white as the brush color. I double-clicked on the Airbrush tool and chose Opacity at 100%. I then went around the image doing a fairly loose painting over of the background. I chose my edges so that the figures and their motion alone were highlighted.

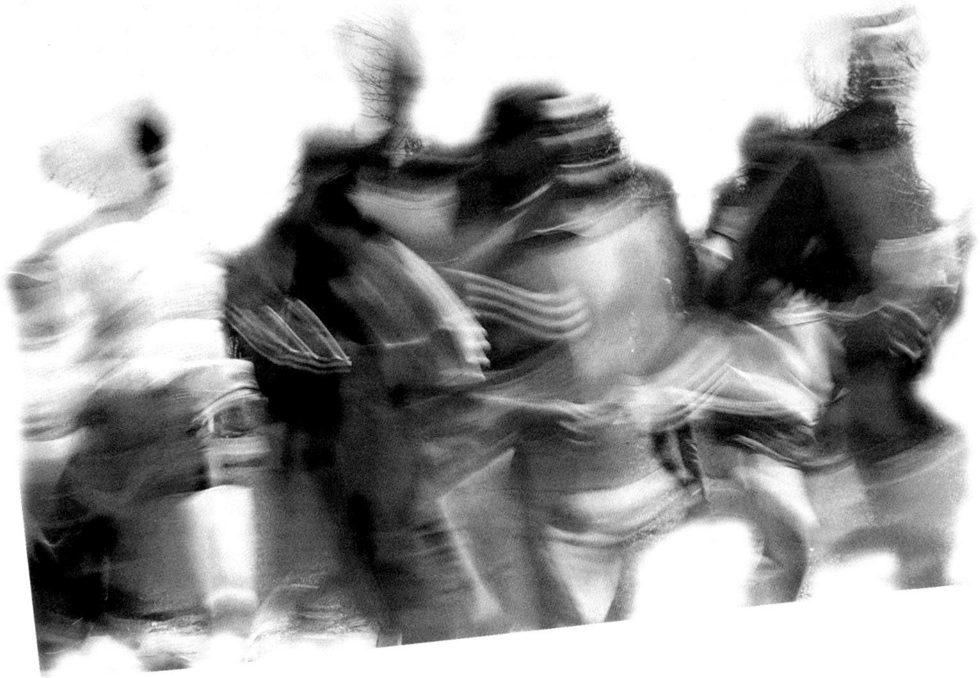

3

IMAGE 3
When I finished airbrushing, I wanted to raise contrast. I chose Filter > Sharpen > Unsharp Mask and 150%, with a Radius of 1 and a Threshold of 0. Every time an image is sharpened its contrast is raised, so I used Unsharp Mask twice. I then chose the History Brush and used a Multiply Blending mode. I placed the History Brush at the first Unsharp Mask state, then painted through the image, making certain areas darker to yield a bit more tonal variety.

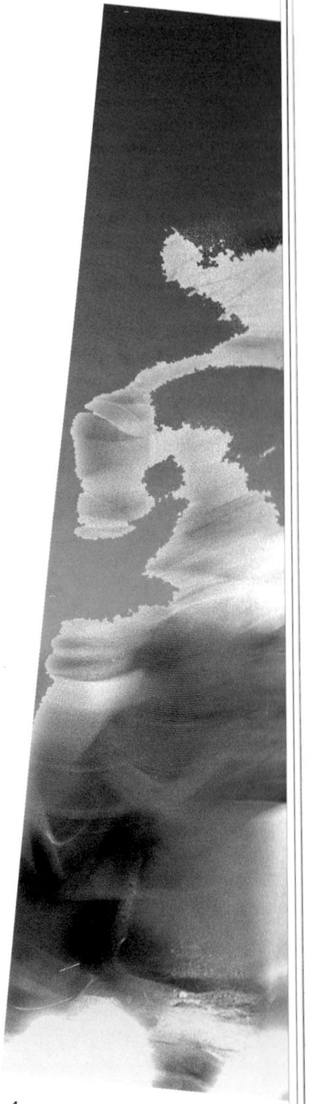

4

IMAGE 4

Once I had the contrast wh
using the Magic Wand tool
Gradient tool and used the d
line down the center of th
became a gradual blend of to

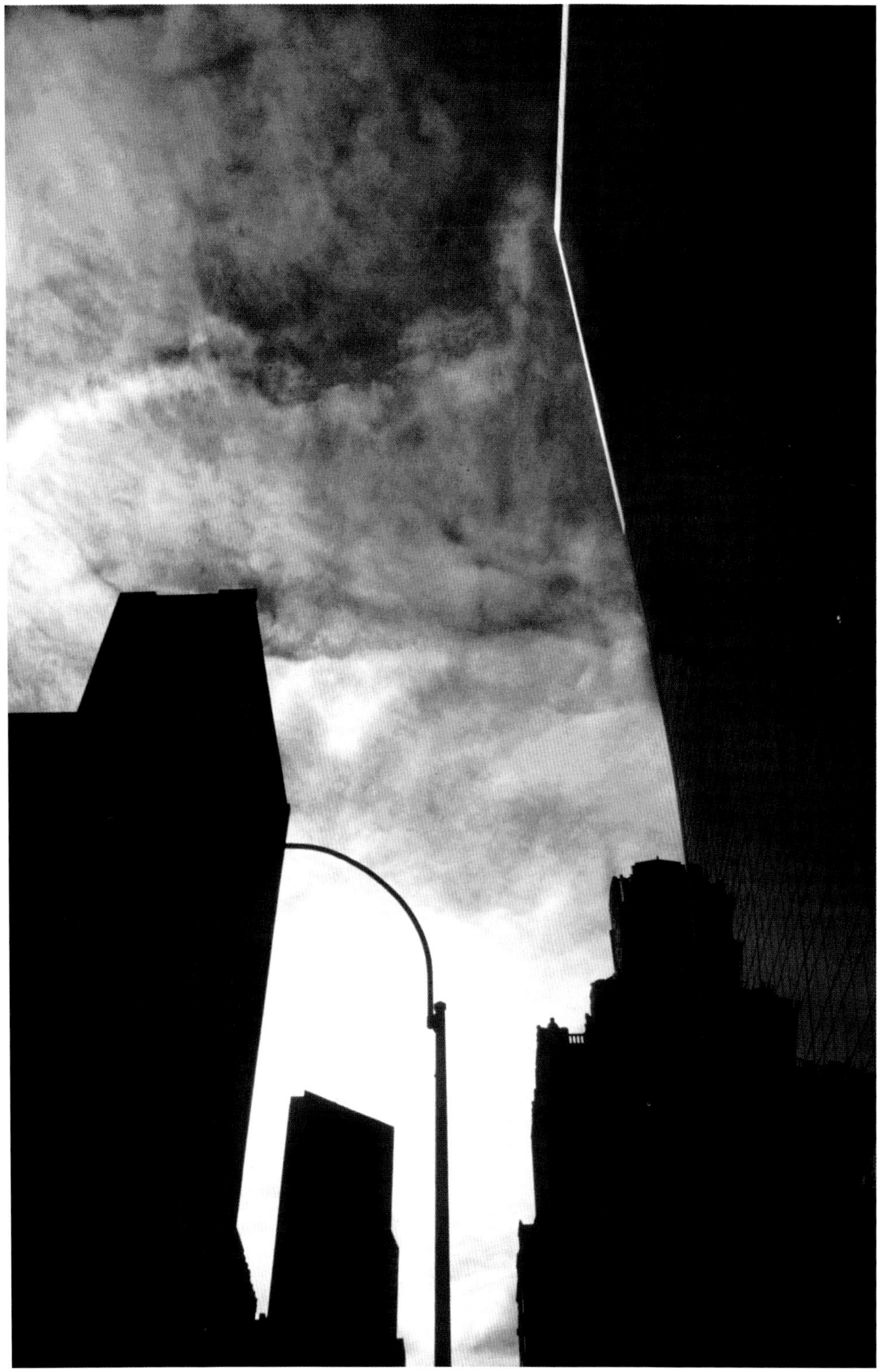

2

IMAGE 2

I then converted the image to Duotone via Image > Mode > Duotone, and chose black and Pantone 168CVC, a brick red. I dodged the edge of the building to increase its separation from the sky.

IMAGE 3

To finish the effect, I used the History Brush placed on the Duotone state and set it to Screen 30%. Every stroke lightened the area where it was applied. I then opened up areas in the building to emphasize the sense of light and the slight solarization of the edges. I also dodged and burned in the sky area to increase contrast.

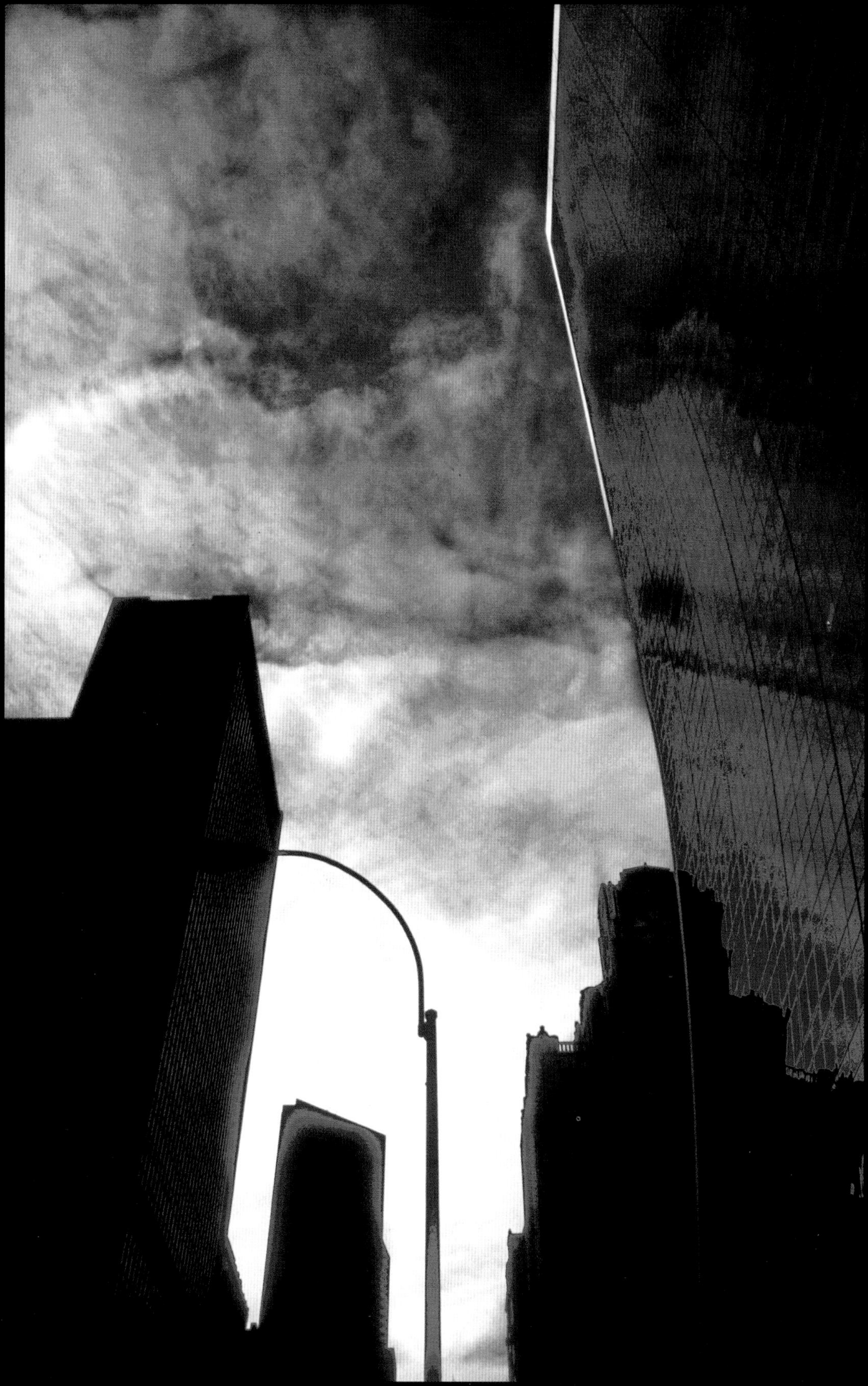

WORKSHOP 6 **PAPER NEGATIVES**

SUNFLOWERS

I have always enjoyed working with paper negatives in the darkroom, as they allow for many broad and interesting effects. Using a lightweight paper with a matte surface permits the use of soft lead pencils and charcoal to add density and various dodging effects. The aim is to create an image that breaks up some of the visual continuity, thus communicating an effect as much as a visual detail. It seems to me to result in a sort of graphic Impressionism; certainly, it draws inspiration from 19th-century photographic prints. Emulating that look in the digital darkroom begins with the choice of image.

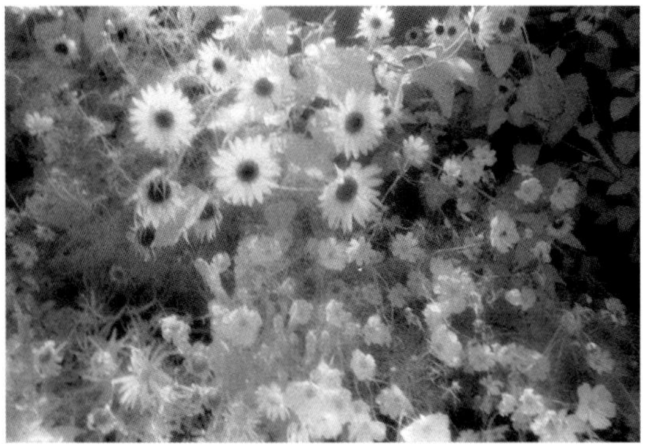

1

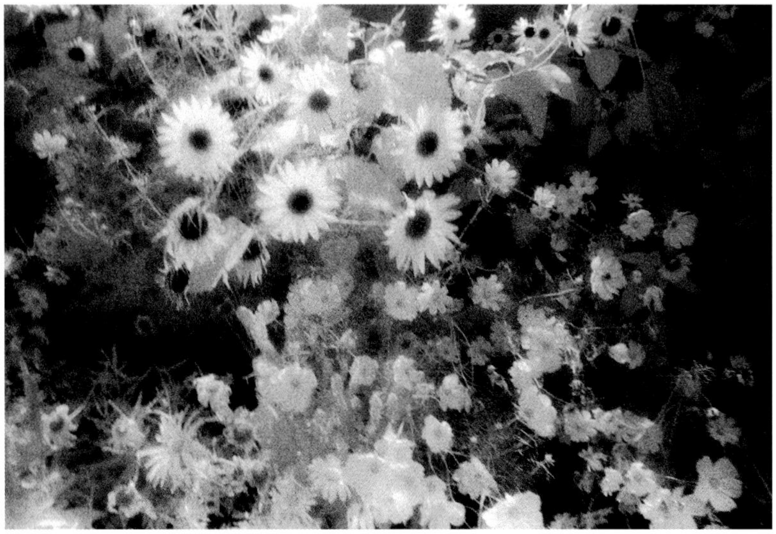

2

IMAGE 1

I made this scan from an infrared black-and-white 35mm negative. It has a soft, gauzy feeling that makes it just right for a paper negative emulation.

IMAGE 2

I wanted to create a block tonal effect to separate the highlights from the midtones and shadows, a kind of visual obscuring that hints at details in the shadows but doesn't necessarily reveal them. I often do this with conventional paper negatives by using a dark pencil and charcoal to mask or eliminate detail. Here, it's done by using Select > Color Range > Highlights. I chose highlights because I wanted to separate both the midtones and shadows. After the selection, I chose Select > Inverse so that the shadows and midtones were selected. I then created an adjustment layer by following Layer > New Adjustment Layer and using Multiply as the Blending mode. I unchecked Show Extras in the View menu to see what was going on and moved the Levels sliders slightly to gain the desired effect. I then burned in some of the brighter areas on the edges because I usually don't like bright highlights on the print edges.

IMAGE 3

To finish the image, I chose an image color that matched the mood by going to Image > Mode > Duotone and selecting Tritone—black, Pantone 1245CVC, and Pantone 392CVC. The look spans paper negatives and Van Dyke brown printing.

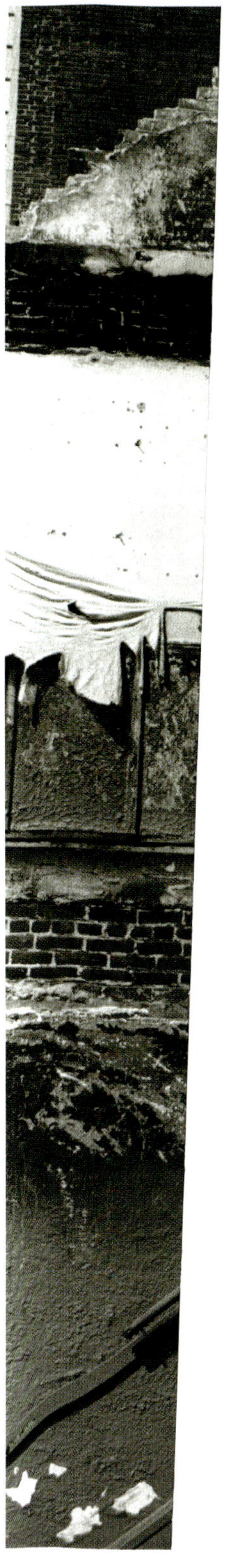

3

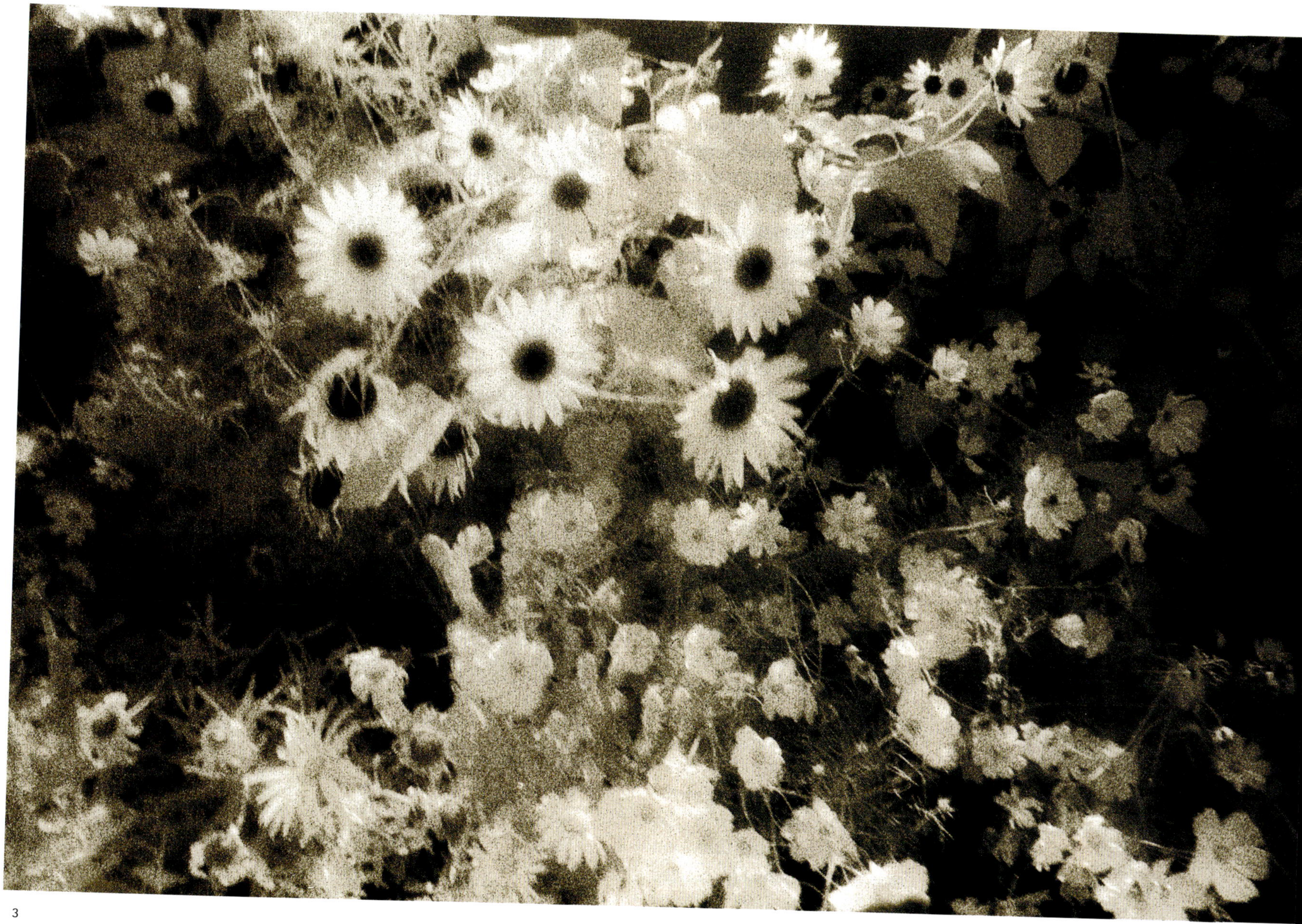

3

WORKSHOP 11 **CREATING MOOD**

FERNS

Printmaking is often about mood. When you choose certain effects you may be guided by a desire to emulate a look you liked, by the way content is reinforced by image treatment, or by some visual instincts that seem to guide us effortlessly in our approach. Digital printmaking is not superior or inferior to any type of photomechanical printing; it is what it is. The difference for me is the way it seems to encourage experimentation. I feel quite strongly about this because of the years I spent printing with both conventional and alternative processes. Although the process of trial and error is important to any creative work—and it is often the way you discover new forms of expression—there is no inherent reason that process must waste materials and excessive amounts of time in the bargain.

The digital darkroom encourages experimentation because of the very nature of the Preview and Variations functions in Photoshop. You can examine each step through use of the History palette and even follow your progress by clicking your way through the states. You can take all the time you like in the process, as there is no set time in which a print must be done and no chemicals that will oxidize if you break for a few hours of sleep. The idea is to remain open to different paths of expression and let unrestricted experimentation be your mentor and guide. Such is the case with this image, which sat on my screen a good half-hour before I did any work to it. Then, as I made changes to it, each choice modified the way the scene was expressed—with no waste, and great flexibility.

IMAGE 1

I made the scan from a 35mm color slide. I first tried to convert via Mode to Grayscale, but it was too contrasty so I used the custom converter, the Channel Mixer—as described in Image 2.

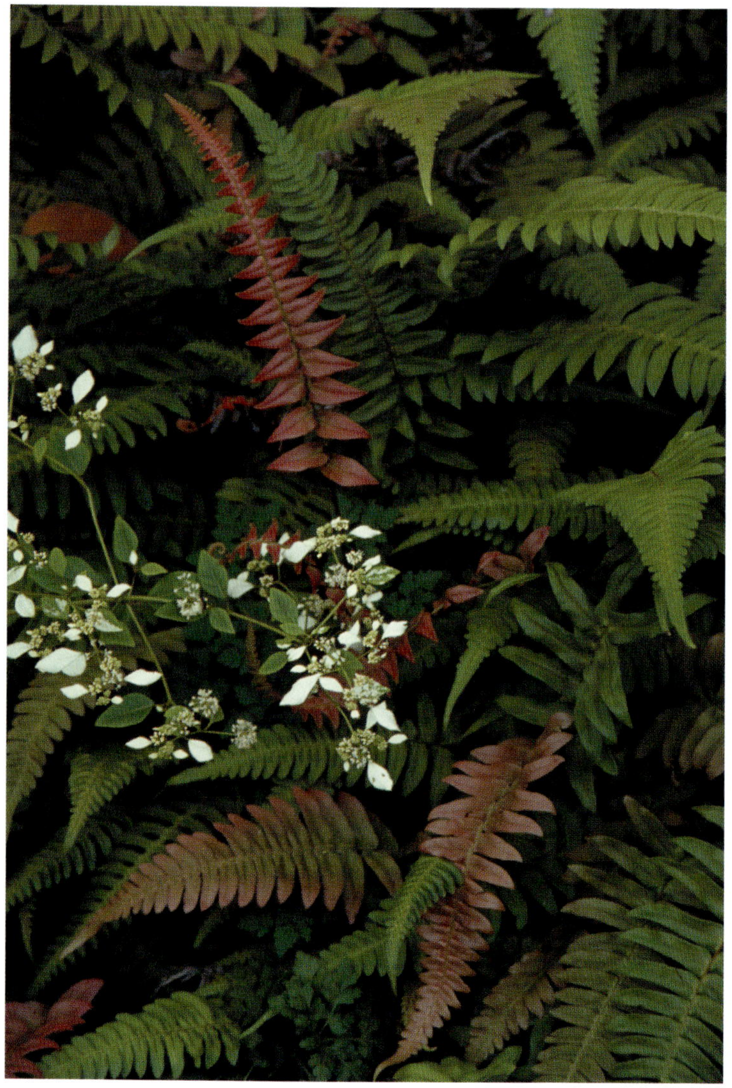

1

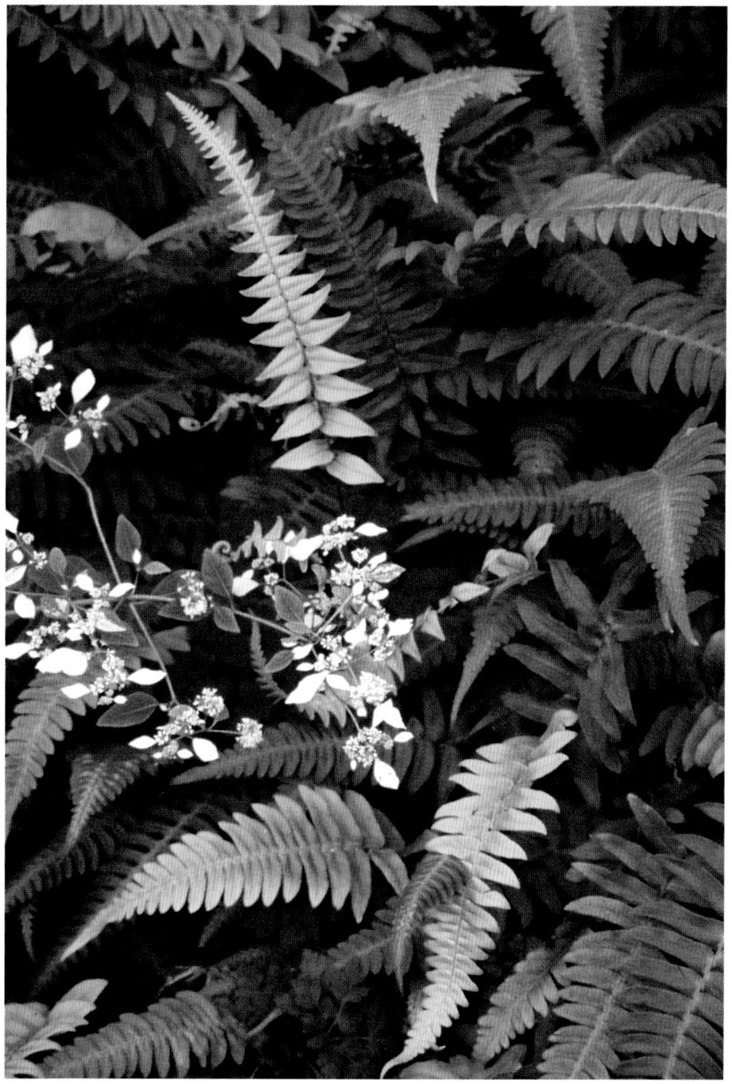

2

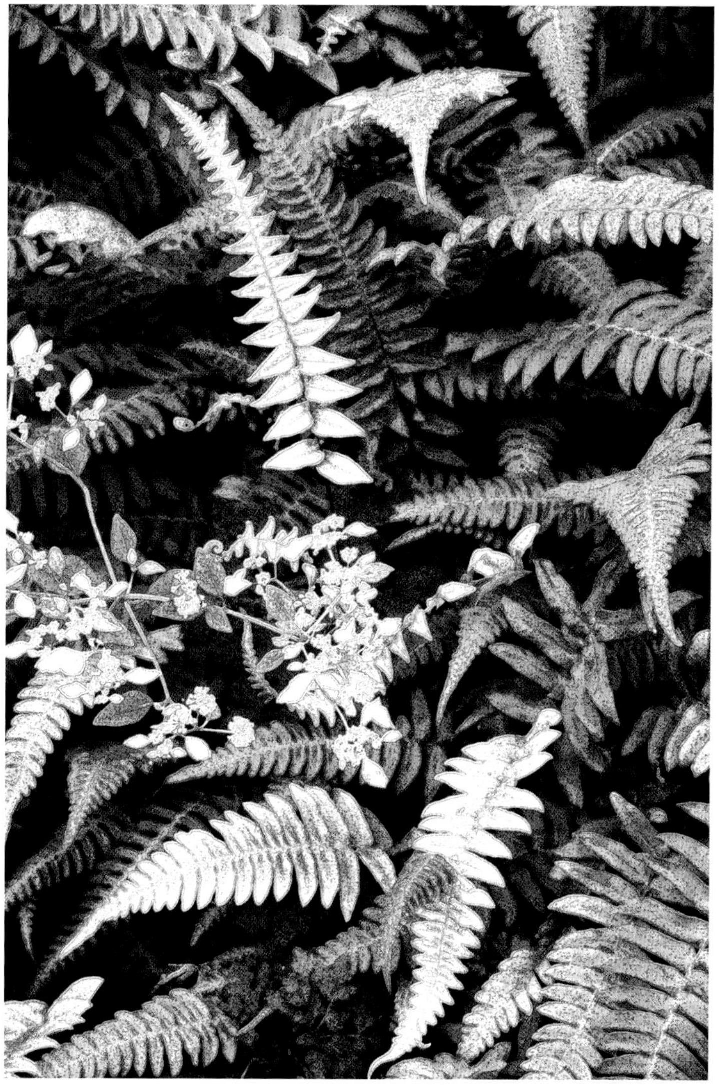

3

IMAGE 2

I accessed the Channel Mixer via Image >Adjust >Channel Mixer. The settings I chose were Red +100, Green +8, and Blue -4. I then used Layer >New Adjustment Layer, Levels, on Screen Blending mode, Levels to open up the middle tones, then converted the image to Grayscale.

IMAGE 3

I wanted to see how an ink change would affect the values, so I chose Duotone—black and Pantone 426CVC. I then applied the Ink Outlines filter in Filters >Brush Strokes >Ink Outlines.

WORKSHOP 14 **ELECTRIFYING AN IMAGE**

WHITE HOUSE

This scene has a touch of the surreal from the lighting and what had happened a few minutes before I snapped the shutter. I was walking in the fields behind the house and leaned over a wire fence to make a picture. Unknown to me was that the fence was electrified, and I was standing in a puddle of water. The shock sent me reeling, and I felt as if my heart had stopped. My eyes were quite wide open after that. I made this photo on the way back to where my car was parked. I knew that this roll of film would have special meaning so I printed images from it with a heightened tonal value.

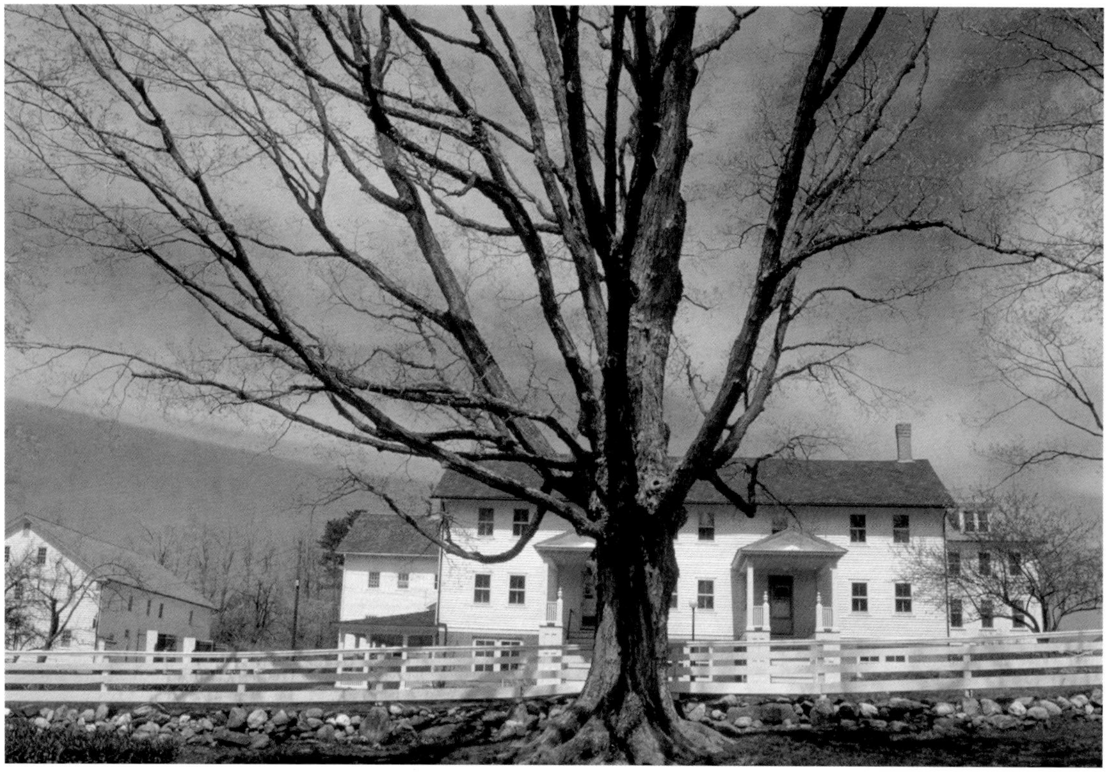

1

IMAGE 1

I made this scan from a 35mm Agfa Scala black-and-white slide. The scan is somewhat flat, but the values are all there. I wanted to give this image a special treatment without veering too far into special effects.

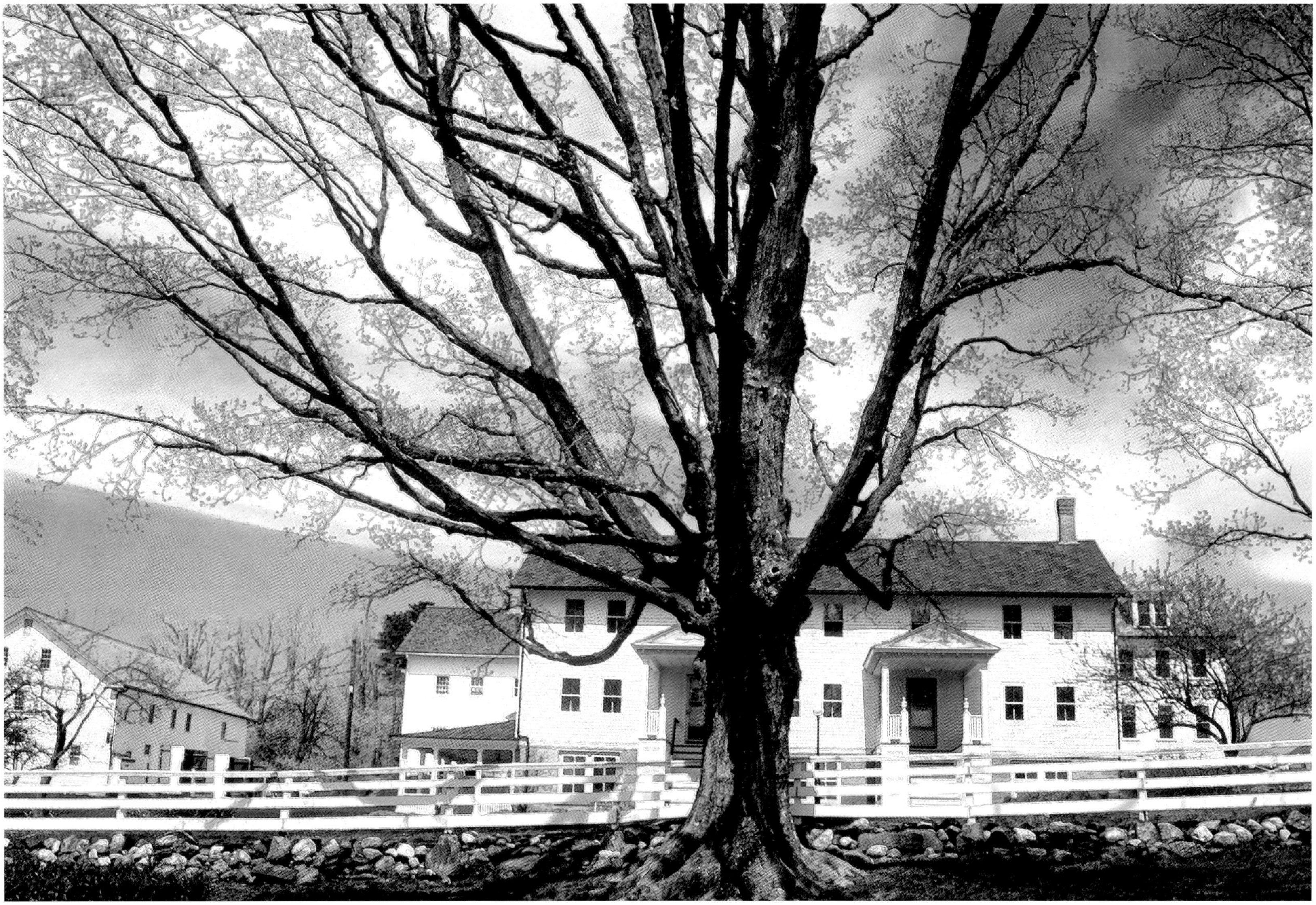

2

IMAGE 2

In one of my rare forays into the Filter menu, I chose Filter >Brush Strokes >Ink Outlines with Stroke Length 4, Dark Intensity 20, and Light Intensity 10. This created a visual edge and kicked up the values of the brighter highlights, giving the scene the electric feel I desired.

IMAGE 3

To finalize the print, I chose Duotone, Tritone—black, Pantone 419CVC, and Pantone 415CVC. This opened up the midtones. Often, you can use the curves in the Duotone settings to play with values as much as you can with Levels or Curves on an adjustment layer

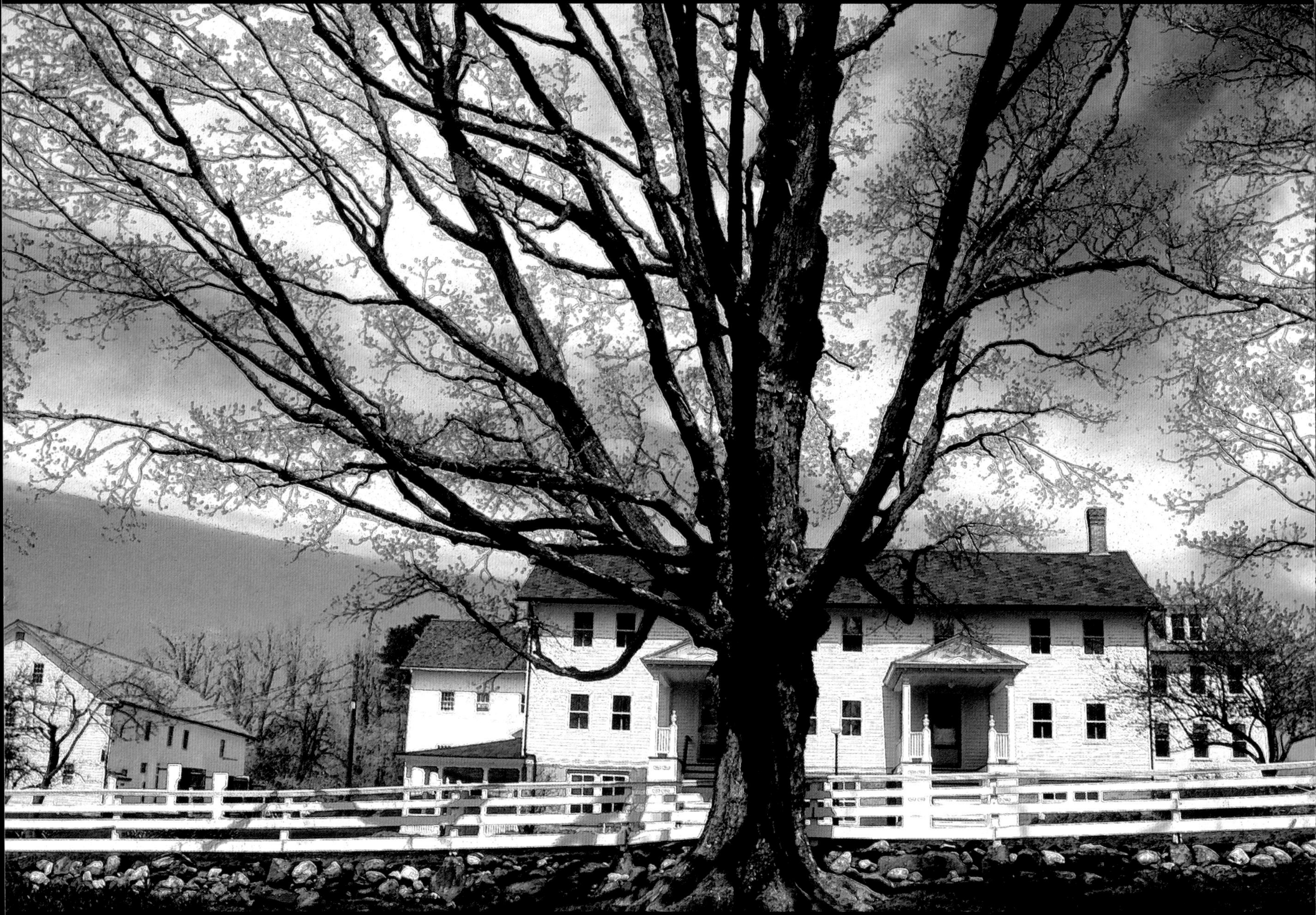